Rightful Resistance in Rural China

How can the poor and weak "work" a political system to their advantage? Drawing mainly on interviews and surveys in rural China, Kevin O'Brien and Lianjiang Li show that popular action often hinges on locating and exploiting divisions within the state. Otherwise powerless people use the rhetoric and commitments of the central government to try to fight misconduct by local officials, open up clogged channels of participation, and push back the frontiers of the permissible. This "rightful resistance" has far-reaching implications for our understanding of contentious politics. As O'Brien and Li explore the origins, dynamics, and consequences of rightful resistance, they highlight similarities between collective action in places as varied as China, the former East Germany, and the United States, while suggesting how Chinese experiences speak to issues such as opportunities to protest, claims radicalization, tactical innovation, and the outcomes of contention. Although the focus of their rich, ground-level analysis is contemporary China, the authors make a compelling argument that wherever a gap between rights promised and rights delivered exists, there is room for rightful resistance to emerge.

Kevin J. O'Brien is Bedford Professor of Political Science at the University of California, Berkeley. His research focuses on popular protest and Chinese politics in the reform era. He is the author of *Reform without Liberalization: China's National People's Congress and the Politics of Institutional Change* and the coeditor of *Engaging the Law in China: State, Society, and Possibilities for Justice*. Currently, he is serving as the chair of the Center for Chinese Studies at UC-Berkeley.

Lianjiang Li is an associate professor in the Department of Government and International Studies at Hong Kong Baptist University. His research focuses on village elections and collective action in rural China. He has published in *Asian Survey, China Information, China Journal, China Quarterly, Comparative Politics, Comparative Political Studies, Journal of Contemporary China*, and *Modern China*.

Cambridge Studies in Contentious Politics

Editors

Jack A. Goldstone   *George Mason University*
Doug McAdam   *Stanford University and Center for Advanced Study in the Behavioral Sciences*
Sidney Tarrow   *Cornell University*
Charles Tilly   *Columbia University*
Elisabeth J. Wood   *Yale University*

Ronald Aminzade et al., *Silence and Voice in the Study of Contentious Politics*
Clifford Bob, *The Marketing of Rebellion: Insurgents, Media, and International Activism*
Charles Brockett, *Political Movements and Violence in Central America*
Gerald F. Davis, Doug McAdam, W. Richard Scott, and Mayer N. Zald, *Social Movements and Organization Theory*
Jack A. Goldstone, editor, *States, Parties, and Social Movements*
Doug McAdam, Sidney Tarrow, and Charles Tilly, *Dynamics of Contention*
Sidney Tarrow, *The New Transnational Activism*
Charles Tilly, *Contention and Democracy in Europe, 1650–2000*
Charles Tilly, *The Politics of Collective Violence*
Deborah Yashar, *Contesting Citizenship in Latin America: The Rise of Indigenous Movements and the Postliberal Challenge*

Rightful Resistance in Rural China

KEVIN J. O'BRIEN

University of California, Berkeley

LIANJIANG LI

Hong Kong Baptist University

CAMBRIDGE
UNIVERSITY PRESS

CAMBRIDGE UNIVERSITY PRESS
Cambridge, New York, Melbourne, Madrid, Cape Town, Singapore,
São Paulo, Delhi, Dubai, Tokyo

Cambridge University Press
32 Avenue of the Americas, New York, NY 10013-2473, USA

www.cambridge.org
Information on this title: www.cambridge.org/9780521678520

First published 2006
Reprinted 2007

A catalog record for this publication is available from the British Library

Library of Congress Cataloging in Publication data

O'Brien, Kevin J., 1957–
Rightful resistance in rural China / Kevin J. O'Brien, Lianjiang Li.
   p.   cm. – (Cambridge studies in contentious politics)
Includes bibliographical references and index.
ISBN 0-521-86131-4 (hardback) – ISBN 0-521-67852-8 (pbk.)
1. Peasantry – China – Political activity.   2. China – Rural conditions.
I. Li, Lianjiang.   II. Title.   III. Series.
JQ156.O27   2006
305.5'633'0951–dc22   2005021714

ISBN 978-0-521-86131-1 Hardback
ISBN 978-0-521-67852-0 Paperback

Transferred to digital printing 2010

For Betsy and Lijuan

Contents

Preface

We first noticed rightful resistance in the summer of 1994, when we were doing fieldwork on village elections in China. As officials and researchers in Shandong, Hebei, and Hubei described the problems rural leaders faced, they told us fascinating stories about "nail-like individuals" (*dingzihu*) and "shrewd and unruly people" (*diaomin*). We soon learned that villagers whom cadres labeled this way were often responsible for launching protests, including actions as small as trying to topple a village leader and as large as organizing an antitax demonstration that drew in thousands of farmers. That first summer, despite some promising interviews, we were not overly hopeful that we could discover a great deal about these people or what they did. After all, rural unrest was (and still is) a sensitive topic in China, on which sources were scarce, anecdotes rare, and fieldwork fraught with complications.

We returned home and started reading. Our initial search for examples of protests did not turn up much, although we did locate some informative articles in out-of-the-way Chinese journals and popular magazines. Still, we felt unsure what to make of these accounts, mainly because we did not have any complete cases that were as detailed as we needed.

This changed when we gained access to our first full episode of rural contention, in which dozens of villagers were struggling to oust a local Communist Party secretary who they were confident was corrupt. With the help of friends and colleagues, we interviewed a number of organizers and community members as well as the accused cadre; we collected letters of complaint and testimonies prepared by protest leaders; we also spoke with several township and county officials who had been drawn into the case. Following one episode of contention from shortly after it began to its conclusion proved more valuable than we could have imagined. It was particularly useful in bringing to light aspects of collective action that Chinese sources usually ignored, such as who the activists were, what tactics they employed, and how important it was to win support outside the village (O'Brien and Li, 1995).

As we continued to gather material on rural protest, it became clear that what we were observing did not fit snugly in the literatures on political participation, popular resistance, or social movements. It was neither as institutionalized as most political participation nor as uninstitutionalized as the "politics by other means" that social movement scholars usually studied. The contention we were hearing and reading about was more noisy, public, open, and consequential than James Scott's (1985) "everyday forms of resistance," yet still fell short of rebellion or revolution. This activity made use of authorized channels without playing exactly by the rules and rested on a familiar rhetorical strategy, but it did not involve quite the same accommodations with existing power relations or assertions of long-standing cultural conventions as "moral economy" claims (Scott, 1976; Thompson, 1971, 1991: 336–51). This type of collective action, we eventually realized, was not political participation, everyday resistance, or a social movement, but something else. Lacking a good term to describe it, we called it "policy-based resistance." At this point, we were working solely in a Chinese context and were content to distinguish "policy-based resisters" from "recalcitrants" and "compliant villagers" (Li and O'Brien, 1996).

Our efforts to figure out what about this contention might be interesting to a wider audience took much longer than we had expected. Once it became apparent that Chinese villagers were struggling to defend rights they had already been granted, or rights they believed could be derived from the regime's policies, laws, principles, and legitimating ideology, we decided that "rightful resistance" (O'Brien, 1996, 2001; O'Brien and Li, 1999; Li, 2004) was a more precise term than "policy-based resistance." But we were continually stymied in trying to gain a more complete understanding of the origins, dynamics, and outcomes of rightful resistance. At this stage, we were not sure whether this type of contention would spread, evolve, and have a significant impact, or if it was an epiphenomenon (characteristic of China in its transitional state) that would vanish without a trace. Owing to the sensitivity of research on social unrest, we found it difficult to arrange fieldwork in locations where we knew major episodes of rightful resistance had occurred. For almost eight years we only inched forward, relying on short stints of field research here and there, some survey work, and irritatingly incomplete accounts of rural contention available in Chinese sources.

Then, in early 2003 good luck came our way. With the help of Yu Jianrong, a researcher at the Chinese Academy of Social Science, we gained access to dozens of protest leaders in Hunan province. In the course of joint fieldwork by Yu and Lianjiang Li in January and March 2003, as well as through transcripts and videotaped interviews that Dr. Yu generously shared with us, much new information came to light and much that we had dimly perceived came into sharper focus.[1]

Making sense of these interviews (and our other evidence) entailed moving from single incidents to general patterns to an underlying logic. Rather than presenting our China findings in great detail, as we have done elsewhere, this book focuses on some of the more theoretical implications of rightful resistance: how, in particular, this form of protest speaks to the literature on contentious politics.

This study is organized like an episode of collective action: it works its way from origins to dynamics to consequences. Chapter 1 defines rightful resistance and explains its relationship to other types of popular contention. In Chapter 2 we explore the onset of rightful resistance by examining opportunities for protest in rural China and how activists perceive them. Chapters 3 and 4 highlight the boundary-spanning nature of rightful claims and tactics and discuss a trend toward claims radicalization and tactical escalation.[2] In the last two chapters we consider the significance of rightful resistance: Chapter 5 examines its effects on policy implementation, protest leaders, and the wider community, whereas Chapter 6 investigates possible consequences for Chinese state-society relations and political change, particularly those related to policy innovations, institutional reforms, and the spread of citizenship practices.

Although this book dips into many topics, it is in no way comprehensive. Among other things, we do not spend much time worrying about regional variation; nor do we provide an all-around treatment of rightful resistance (and its analogues) in Chinese history. The book is largely conceptual and "universalizing" (Tilly, 1984: 97, 108) rather than causal and variation

---

[1] For more on the interviews in Hengyang county, Hunan, see Appendix B.

[2] Throughout the book, our time frame is the post-Mao era. When we refer to "recent" trends or "new" developments, the point of reference is typically the 1980s or early 1990s. Claims radicalization and tactical escalation have, of course, occurred many times in China's past, including just before the 1911 Revolution and again during the "Great Revolution" of 1925–27.

seeking.[3] For readers interested in the reach of our findings in China, we encourage them to investigate whether our hunches and survey results (often summarized in long footnotes) hold up in different regions, for different policies, at different times.[4]

We have also not been able to examine as many concepts as we had hoped to. We had thought about including chapters on framing, mobilizing structures, high-risk activism, repertoires of contention, grievances, leadership, and elite allies. But we just did not have enough data to do them justice. The hooks we did end up with were chosen according to two simple principles: where did we have the most to say to students of contentious politics, and where was the lowest-hanging fruit to be found? There are certainly many other points of entry for Sinologists who wish to engage the contentious politics literature, and we are delighted to see that a number of our fellow China scholars, using their own fieldwork and findings, have begun to exploit them.[5]

Nearly all the questions addressed in Chapters 2 through 5 are drawn from the contentious politics literature, and we discuss (often in glancing fashion) many familiar concepts and theories. But we have seldom found it necessary to jump in decisively on one side or the other in ongoing debates.[6] Instead, our approach has been to position the China case in relation to the literature by appropriating whatever explained our findings

---

[3] On "the parallel demonstration of theory" and using comparison to group cases, highlight similarities, and refine theories, see Skocpol and Somers (1980). O'Brien (2004) suggests how concepts drawn from the comparative literature can be used to understand the significance of interviewees' comments, place findings in relation to others, and generalize (ever so modestly), as China scholars repackage their ground-level evidence for disciplinary colleagues who have been working with grand theories that only apply in a limited context.

[4] The appendixes also present a number of testable hypotheses and some additional survey findings.

[5] Examples of this are becoming too numerous to list. On framing, see F. Chen (2003), Hurst (2004), Lee (2000), and Thornton (2002). On mobilizing structures, see Cai (2002) and Hurst (2004). On the repertoire of contention in China and its historical roots, see X. Chen (2004), Perry (1985, 2003a, 2003b), and Thornton (2004). On grievances, see F. Chen (2000, 2003), Hurst (2004), Landry and Tong (2005), and Michelson (2004, 2005). On elite allies, see Bernstein and Lü (2003), Cai (2003), and Guo (2001). On collective memories, see Lee (2000) and Perry (2003a, 2003b). On emotions, see G. Yang (2000a). On the biographical consequences of contention, see G. Yang (2000b). On leadership, see Bernstein and Lü (2003), Cai (2002, 2003), and Thornton (2004). On policing protest, see Tanner (2005). On the spatial origins of mobilization, see Zhao (2001). On political opportunities in comparative perspective, see Wright (2001).

[6] Our discussion of the consequences of contention in Chapter 5 is an exception in that it is openly hortatory. Chapter 2 also adopts a largely structuralist orientation to "political opportunity" and then shows how perceptions might be layered into such an account. In

best. This has enabled us to underscore commonalities between protest in China and protest elsewhere, while suggesting bridges between different theories and perspectives. It also means that readers hoping to find clear-cut statements that, for example, failures are more crucial than opportunities in spurring tactical innovation, or perceptions of opportunity are more important than structural opportunities, may be disappointed. Instead, they will have to settle for seeing what rightful resistance in the Chinese countryside can tell us about tactical innovation, radical flank effects, the strategic dilemma, object shift, venue shopping, unpacking political opportunity, blame attribution, transgressive versus contained claims, the biographical consequences of protest, the pleasures of protest, and so on, as we learn what evidence from China and theory can offer each other.[7]

Looking back over our decade-long collaboration, we feel fortunate and grateful for many reasons. Beyond what we have learned, our work has deepened our ties immeasurably, as we evolved from adviser and advisee into frequent travel companions, daily sounding boards, and close friends. Writing in tag-team style, usually nine time zones apart, enabled us, as Marc Blecher once put it, to reap the benefits of a "globalized production system." It also ensured that each of us would wake up nearly every morning to find an inbox filled with an improved version of the muddled, question-laden text we had e-mailed across the Pacific the night before.

Our field trips and surveys were made possible by generous financial support from the Asia Foundation, the China Times Cultural Foundation, the Harry Frank Guggenheim Foundation, the Henry Luce Foundation, Hong Kong Baptist University, the John D. and Catherine T. MacArthur Foundation, Ohio State University, the Pacific Cultural Foundation, the Research Grants Council of Hong Kong, the Sun Yat-sen Culture & Education Foundation, and the Institute of East Asian Studies, Center for Chinese Studies, and Department of Political Science of the University of California at Berkeley. For able research assistance in the nooks and crannies of the contentious politics literature, we thank Kevin Wallsten. Margaret Boittin skillfully wrestled the Word indexing tool to a draw and responded (with unfailing cheer and frightful speed) to our requests to add just one more

general, we feel that "debates" in the field are often overstated and that many theorists are not as strange bedfellows as the introductions of countless articles and books would suggest.
[7] On Chinese politics, perhaps being "on the verge of maturing from a 'consumer field' (dependent for its analytical insights upon imports from the study of other countries) to a 'producer field' (capable of generating analyses of interest to comparativists in general)," see Perry (1994).

set of subcategories. As we shared thoughts and papers with colleagues over the past decade, we benefited greatly from comments by Thomas Bernstein, Lucien Bianco, Marc Blecher, Anita Chan, Donald Clarke, Neil Diamant, Maria Edin, Randle Edwards, Edward Friedman, Thomas Gold, Peter Gries, Lei Guang, Kathy Hartford, Daniel Kelliher, Stanley Lubman, Ching Kwan Lee, Kenneth Lieberthal, Xiaobo Lü, Melanie Manion, Ethan Michelson, Andrew Nathan, Michel Oksenberg, Stanley Rosen, James Scott, Tianjian Shi, Dorothy Solinger, Ralph Thaxton, Stig Thøgersen, Jonathan Unger, Lynn White III, Tyrene White, Brantly Womack, Dali Yang, Guobin Yang, Dingxin Zhao, and David Zweig. We owe a special debt of gratitude to Elizabeth Perry and Charles Tilly, both of whom read the manuscript from front to back, and both of whom provided a host of helpful suggestions that improved the book in ways we could never have come up with on our own.

Among our Chinese friends and colleagues, we are particularly thankful to Bai Gang, Bai Yihua, Che Mingzhou, Cheng Tongshun, Fu Xizhong, Gao Shan, Guo Zhenglin, Hu Rong, Jean Hung, Li Changping, Li Changqing, Li Fan, Li Kang, Liang Jun, Mi Youlu, Qiao Riyong, Shi Weimin, Tang Jinsu, Wang Aiping, Wang Jiexiu, Wang Jingyao, Wang Zhenhai, Wang Zhenyao, Wang Zhiquan, Wu Bin, Xiang Jiquan, Xiao Tangbiao, Xin Qiushui, Xu Fuqun, Xu Yong, Yan Tiezheng, Yang Aimin, Yang Wenliang, Yao Dongfang, Yu Xin, Zhang Guang, Zhang Houan, Zhang Jianxin, Zhang Jinming, Zhang Yinghong, Zhao Shukai, Zhu Guanglei, and, especially, Yu Jianrong. To our interviewees and survey respondents we are most grateful of all.

At Cambridge University Press, we would like to thank our editor Lew Bateman for keeping us moving toward the finish line; our production editor Brian MacDonald; and Sidney Tarrow, in his dual capacity as coeditor of Cambridge's book series, Studies in Contentious Politics, and sure-handed guide through the social movement literature. We owe Sid more than he realizes for his encouragement, his suggestions, and the efforts he has made (with Charles Tilly and Doug McAdam) to open up the field of contentious politics and welcome in those of us who do not study industrialized democracies.

Chapters 1, 3, and 5 draw to varying degrees on our previously published articles: "Rightful Resistance," *World Politics*, 49(1) (October 1996), 31–55; "Neither Transgressive Nor Contained: Boundary-Spanning Contention in China," in Peter Hays Gries and Stanley Rosen (eds.), *State and Society in 21st Century China: Crisis, Contention, and Legitimation* (New York:

RoutledgeCurzon, 2004), pp. 105–22; and "Popular Contention and Its Impact in Rural China," *Comparative Political Studies*, 38(3) (April 2005), 235–59. Several pages in Chapter 6 were adapted from "Villagers, Elections, and Citizenship in Contemporary China," *Modern China*, 27(4) (October 2001), 407–35. We are grateful to Johns Hopkins University Press, Taylor & Francis Books Ltd., and Sage Publications Inc., for permission to use copyrighted material.

For our wives and daughters, Betsy, Lijuan, Brenda, Joyce, and Molly, we hope this book provides a small return on the many sacrifices they made while we were working, either in China or tethered to our computers at home. And yes, Molly, you're right: "That's enough work for today. Going to the park is much more fun."

Rightful Resistance in Rural China

1

Rightful Resistance

The words "popular resistance" typically bring to mind images of negation, usually of the legitimacy of something, and actions by people who lack recourse to institutional politics. When considering examples of popular resistance, we are drawn to accounts of marginalized workers and peasants rejecting the claims of political and economic elites – of efforts by the poor and weak to upset the plans of those with more power and status. Whether it is furtive, everyday resistance to changes in village norms and charitable practices, or open defiance of national rule, it is uninstitutionalized acts that spring from a deeply felt (if sometimes artfully undeclared) denial of legitimacy that tend to attract attention.

Much popular resistance surely fits this description. Struggles to tame political and economic power are often waged by the utterly excluded and rest on feelings of disavowal, even outrage. At the same time, however, other episodes of resistance exhibit a somewhat different logic. Contentious politics is not always a story of neatly divided antagonists, with representatives of the state or dominant classes posed on one side and members of the popular classes on the other. Sometimes resistance depends on the discontented locating and exploiting divisions within the state. In these circumstances, setting up subordinates (in society) in opposition to superordinates (in the state) can obscure how people actually go about warding off appropriation and political control. Thinking in terms of two parties can be especially misleading in those cases when aggrieved persons employ government commitments and established values to persuade concerned elites to support their claims. When receptive officials, for instance, champion popular demands to execute laws and policies that have been ignored elsewhere in the hierarchy, unexpected alliances often emerge and simple dominant-subordinate distinctions break down. On these occasions, popular resistance operates

1

partly within (yet in tension with) official norms; it depends on a degree of accommodation with a structure of power, the deft use of prevailing cultural conventions, and an affirmation – sometimes sincere, sometimes strategic – of existing channels of inclusion.

More than a decade ago, Jeffrey Herbst (1989: 199) pointed to the importance of opportunities afforded by the wider environment to dissatisfied members of the popular classes. He advised against turning the state into a "forbidding monolith" and recommended recognizing that "certain institutional arrangements and political goods may be particularly amenable to the type of political pressure that only weak, unorganized groups can bring to bear." At about the same time, James Scott (1990: 101, 106) called attention to forms of resistance that occur "within the official discourse of deference," inasmuch as they rest on ethical claims legitimated by official ideologies. Such resistance, Scott explained, can hamstring elites because it is couched in the language of loyal intentions; it can reveal when members of powerful groups have dared to take liberties with the symbols in which they are most invested. Meanwhile, other students of contentious politics have used terms such as "in-between forms of resistance" (Turton, 1986), "consentful contention" (Straughn, 2005), "reformist activism" (Anderson, 1994), and "reasonable radicalism" (McCann, 1994) to describe petition drives in Thailand and East Germany, struggles to reclaim appropriated land in Latin America, and the use of antidiscrimination laws to agitate for equal pay in the United States. What is to be made of individuals or groups who dispute the authority of certain political authorities and their actions while affirming (indeed relying upon) other authorities and established values to pursue their ends? How should we understand contentious acts that are intended both to open channels of participation and to make use of existing channels, that straddle the border between what is usually considered popular resistance and institutionalized participation?

This chapter begins the task of defining rightful resistance, first rather abstractly, then on the ground in rural China and elsewhere. Rightful resistance is a form of popular contention that operates near the boundary of authorized channels, employs the rhetoric and commitments of the powerful to curb the exercise of power, hinges on locating and exploiting divisions within the state, and relies on mobilizing support from the wider public. In particular, rightful resistance entails the innovative use of laws, policies, and other officially promoted values to defy disloyal political and economic elites; it is a kind of partially sanctioned protest that uses influential allies and recognized principles to apply pressure on those in power who have failed to live up to a professed ideal or who have not implemented some beneficial measure.

Rightful resisters normally frame their claims with reference to protections implied in ideologies or conferred by policy makers. Because they often demand little more than scrupulous enforcement of existing commitments, theirs is a contention based on strict adherence to established values. In their acts of contestation, which usually combine legal tactics with political pressure, rightful resisters typically behave in accord with prevailing statutes (or at least not in open violation of them). They forgo, for example, violence or other openly criminal behavior,[1] which might weaken their standing and alienate their backers. Instead, rightful resisters assert their claims largely through approved channels and use a regime's policies and legitimating myths to justify their challenges. Rightful resisters act as if the instruments of domination that usually facilitate control can be turned to new purposes; they have an aspirational view of government measures and elite values and recognize that the very symbols embraced by those in power can be a source of entitlement, inclusion, and empowerment (in other contexts, see Goldberg, 1986: 14–15; Matsuda, 1987; McCann, 1994: 232–33).[2]

Rightful resistance resembles other forms of popular contention, though at some remove. Like a full-fledged social movement, rightful resistance involves a collective, public challenge, based on common purposes and group solidarity (Tarrow, 1998: 4). It also harks back to Gramsci's (1971: 229–39) "war of position," in that it involves probing for vulnerabilities in a facade of power, and because it offers the marginalized a way to work the system to their minimum disadvantage (Hobsbawm, 1973: 13). In their search for patrons, rightful resisters also bear some likeness to "rebels in the name of the tsar" – Russian peasants who employed the myth of the tsar-deliverer to mobilize others, protect themselves, and reject claims made by "faithless" officials (Field, 1976). At the same time, rightful resisters have a certain affinity with "everyday resisters" (Scott, 1989: 8) insofar as their challenges are opportunistic and measured and because, at least at first, they almost always lack the organizational resources and collective consciousness shared by members of well-formed groups.

---

[1] We exclude violent acts by definition, although rightful resistance can escalate into violence, after, for instance, repeated failures or local repression.

[2] On the use of official symbols and practices as a base for protest in China, see Perry (2003a: xxiii), Thornton (2002), and Wasserstrom (1992: 135–36).

As should be clear, however, rightful resistance is not simply a specific kind of social movement, everyday resistance, or not-so-naive monarchism. Unlike a typical social movement, rightful resistance is often episodic rather than sustained (Tarrow, 1998: 4–5), within-system as much as extra-institutional (Burstein, Einwohner, and Hollander, 1995: 277; Gamson, 1990; McAdam, 1982: 25; but cf. Goldstone, 2003: 2), and local or regional rather than national or even transnational (Tarrow, 2005; Tilly, 1986: 392). Unlike rebels in the name of the tsar, rightful resisters stop short of violence and are not limited to wishfulness and willful misinterpretation of imaginary protections. Their insubordination is in fact nurtured by authoritative pronouncements, and they have evidence (or at least good reason to believe) that powerful and sympathetic advocates exist. And unlike everyday resisters, rightful resisters seek rather than avoid the attention of elites: whereas foot dragging, poaching, sabotage, and other "weapons of the weak" are invariably quiet, disguised, and anonymous, rightful resistance is invariably noisy, public, and open. Rightful resisters aim to mitigate the risks of confrontation by proclaiming their allegiance to core values rather than by opting for disguised dissent. Indeed, because they work the territory between officials and challenge misconduct using an approved discourse, rightful resisters do not subscribe to the view that "the state and its laws are typically inaccessible, arbitrary and alien" (Scott, 1989: 28). To the contrary, they have learned how to exploit the potent symbolic and material capital made available by modern states. Rightful resistance is thus a product of state building and of opportunities created by the spread of participatory ideologies and patterns of rule rooted in notions of equality, rights, and rule of law. It derives as much from the "great tradition" of the powerful as the "little tradition" of the powerless and is a sign of growing rights consciousness and a more contractual approach to political life. It appears as individuals with new aspirations come to appreciate common interests, develop an oppositional consciousness,[3] and become collective actors in the course of struggle.

For rightful resistance to emerge, discontented community members must learn that they have been granted certain protections, often in the course of prior "contentious conversation" (Tilly, 2002: 111–22). For it to be effective, its practitioners must craft effective tactics, mobilize followers, and win a measure of sufferance, even support, for their contention. That

---

[3] On the development of an oppositional consciousness that only partly rejects a would-be hegemonic consciousness, see Morris (1992: 363–64).

rightful resisters often engage in deliberately disruptive but not quite unlawful collective action inevitably attracts the attention of officials responsible for preserving order and administering justice. That they use the vocabulary of the regime to advance claims can help them locate advocates among the powerful and may afford a measure of protection when their plans go awry.

Rightful resistance, with its slightly oxymoronic sound, is the quintessential "critique within the hegemony" (Scott, 1990: 106). Those who pursue it act as if they take the values and programs of political and economic elites to heart, while demonstrating that some authorities do not. They launch attacks that are legitimate by definition in a rhetoric that even unresponsive authorities must recognize, lest they risk being charged with hypocrisy and disloyalty to the system of power they represent (see Scott, 1990: 90–107; Straughn, 2005).

Rightful Resistance in Rural China

Rightful resistance can appear in many settings; it happens, however, that the concept was derived from research in the Chinese countryside. In the next part of this chapter, we turn to examples of collective action in rural China to shed light on the claims, origins, and dynamics of rightful resistance. Individually, each episode illuminates at least one feature of rightful resistance.[4] Together, they trace what can happen when villagers frame their claims around Communist Party policies, state laws, and official values; solicit assistance from influential allies; and combine legal tactics with collective action to defend their "lawful rights and interests" (*hefa quanyi*).

Rightful Claims

The roots of Chinese rightful resistance lie in the rich soil of central policy. To appreciate how the programs of an unaccountable national leadership provide openings for rightful resisters, the term "central policy" must be understood in its broad, Chinese sense. Central policies, in this usage, include essentially all authoritative pronouncements, ranging from Party documents, laws, State Council regulations, and leadership speeches

---

[4] Given the sensitivity of rural contention and the limitations of Chinese sources, full ethnographic detail for each episode was not always available.

to editorials by special commentators in prominent newspapers. Central policies can be both as general as "guidelines" (*fangzhen*) that cadres should "develop the economy" or be "clean and honest" or as specific as regulations prohibiting local fees from exceeding 5 percent of a village's net per capita income the previous year (Nongmin chengdan feiyong, 1991; see also Bernstein and Lü, 2003: 167–68). At the same time, central policies may be formally ratified, like the State Constitution, or only informally publicized, like Deng Xiaoping's remark that "some people should be allowed to get rich first." The scope of central policy in China thus encompasses what constitutes law in most other nations but also reaches into far murkier realms, such as pledges made by officials on inspection tours, Party propaganda, and the "spirit of the Center" (*zhongyang jingshen*).

In the Chinese countryside the number of grievances amenable to rightful resistance has been rising. In contrast to the early reform era, discontented villagers increasingly cite laws, regulations, and other authoritative communications when challenging all sorts of cadre malfeasance, including misconduct related to economic appropriation, grass-roots elections, village finances, land use, cadre corruption, and the use of excessive force (Bernstein and Lü, 2003; Cai, 2003; Guo, 2001; Howell, 1998; Jennings, 1997; Li and O'Brien, 1996; Liu, 2000; O'Brien, 2002; Wedeman, 1997; Zweig, 2000). They often claim a right, for instance, to withhold grain tax payments because they have not received fertilizer or diesel fuel that government authorities were contractually obliged to provide (Shixin haiyao feili, 1993). On even firmer ground, rightful resisters sometimes point to regulations limiting "farmers' burdens" (*nongmin fudan*) to fend off unapproved fees or demands for grain that exceeds amounts previously agreed to (Bernstein and Lü, 2003). In one of the poorest villages in Henan's Sheqi county, for example, a group of plucky villagers presented county officials with State Council regulations distributed by the prefectural government when protesting thirty-seven fees that far exceeded the 5 percent limit (Cheng Tongshun, 1994: 11–12). The complainants' unspoken threat was that if county officials dared to rebuff them, they would take their case up the hierarchy and insist that prefectural officials enforce central regulations they themselves had publicized.

Contractual ways of thinking and a growing fluency in rights talk appear to underlie much of the rightful resistance present in rural China (Brandstädter and Schubert, 2005; S. Chan, 1998; Diamant, Lubman, and O'Brien, 2005; Interviews 4, 11; He, 2005: 217; Jakobson, 2004; Jing, 2000; Johnson, 2004; Liebman, 1998; O'Brien, 2001, 2002; Pei, 1997; Tanner,

1994; Zweig, 2000). Censorious villagers are demanding fidelity to values and rights embodied in the contract responsibility system of farming (which has been promoted by the central government since the early 1980s), and they are finding fault with local power holders who fail to respect the sanctity of agreements (Blecher, 1995: 106; Zweig, 1997: 151–82). These exacting critics know that the Center seeks to encourage economic growth and head off unrest by creating webs of mutual obligation, and they are prepared to hand over whatever grain, taxes, and fees they lawfully owe, provided the local representatives of state power treat them equitably, respect their rights, and deliver on promises made by officials at higher levels.

When, however, grass-roots leaders neglect the letter of the law or sidestep limits on their discretion, eagle-eyed villagers are quick to step in and to accuse them of engaging in prohibited behavior. Aggrieved farmers say things such as, "Failing to carry out the 'three-linkage-policy' [concerning supply of agricultural inputs] amounts to unilaterally breaking a contract. I have the right not to pay the grain tax. You have broken the contract, so how can you ask me to honor it?" (Shixin haiyao feili, 1993: 41). Or, "central policy says that after farmers fulfill their contractual obligations, we can sell our grain freely on the market, so why don't you obey? If you don't listen to the Center, then we won't listen to you. . . . Why do you always oppose the Center? Why do you always oppose us? Are you cadres of the Communist Party?" (Tang Jinsu and Wang Jianjun, 1989: 4). Employing authorized symbols to pose inconvenient rhetorical questions, these villagers wrap their resistance in sweet reason and tender impeccably respectable demands; at the same time, their rebukes reflect growing rights consciousness and a claim to equal status before the law.

In addition to inspiring challenges to unauthorized financial demands, a contract-based understanding of accountability is also apparent in China's rural areas as villagers turn a disapproving eye toward "unqualified" (*bu hege*) cadres and the undemocratic methods by which they are often selected. Delegations of rightful resisters, for example, frequently lodge complaints about rigged village elections, demand greater responsiveness, and request the removal of imperious local leaders (Howell, 1998: 103–4; Li, 2001; Liu, 2000: 30–34; Jennings, 1997: 366; O'Brien, 2001, 2003; O'Brien and Li, 2000, Zhongguo Jiceng Zhengquan Jianshe Yanjiuhui, 1994). Relying mainly on the Organic Law of Villagers' Committees (1987, revised 1998) and provincial regulations governing its implementation, some villagers make much of procedural violations (e.g., snap elections, stuffed ballot boxes, nomination abuses, annulled elections) concerning one of the more delicate issues in rural China: rules mandating how the village political elite is constituted.

While infractions of laws that stipulate election procedures, fee limits, land use, detention limits, and so on are generating rightful resistance in many locations, Chinese villagers also base their challenges on Party policies that have not been formalized in legislation. These include, for example, a circular on transparency and democratic management of village affairs, which entitles villagers to make claims related to financial disclosure (Zhonggong Zhongyang Bangongting and Guowuyuan Bangongting, 1998, June 1: 1); cadre responsibility systems, which set targets for cadres but also oblige them to respect villagers' rights (Edin, 2003; O'Brien and Li, 1999; Wedeman, 2001; Whiting, 2001: 100–18); minutely detailed village compacts and codes of conduct, which codify rights and responsibilities and provide standards for cadre supervision (Anagnost, 1992: 178; Bøckman, 2004; O'Brien, 1994b: 43–44);[5] and birth control regulations – not the policy itself, which is of course impervious to rightful resistance, but improper favoritism in allocating village-level quotas and other enforcement issues, such as the use of coercion, arbitrary fines, and the destruction of homes (O'Brien and Li, 1995; White, 2003: 189).[6]

---

[5] Such rules are, of course, also designed to control ordinary villagers. On the "10 Stars of Civilization," see Thøgersen (2000: 138–40) and O'Brien (2004). Village compacts date back to the eleventh-century Neo-Confucian ideas of Lü Dafang and were promoted by Wang Yangming in Jiangxi during the sixteenth century as a way "to ameliorate social duress or political unrest" (Bøckman, 2004: 7). Village compacts in late imperial China often stipulated tax regulations, corvée labor responsibilities, timber rights, and so on. During the Ming and Qing dynasties, the reading aloud of imperial edicts (at periodic meetings held to discuss compacts) made many villagers aware of central policies (Bøckman, 2004; also Elizabeth Perry, personal communication, 2005).

[6] In December 2001 a national law on population and birth planning was finally enacted. Although it states that officials must "enforce the law in a civilized manner, and must not infringe upon citizens' legitimate rights and interests" (art. 4), and calls for punishments for "abusing citizens" (art. 39), analysts (e.g., Winkler, 2002: 395–98) have noted that it does not fully define "legitimate rights and interests" or provide strong enforcement mechanisms. Popular contention surrounding this law has begun to occur. In rural Linyi, Shandong province, for example, a collective lawsuit was filed in 2005 against local authorities who demanded that families with two children permit one parent to be sterilized. A self-trained lawyer pressed the villagers' case until he was seized in Beijing by local authorities and spirited back to Linyi. Prior to the activist's detention, Yu Xuejin, a senior official with the National Family Planning Commission, applauded the villagers for asserting their rights and said that the practices they described in their lawsuit were "definitely illegal." He added that, if the 2001 Law's provisions on "informed consent" had been violated, "I support the ordinary people. If they need help, we'll help them find lawyers" (Pan, 2005, August 27; Pan,

All these protections offer ready-made rationales for demanding rights offered by the Center but denied at lower levels. When such well-grounded appeals do not meet with success, however, another set of somewhat more equivocal commitments provides a different sort of ammunition – usually less potent, but occasionally quite effective. Since the 1980s, villagers have been linking their claims with seemingly halfhearted campaigns "to clean up the government" (*lianzheng*), "to struggle against corruption" (*fan fubai douzheng*), "to build socialist democracy" (*jianshe shehuizhuyi minzhu*), "to build a country ruled by law" (*jianshe fazhi guojia*), and even to promote "citizenship rights" (*gongminquan*)[7] and "to protect human rights" (*baohu renquan*). Venturing forth in the name of unimpeachable ideals and in response to the Center's "call" (*haozhao*), they use the regime's own pledges to assail corrupt, predatory, and coercive cadres. At the same time, some villagers have also given new life to Maoist norms and buzzwords by summoning "communist values" to support demands that cadres "work hard and live plainly" and be willing to "serve the people" (Interviews 4, 6, 7, 8, 35). Acting now in the name of loyalty to the revolution and its founder, they "search for the real Communist Party" and level charges against "commandist" and grasping cadres who "oppress the masses" and are not "authentic communists" (e.g., Interviews 7, 22, 36, 37; Wang Wanfu, 1992: 33).[8]

Origins and Dynamics

Rural resistance is, of course, far from new in a nation where peasant rebellions have occurred for thousands of years and no decade since the fall of the Qing Dynasty has been entirely free of rural unrest (Bernhardt, 1992; Bianco, 2001; Perry, 1984, 1985; Thaxton, 1997; Unger, 2002: 49–72; Wong, 1997; Zweig, 1997: 130–50). Even more germane to our discussion, petitioning and appeals have long been elements in the Chinese

---

2005, September 7). Whether this law leads to an upsurge of rightful resistance surrounding reproductive policy remains to be seen.

[7] This discourse is particularly relevant to rightful resistance (Goldman and Perry, 2002; Gray, 2001; Keane, 2001; McCarthy, 2000; O'Brien, 2001; Parris, 1999; Solinger, 1999).

[8] Perry (2003b: 266, 270) underscores protest legacies that date to the Cultural Revolution and a "continuing reverence for certain Maoist values." Thornton (2004: 87–104) focuses on contemporary, rural tax resisters who have mounted "protest[s] that invoke the revolutionary language and class-based oppositions of the Mao era." Among state-owned workers, the laid-off, and retirees in China's cities, claims based on the "sacred rights" of the past are even more common (F. Chen, 2003; Hurst and O'Brien, 2002; Lee, 2000, 2001; but cf. Blecher, 2002).

repertoire of contention (Esherick and Wasserstrom, 1990; Minzner, 2005; Rankin, 1982; Ocko, 1988; G. Zhou, 1993), and it was Mao himself who launched mass campaigns against corrupt and unreliable grass-roots cadres and said "to rebel is justified" (Perry, 2003b). Throughout history, resourceful protest leaders have been conscious of central government rules and adept at seizing on official rhetoric – whether framed in terms of Confucianism or class struggle – to press claims against local power holders. In late imperial China, for example, tenants sometimes used government rulings as grounds to withhold rent payments, and villagers also objected to taxes when they felt local authorities had ignored proper collection procedures and were likely to back off when faced with complaints. Such challenges typically rested on appeals to equity and fairness, focusing on how the tax burden was apportioned or adjusted for harvest conditions and on the use of biased measures and conversion ratios (Bernstein and Lü, 2003: chap. 2; Wong, 1997: 235–37).[9] Some of these claims were even based on explicit references to tax codes and other government regulations (Bernhardt, 1992; Bianco, 2001).

Still, the rural rightful resistance we focus on in this book is not merely a recrudescence of routines that have existed since time immemorial, or an echo of the mobilized participation of the Maoist era, or a simple borrowing of legalistic tactics pioneered by Chinese workers and intellectuals.[10] For it is only with recent socioeconomic and political reforms that country folk have begun to blend traditional tactics with self-directed, legalistic, and arguably proactive struggles to assert their lawful rights and reconfigure

[9] Although this book highlights the upsurge in rights-based contention in recent years, rules consciousness and a sensitivity to the power of government discourse are, of course, not unprecedented in China. In the Laiyang tax revolt of 1910, for example, peasants considered the regular rates to be fair enough and employed them to fend off irregular levies. Like the rural complainants of a later era, their resistance was not purely a reactive effort to restore what they had. Beyond demanding the removal of exploitative tax farmers, the Laiyang protesters "also proposed a system to help ensure that corrupt power was not regenerated – namely, the public election of new functionaries to administer reform programs" (Prazniak, 1980: 59).

[10] Perry's (2003b: 265–66, 274) position is complex. Despite her emphasis on "continuations," she agrees that recent unrest is also partly a by-product of post-Mao reforms. Heilmann (1996) underscores the adaptation of old repertoires to new concerns and shows how borrowing slogans and tactics from the government arsenal to express heterodox views was a common tactic during the Cultural Revolution. We agree that Maoist practices set the stage for the partly institutionalized, partly legitimate resistance evident today, not least by altering popular expectations, inspiring innovation at the edge of the repertoire of contention, and making villagers more likely to act up when faced with official misconduct.

rural governance. Post-Mao reforms have shifted resources toward societal actors (K. Zhou and White, 1995) and have offered rural residents unparalleled opportunities to press new claims. As decollectivization and marketization have made villagers wealthier and less dependent on grass-roots cadres, the end of class labeling and mass political campaigns have made them less fearful. As increased mobility and media penetration have made them more knowledgeable about their exploitation and protest tactics devised elsewhere, so too administrative, electoral, and legal reforms have given them more protection against retaliation and more violations to protest.

These changes taken together have nurtured the recent upsurge of rightful resistance, rendering it less risky (O'Brien and Li, 1995: 761–67; Oi, 2004: 273)[11] and making it more effective than conventional petitioning and appealing to higher levels. Bottom-up initiative has become more viable because restive villagers are more aware of conflicts of interest with local cadres and more able to act without mobilization from above. Emboldened by what often seems to be a genuine belief that their "lawful rights" have been abridged, rural people are quite willing to invoke provocative symbols and mount high-profile protests.[12] Even in places where grass-roots cadres broker economic relationships and still control access to vital resources, villagers are better placed to defy corrupt or arbitrary rule and unsanctioned appropriation.

Of course, increased leverage over structurally weakened cadres does not automatically translate into effective contention. In today's China, rightful resisters seldom win the day uncontested. For one, "rural cadres generally do not welcome the diffusion of political information, especially about personal rights" (Yan, 1995: 235; also Interview 52; Ma Zhongdong, 2000; Yu Xin, 1993; Zhang Cuiling, 2002), and some openly try to sabotage central efforts to foster "popular legal education" (*pufa*) (Chen Lumin, 2001; Xi Ling, 1993). Grass-roots leaders typically feel that more knowledgeable

---

[11] These risks are, of course, still substantial. See Chapter 4, Bernstein and Lü (2003), Bianco (2001: 251–53), Guo (2001: 434–35), and O'Brien and Li (1995: 776–77).

[12] In a seven-year dispute over the illegal renaming of a township, hundreds of Shanxi villagers demonstrated in front of a county office building, demanding that the responsible officials come out. A group of the complainants marched carrying lit lanterns and candles (in broad daylight!) to prove that they could not "see" under the township's dark rule (Li Renhu and Yu Zhenhai, 1993: 32–36). This case is a textbook example of rightful resistance because the villagers based their claims on two State Council regulations, sought to locate allies in the county and provincial government, and engaged in arguably lawful collective action.

villagers are harder to control, and they sometimes detain or rough up villagers for publicizing central policies (Ding Guoguang, 2001: 433–34; Interviews 4, 7, 17, 19, 21).

At the same time, equally established principles support existing power relations and serve to delegitimize even well-grounded rightful resistance. Chinese villagers, for example, may speak of "democracy" and their right to "reflect problems and expose bad cadres," but cadres can often trump them by invoking "Party leadership" and the need to maintain "stability above all" (e.g., Interview 53). Or when farmers charge that it is unlawful to lock them up simply because a family member has violated the birth control policy, a public security officer may just as persuasively counter that forcing relatives to attend full-time, daily "study sessions" is warranted because a "national policy" (*guoce*) like family planning takes precedence over any law and every citizen has an obligation to assist in its enforcement (Interview 53; also Yu Jianrong, 2001: 474–88).

For their part, accused cadres typically try to discredit and disrupt rightful resistance by pointing to norms sanctioning coercion and also to political expediency. Most grass-roots leaders are proficient at casting all contention in the ominous light of "rebellion against the government" (*fan zhengfu*) or even "organizing a counterrevolutionary group" (*zuzhi fangeming jituan*), and at countering legal tactics and smothering collective action by winning support from officials at higher levels (Interviews 4, 21). Township- and county-level Party secretaries, for example, frequently side with notoriously high-handed village cadres so long as they enforce birth control regulations and induce villagers to pay their taxes and fees (Interviews 4, 21, 36, 37; Zhang Chenggong, 1993; Zeng Yesong, 1995). County leaders, in particular, tend to be receptive to pleas from township officials that they face dozens of genuinely incompatible demands that even the most conscientious cadre could never meet (O'Brien and Li, 1999: 179; on prioritizing, see Edin, 2003: 51–52; Frazier, 2004: 47–48).

Many cadres use these conflicting norms and expectations to make rightful resisters appear unreasonable and to justify not implementing a popular measure or institutional protection. When all is said and done, officials at higher levels often end up dispatching the police to suppress villagers who disrupt a rigged election or lodge a collective complaint about excessive appropriation – particularly if the targeted cadre lubricates a request for protection with a generous bribe (Interviews 14, 21, 54, 55). And even if they find it impolitic to defend a cadre openly, township and county leaders can often convince judicial authorities to conduct perfunctory investigations of highly credible charges, or spend years taking testimony and auditing finances (Interview 14).[13] In present-day China, a strong legal case and the use of compelling normative language is merely the ante for rightful resisters; to overcome the many advantages local cadres still enjoy, protest leaders must also secure support from allies who have more clout than their adversaries.

In this regard, some protest leaders have proved themselves to be adept at finding advocates (including journalists)[14] who are willing to investigate their charges and champion their claims.[15] Enterprising protest leaders skillfully ferret out supporters and sympathizers in various bureaucracies who have a stake in seeing their appeals addressed and in upholding the policies they invoke. Officials in the Ministry of Civil Affairs and its local offices, for instance, have frequently received delegations of villagers protesting infractions of the Organic Law of Villagers' Committees – a law the ministry is entrusted to implement.[16] Discipline Inspection Commissions, for their part, have become a focus for collective complaints concerning violation of Party discipline, whereas local people's congresses, in the course of promoting "rule by law" and "socialist democracy," often attract groups of villagers who point to the villagers' committee law and local implementing regulations when combating election irregularities.[17] Newspapers' "mass work departments" (*qunzhong gongzuo bu*) may refer popular complaints to

---

[13] In Hebi city, Henan, about 60 percent of the collective complaints lodged in 1993 demanded an audit of village financial records, sometimes up to ten years' worth (Fang Guomin, 1993: 36). Rigged and delayed audits were also a major concern of interviewees 54 and 55.

[14] On "activist journalists" who seek to pressure officials and solve problems informally by threatening media coverage, see Liebman (2005: 110–13). In one village where we have conducted research, a group of complainants has raised a collection to hire a journalist (preferably from the national television program *Focus*) to investigate its charges. See Chapter 4 for a discussion of new tactics that have been developed in response to difficulties locating allies who will follow through on their promises.

[15] Hobsbawm (1973: 15) writes: "It is as though the villagers, always conscious of potential strength even within their subalternity, required only the assurance of goodwill or even mere toleration from the highest authorities to straighten their backs."

[16] Jean Oi (2004: 278) reports that one indicator of the importance that the ministry attaches to popular complaints is that it has assigned a staff member to be available twenty-four hours a day to handle emergencies concerning petitioners.

[17] Local people's congresses have also become a common venue to level charges that the Administrative Litigation Law has been subverted (Li Chao, 2002; Lian Jimin, 2000; O'Brien and Li, 2004: 87–88; Peng Fei, 2000).

reporters or to the authorities and occasionally publish them openly or in internal editions (Liebman, 2005: 102–10).[18] Even the many government-run "letters and visits offices" (*xinfang ban*) that dot the country can serve as a clearinghouse for grievances, and at times they have roused ranking officials to investigate accusations of wrongdoing (Cai, 2004; X. Chen, 2003; Luehrmann, 2003; Thireau and Hua, 2003).

Given the limited institutionalization of Chinese politics and because their opponents usually have protectors among the local notables who matter most, rightful resisters typically find it advantageous to press their claims wherever they can.[19] They recognize that state power nowadays is both fragmented and divided against itself, and, if they search diligently, they can often locate pressure points where elite unity crumbles. They are perfectly aware that their contention hinges on exploiting the divergent interests of officials in both different "systems" (*xitong*) and at different levels in the same system, and they astutely align themselves with "benefactors" (*enren*) who they believe are disposed to take their charges seriously and who have the authority to ensure that a cadre is disciplined or prosecuted.

Rightful resistance, in the final analysis, is a way for villagers to attack abusive cadres with rights claims rather than with their "shoulder poles."[20] It is pursued by those who (at least outwardly) accept Party rule and who go along with many unwelcome measures (e.g., birth control and legal taxation) in exchange for unflinching execution of all beneficial policies.[21] Such individuals cede the high ground to official values, shape their challenges from materials made available by the structure of domination, and appeal to elites who recognize that their claims are consistent with established principles. Aware of the risks involved in other, less dependent forms of contention, they forgo revolutionary demands and offer consent (and

---

[18] Liebman (2005: 106) reports response rates of approximately 25 and 40 percent, respectively, for popular complaints forwarded from *Worker's Daily* and *People's Daily*.

[19] Minzner (2005) recounts a petition campaign in Faxi county, Shaanxi, in which hundreds of villagers from 1996 to 2001 did not focus on a single organ but instead sought attention and support from a range of higher-level Party and government departments, including Party committees, letters and visits offices, National People's Congress deputies, and procurators. Their strategy was underpinned by a belief that these potential allies could draw in key leadership figures and enhance the odds their grievances would be addressed.

[20] On concerns that angry villagers may one day attack grass-roots leaders with their shoulder poles, see Peng Zhen's speech to the Law Committee of the National People's Congress, April 6, 1987, excerpted in Bai Yihua (2002: 20–25).

[21] For data on the demographic background of protest leaders in rural China, see Appendix A.

14

even support) to rulers who control their agents and enforce their commitments.[22] Their claims do not always fall on deaf ears because some members of the elite believe that offering redress may help placate the discontented and reduce the likelihood of unrest while improving policy implementation and cadre oversight (Interviews 1, 2, 56; Zhou Qingyin and Wang Xinya, 2000a, 2000b).

That rightful resistance is turning up in the Chinese countryside is perhaps not a great surprise, given the chasm between what the Center offers and what local officials deliver. But rightful resistance does not appear only where accountability is advocated but weakly institutionalized and rights are granted but weakly guaranteed. Elites in other settings may also be encouraged by rights talk and political pressure to surrender advantages in accord with principles that usually favor them. In places far from rural China, different established values, legitimating myths, and government commitments may also provide a basis for rightful resistance.

Comparative Perspectives

Most social scientists would agree that the value of a concept is closely related to how well it travels (Collier and Levitsky, 1997; Collier and Mahon, 1993; Gerring, 2001).[23] A truly useful construct has to survive applications beyond its original context; it must continue "to yield defensible interpretations as new social phenomena swim into view" (Geertz, 1973: 27).

With this in mind, this section looks to research by others to explore possible instances of rightful resistance outside of China. Three of the examples presented are partial and illustrate only elements of rightful resistance. One is more complete. Our aim here is to highlight a common dynamic: to identify "deep analogies" (Tilly, 1981: 8) or "conceptual equivalencies" (Rueschemeyer, 2003: 328) that can help us "make sense of numerous details that otherwise would seem purely accidental" (Sewell, 1996: 262). Without glossing over dissimilarities, we can try to locate parallels that help "break

---

[22] Many students of protest have noted that "even while resisting power, individuals or groups may simultaneously support the structures of domination that necessitate resistance in the first place" (Hollander and Einwohner, 2004: 549). This pattern of resistance paired with accommodation allows protesters to "challenge their own positions within a particular social structure, while not challenging the validity of the overall structure (Hollander and Einwohner, 2004: 549).

[23] In Gerring's (2001: 54) words: "A concept that applies broadly is more useful than a concept with only a narrow range of application. A good concept stretches comfortably over many contexts; a poor concept, by contrast, is parochial – limited to a small linguistic turf."

out the relevant part of the narrative" (Stinchcombe, 1978: 15, 21). And while remaining attentive to variation stemming from a host of factors,[24] and doing our best to avoid "theory-drivenness" (Shapiro, 2002: 597),[25] we can begin to gauge the generality of the findings from China and avoid wrapping a concept around a single case.

One example of the boundary-spanning claims characteristic of rightful resistance is the "censoriousness" of Norwegian prison inmates, who base their demands for better treatment on prison regulations and recognized principles of justice (e.g., equality). According to Thomas Mathiesen (1965: 13), such prisoners "argue with the ruler on the basis of norms that the ruler also agrees with, trying to convince the ruler that he has not correctly adhered to these principles." These expert faultfinders employ the rhetoric and values of the wider society and the legal system their jailers represent while targeting "personal regimes" and a demanding "bureaucracy" (Mathiesen, 1965: 178, 187). In their efforts to domesticate power and render it predictable, they fall short of rightful resistance mainly because few inmates are able to locate elite advocates and because their potential for nonviolent political pressure is subject to obvious limitations.

In contrast to an actual prison, apartheid-era South Africa offered somewhat greater scope for using official values to goad concerned authorities into action. In Richard Abel's (1995: 23–65) account of opposition to the "pass laws," black plaintiffs and their legal advisers pointed to inconsistent and ambiguous regulatory structures and demanded that the government prove its commitment to the rule of law. Invoking South Africa's "liberal tradition" and Nationalist boasts about judicial independence, they contested racial discrimination "on the terrain of ideology" and "honored the regime's pretensions by judging it in terms of legality" (Abel, 1995: 12, 541, 13). By framing their claims with reference to official values (including the sanctity of the family) and stressing misimplementation of judicial decisions, they won over key insiders (including some government attorneys, large employers, and judges) who endorsed their appeals and urged obstructionist enforcement agencies to heed the law. Although their foes hid behind procedural maneuvers and principles that condoned apartheid, workers and

---

[24] Some relevant factors include which government commitments resisters invoke, which elite allies are available, which opponents are targeted, how political pressure is applied, and how willing authorities are to resort to ruining rightful resisters outside the law.

[25] Shapiro (2002: 603) compares the search for "general theories of everything" to "looking for a general theory of holes."

their families were able to use the language of power to win residency rights when obliging judges invalidated local rulings and condemned stalling tactics (Abel, 1995: 28–43, 61–62, 539). Accommodating elites played a central role in this contention, unlike the Norwegian example, but this case still falls short of rightful resistance because, by the 1980s, opponents of influx controls focused on single-client legal challenges, while less institutionalized forms of political pressure (with the exception of a small amount of squatting) were not employed.

State socialist regimes, as we might expect, have proved to be a fertile ground for claims and tactics that call to mind rightful resistance. In Jeremy Straughn's treatment of "consentful contention" in East Germany in the 1960s and 1970s, young men who refused to be inducted into the military and cultural figures who protested the expulsion of a satirical singer-songwriter appealed to the state's legitimating principles to resist decisions that they felt were opposed to those principles (Straughn, 2005). Using artful arguments or group petitions, they adopted the role (or pose) of a "dutiful citizen" (Straughn, 2005: 1601, 1604, 1641) and sought "to test the sincerity of the state's adherence to formally guaranteed rights" (Straughn, 2005: 1604). By "taking the state at its word" (Straughn, 2005: 1602), they displayed loyalty and deference to the powers-that-were, while also plumbing the limits of the permissible. Their contention did not challenge the official value system as a whole, and so long as their claims and tactics did not cause an undue loss of face for those in power, they found some room to operate and a cautious tolerance for their actions (Straughn, 2005).

Like Chinese rightful resisters, practitioners of consentful contention often displayed "exceptional agency, creativity and skill" in an attempt to "beat the authorities at their own game" (Straughn, 2005: 1607, 1626). Their rhetorical strategy involved insisting that the powerful comply with their demands or be seen as hypocritical, and their stated mission was to close the gap between real-existing socialism and its legitimating claims (Straughn, 2005). As in China, their intentions and behavior were not easy to categorize as loyal or oppositional, not least because a cautious style of claims making and measured tactics provided a ready cover story and a degree of plausible deniability when events turned against them (Straughn, 2005: 1608).

Straughn's "consentful contention" differs from rightful resistance in rural China mainly because the central-local divide does not figure in generating grievances or in providing openings for protesters to exploit, and because rights claims were not as central as they have become in China.[26] Protesters in East Germany instead pointed to a broad range of values, interests, and vulnerabilities in the regime's legitimation project, including the defense of socialism, the reputation of the GDR as the incarnation of German socialism, and the state's promise to provide basic material security for its citizens (Straughn, 2005).[27]

In the most repressive regimes, resistance is largely limited to "weapons of the weak" (Scott, 1985). In slightly less controlled settings, one or more features of rightful resistance may appear. As sanctioned coercion diminishes further and partial inclusion is formally extended, cases of more complete rightful resistance become possible, as in rural China. But what about further along the spectrum? In circumstances where numerous rights are guaranteed, the rule of law is established, and political participation is unquestionably legitimate, is rightful resistance still viable and effective? Consider Michael McCann's analysis of how women workers in the United States employed legal strategies and collective action to press for wage reforms.

According to McCann (1994: ix), several familiar approaches to law and social change all share a skepticism "about the value of law for empowering marginalized and even ordinary citizens." Modern neorealists, he explains, often portray litigation (concerning civil rights, women's rights, environmental protection, and so forth) as a "hollow hope" (Rosenberg, 1991) – a strategy flawed by the limited resources that even congenial judges can muster to implement their decisions (McCann, 1994: 290–93). Structuralists, on the other hand, stress the limited resources possessed by disadvantaged citizens themselves and the unlikelihood these resources will be well spent on quixotic legal battles where the probability of success is low (McCann, 1994: 293–95). Even many Marxist scholars emphasize how law can mystify the powerless and disguise domination, largely by imposing definitions of property advantageous to ruling groups and by

---

[26] This is not to say that all rightful resistance in China is strictly rights-based. Especially in the early post-Mao years, when few laws existed and most policies were broadly framed and open to interpretation, some villagers' claims hinged on "communist values" and Maoist norms, such as equality, the mass line, "the four freedoms," and cadres "working hard and living plainly," "being honest and clean," and "serving the people" (Li and O'Brien, 1996: 45–46; O'Brien, 1996: 40; Perry, 2003b; Thornton, 2004). Rightful resistance in this period was, in other words, even closer to Straughn's "consentful contention."

[27] We regard consentful contention and rightful resistance to be members of a family of contention. Both share resemblances but it is impossible, without developing many more cases, to say which is more typical of the family (Wittgenstein, 1958).

sustaining dubious claims to legitimacy (for a critique, see Thompson, 1975: 258–61).

Nonetheless, as McCann found in his study of the pay equity campaign in the United States, ordinary workers and movement organizers had more access to the law than he had ever anticipated (McCann, 1994: ix; also Schultz, 1998). Although prevailing legal discourses and practices were at times forces that obstructed challenges to the status quo, they too could be a source of disorder and egalitarian reordering. Litigation and other legal tactics, in other words, were potent and flexible tools that enabled women's rights activists to employ existing statutes and recognized legal symbols while still remaining somewhat separate from the prevailing legal order. By the end of his research, McCann had come to question many assumptions about the conservative impact of established legal practices and was instead drawn to evidence of inventive tactical maneuvers and "site-specific accommodations between domination and resistance" (McCann, 1994: 9).

These tactical maneuvers originated on precisely the "old ground" (Hunt, 1990: 313, 320, 324) on which rightful resistance appears. In the United States this meant appropriating a "rights talk" that had long offered reform activists a normative language for identifying, interpreting, and challenging discrimination. In particular, comparable worth advocates borrowed from a decades-old discourse about equal rights, discrimination, and segregation that had become part of everyday understandings and expectations. They then used this language to express their demands for reworked wage scales, draping calls for reform in evocative and comparatively uncontroversial appeals to fairness and equity (McCann, 1994, 49, 101, 245–58).[28]

In the course of mastering a new tongue, pay equity activists found it advantageous to couple broad references to widely accepted values with appeals to specific laws and regulations, at both the state and the federal levels. Accordingly, movement participants drew on explicit comparable worth, pay equity, and equal pay statutes, as well as more general equal rights, antidiscrimination, civil service, and fair employment measures. Most notably, several Supreme Court decisions, the Equal Pay Act of 1963, the 1964 Civil Rights Act, and various executive orders were all repeatedly

---

[28] "Openings for resistance derive from the regular exercise of power. . . . Resistant acts use, in unforeseen and inventive ways, the resources that are at hand, the very same aspects of social structure that support power and domination" (Ewick and Silbey, 2003: 1330, 1336).

cited when attacking wage discrimination in the courts (McCann, 1994: 41, 48–50).

Established law thus offered a framework for equity activists to make sense of their circumstances and to ground their contention. At the same time, evolving antidiscrimination norms made it possible to take advantage of the flexibility of the American rights tradition to cloak new claims in old cloth. By urging, for instance, that job evaluation methods previously used to justify hierarchy be reinterpreted to support salary increases for low-ranking workers, rights activists appropriated "the master's tool to challenge the master" (McCann, 1994: 185). In their actions on the courtroom steps and in the courtroom alike, pay equity proponents shrewdly framed even their more radical demands in terms of loyalty to established principles while professing little more than a desire to make the legal system "live up to what it was supposed to be" (McCann, 1994: 234; also see 298–99).

Breaking through the silence and pursuing their claims depended on a series of timely events – some of which occurred apart from the movement, some of which were engineered by campaign activists themselves. In the first place, the overarching political opportunity structure had to shift in ways that supported, or at least allowed, articulation of new claims by individuals concerned with gender justice. At the same time, early arrivals had to become aware that the political landscape had become more advantageous, and they then had to exploit this realization to draw in additional participants who were willing to devote time, energy, and resources to the campaign. Both of these conditions were effectively met by the late 1970s, as more women entered the work force, the women's movement matured, and an accommodating Carter administration made it possible for participation in the campaign to appear sensible to prospective participants (McCann, 1994: chap. 4).

With awareness, expectations, and organizational resources mounting, a few high-profile legal victories then helped convince even more recruits that wage structures could be altered and that a meaningful space for grass-roots action had opened up. Buoyed by their successes, organizing national legal challenges and local pressure on employers became easier, as previously uninvolved workers and long-standing activists came to believe they were acting at a particularly auspicious moment, ripe with possibilities for reform (McCann, 1994: 64, 74, 89).

To increase their leverage and institutionalize their gains, activists also sought out influential backers, particularly ones who would take up the cause within the federal and state governments. Among the movement's champions were a handful of government administrators who were responsive to the campaign's "realistic radicalism." Some federal officials had in fact endorsed pay equity reform from an early date: lawyers and officials in the Department of Labor and the Equal Employment Opportunity Commission were instrumental in developing and initially publicizing the notion of comparable worth, whereas committees on the status of women and elected female representatives and their staffs had pressed pay equity reform in several dozen states and the U.S. Congress (McCann, 1994: 276, 52, 123–29). Other officials, however, opposed reform from the start, and withdrawal of support was not uncommon. The Equal Employment Opportunity Commission and federal judges, for example, were generally receptive to pay equity claims during the Carter administration, but the Reagan years brought a response more hostile to litigation and political pressure.

To their credit, movement activists found ways to endure and even exploit their fair-weather friends in the federal government. The pay equity campaign grew, even though not a single, unambiguous judicial endorsement of its underlying comparable worth theory managed to survive appellate review. Resourceful equity advocates needed only a tiny opening for their resistance to develop a momentum of its own. Even after judicial defeats became commonplace during the 1980s, movement organizers persevered. In fact, frustration with Reagan-era interpretations of civil rights law led to a redeployment of organizational resources from legal campaigns to collective bargaining, lobbying, and other forms of grass-roots collective action. And this strategic retreat seems to have catalyzed rather than retarded the movement (McCann, 1994: 58, 53, 64, 85–86).

In the end, the campaign's limited successes arose from using "law as a club" and "bargaining in the shadow of the law." A range of tactics heightened uncertainty and posed risks to employers while creating a favorable environment for negotiation. Although more confrontational, openly transgressive forms of contention were rendered impractical by the reliance on prevailing channels of inclusion and on advocates within the executive and judicial branches, the campaign did help alter workplace practices and promoted other efforts to enhance workplace rights, even as the movement itself was contained (McCann, 1994: 140, 143, 220, 285, 232, 281–82).

To imagine that rightful resistance, in the United States or anywhere, can remake a political system from top to bottom is a lot to expect from a form of contention that is, by its nature, accommodating and circumscribed. Lasting impacts are more likely to be a consequence of intensified rights consciousness in populations that are experiencing "cognitive liberation"

(McAdam, 1982: 34) and in people who recognize that their capacity for action is growing.[29] In the United States, McCann notes, the legacy of pay equity reform included other, more significant advances that "matched or exceeded wage gains" (McCann, 1994: 281). The movement, for instance, increased sensitivity to social wrongs and strengthened organizational ties, as pay equity became a "symbol for a broad and growing political agenda of gender based reform in the workplace" (McCann, 1994: 269, 271). The cohesion and solidarity forged in one struggle swiftly spilled over to other, often more successful campaigns for improved child care, sexual harassment regulations, parental leave, and health care for pregnant women (McCann, 1994: 268).

The greatest impact of the pay equity campaign, however, was probably on the activists themselves: participation in the movement affected their "hearts, minds, and social identities" by transforming their "understandings, commitments, and affiliations" (McCann, 1994: 230). As previously unvoiced or whispered objections grew into loudly asserted claims, thousands of working women became proficient at generating pressure on employers and "mobilizing rights as a political resource" (McCann, 1994: 276). Rather than being lulled by the law and its ability to confer legitimacy, they broke its spell and used legal practices and institutions to create protected spaces in which to act. In the end, taking rights seriously "opened up more than closed debates, exposed more than masked systemic injustices, stirred more than pacified discontents, and nurtured more than retarded the development of solidarity" (McCann, 1994: 232). Instead of reinforcing prevailing power relations, rights advocacy sparked dialogues, validated new ways of thinking, posed troubling questions, and spurred a desire for political change (McCann, 1994: 269).

The effort to win equal pay for women workers in the United States nicely exhibits the main attributes of rightful resistance:

- Reliance on established principles to anchor challenges
- Use of legitimating myths and persuasive normative language to frame claims
- Deployment of existing statutes and commitments when leveling charges
- Recognition and exploitation of congenial aspects of a shifting opportunity structure
- Importance of allies, however uncertain, within officialdom

---

[29] On the outcomes of rightful resistance in rural China, see Chapters 5 and 6.

- Combination of legal tactics with grass-roots collective action
- Disavowal of overtly revolutionary alternatives
- Partial victories and built-in limitations of a form of resistance that embraces values endorsed by conscientious political and economic elites

Rightful resistance in a democracy, as illustrated by McCann, is one way that dissatisfied citizens try to make officials and business leaders "prisoners of their own rhetoric" (see Thompson, 1975: 263). It is a form of contention ideally suited to bargain for rights vis-à-vis local authorities and pursue new rights claims, because at its heart lies the eminently reasonable expectation that rules and norms that usually reinforce dominance should be equitably and universally enforced. Enterprising rightful resisters in a nation such as the United States have astutely recognized that legal symbols and norms create practical obligations that can be used to mobilize the discontented and to limit the abuse of power (McCann, 1994: 297–98). They know, along with E. P. Thompson (1975: 263), that for the law and other official norms to appear just, they must, sometimes, be just.[30]

Rightful resisters may act out of conviction or they may strategically manipulate official norms. Most often, their motivations probably combine elements of both sincerity and cynicism.[31] As Straughn (2005) points out in his study of East German popular contention, it is not easy to pin down the extent to which a specific instance of contestation was dissimulative, opportunistic, and context dependent, or an authentic and honest effort to make socialism real.[32] Whatever the case, rightful resisters are adept at picking out where claims to authority lie and at maneuvering within systems that otherwise control them (in a different context, see Willis,

---

[30] Hunt (1990: 311) has also noted, in discussing Gramsci's understanding of the relationship of law to social change, that "for a hegemonic project to be dominant it must address and incorporate, if only partially, some aspects of the aspirations, interests, and ideology of subordinate groups."

[31] Analysts have underscored the sincerity of "moral economy" and law-related claims made by laid-off, urban workers and unpaid pensioners in China (F. Chen, 2003; Hurst, 2004; Hurst and O'Brien, 2002; Lee, 2000: 219, 225–28; Lee, 2001: 215; Thireau and Hua, 2003) – without denying they also have a strategic element. On Chinese workers who are subject to the hegemony of the market and the state, see Blecher (2002). In the contemporary countryside, many rightful resisters appear to be "true believers" at first (Li, 2004), who become increasingly cynical and instrumental as various levels of government fail them (Interviews 4, 5, 6, 13, 21, 36, 37). On dissimulators "piggybacking" on the sincere, see Straughn (2005: 1609).

[32] On difficulties in gaining access to the "internal states" of protesters, see Hollander and Einwohner (2004: 542).

1977: 26–27). They have partly cast off the "mind-forged manacles" (Hay, 1975: 49),[33] through which law and other established values reap obedience and deference, and have recognized that the weaknesses of any would-be hegemonic ideology provide grounds for resistance.

Rightful resistance is a hardy perennial that can sprout wherever the authorities make commitments they cannot keep. A partly institutionalized type of contention, it works largely at the edges of an existing opportunity structure, and it can be more consequential than most "everyday resistance" but still less risky than wholly uninstitutionalized defiance. Its successes come about not because its practitioners remain unobtrusive or because they are insulated from hegemonic penetration,[34] but because they openly and opportunistically engage the structure of domination (and pierce the hegemony) at its weakest point. Using the materials at hand, rightful resisters align themselves with lawful authority, however it is constituted, and confront power holders who compromise the ideals that justify their rule. So long as a gap exists between rights promised and rights delivered, there is always room for rightful resistance to emerge.

[33] Although Hay (1975: 34) allows for resistance based on law, he focuses on the persuasiveness of law as ideology and its contribution to legitimacy.

[34] On the advantages of insulation from hegemonic discourses, see Scott (1977). Our treatment of engaging the hegemony is closer to that developed in Scott (1990: 94–107) and Lazarus-Black and Hirsch (1994).

2

Opportunities and Perceptions

Is there truly a gap between the Center and lower levels that Chinese villagers can exploit? Rightful resistance cannot appear without divisions in the state or, put more simply, without patrons and villains. Potential activists must blame their troubles on misconduct by local officials and believe they have allies at higher levels whom they can turn to for help. The emergence of rightful resistance in rural China is thus a story about both opportunities and perceptions. There must be openings to exploit and villagers who can locate them and make the most of them.

Understanding Opportunities

Studies of political opportunity have become much more nuanced of late (Meyer and Minkoff, 2004; Tarrow, 1996). Researchers have moved beyond discussions of a single, national "opportunity structure" to examine under what conditions a particular opportunity inspires or discourages mobilization (e.g., Suh, 2001: 456). Students of movement origins increasingly appreciate that windows for action are often not open or closed but are partly opened (Sawyers and Meyer, 1999: 189), and that opportunities may vary by policy or group (Gamson and Meyer, 1996: 289; Tarrow, 1996: 42–43). When accounting for protest, there is new attention to contradictory trends and the complexity of external environments (Goodwin and Jasper, 1999: 53; Meyer and Minkoff, 2004: 1484). Reflecting calls to do more splitting to balance the lumping (Goodwin and Jasper, 1999: 53; Koopmans, 1999), scholars talk of the need to "unpack political opportunity" (Gamson and Meyer, 1996: 277) and to recognize that mobilization is often a question of "opportunities for what?" (Meyer and Minkoff, 2004: 1484).

At the same time, there has been growing interest in the role that perceptions play in the onset of collective action. By now it is a truism to say that structural openings alone do not generate protest. Outside developments related to repression, institutional access, elite rifts, and influential allies affect the potential for contention, but how people understand their situation always intervenes between opportunity and action (della Porta and Diani, 1999: 224; Gamson and Meyer, 1996: 283; McAdam, 1982: 48; McAdam, McCarthy, and Zald, 1996: 2). For protests to occur, potential activists must recognize that an opening exists (or discover it in action) (Koopmans, 2005: 26–28) and decide that they have the wherewithal to bring about change. For many scholars, perceived opportunities are just as important as structural ones (Goodwin and Jasper, 1999: 52–53; Kurzman, 1996; Suh, 2001) and an unnoticed opening may be no opening at all (Gamson and Meyer, 1996: 283; Koopmans and Olzak, 2004: 201). In more cultural and phenomenological accounts, in fact, there may be no such thing as opportunities prior to interpretation, or none that matter (Goodwin and Jasper, 1999: 33). At the very least, a consensus seems to be emerging that we should view opportunities as subject to attribution – inducements and deterrents that must be perceived if they are to be significant (della Porta and Diani, 1999: 223; McAdam, Tarrow, and Tilly, 2001: 43; Tarrow, 1998: 77).

And this process of attribution is fraught with uncertainty. There need not be a tight fit between perceptions and the "objective" opportunity structure (Kurzman, 1996: 154, 164). Some openings are missed, while others are thought to be present when they are not (Kurzman, 1996: 154; Meyer and Minkoff, 2004: 1463–64; Sawyers and Meyer, 1999). Elite signals are often misread and invitations to mobilize may be more hedged than protesters realize. Although external factors provide incentives and affect expectations (Tarrow, 1998: 76–77), the cues the aggrieved heed are inevitably filtered through shared understandings and interpretations (della Porta and Diani, 1999: 224; McAdam, McCarthy, and Zald, 1996: 8; Suh, 2001: 437). Whatever structural openings exist, agency, cognitive processes, and choice are involved in every decision to take to the streets (della Porta and Diani, 1999: 224; Goodwin and Jasper, 1999: 53).

A Preview of the Argument

In the rest of this chapter, we first explain the structural opening that makes rightful resistance possible in rural China. This opening is not so much issue- or group-specific as one that crops up because officials in a multilevel hierarchy have encountered monitoring problems and have turned to the public to help control their underlings. After defining the opening, we explore several crosscurrents that limit it. Disgruntled individuals in rural China are faced with a dizzying array of open, closed, and partially open doors. "Unpacking political opportunity" reveals conflicting trends at work and reminds us that elite allies can be fickle friends or even two-faced (Lipsky, 1968: 1158; McAdam, 1982: 27–29; Tarrow, 1998: 89).

Then we turn to perceptions of opportunity. We find that mixed signals from inside the state shape the expectations and feed the hopes of both protesters and their targets. A host of conflicting cues have made it difficult for villagers to determine if there is a gap between the Center and lower levels, how big it is, and how safe and effective it is to try to exploit it. Here, we underscore the role of information. Information about beneficial policies spurs rightful resisters into action, but this information is often neither perfect nor complete, nor is the interpretation of it infallible. This is the key reason why there often is a poor fit between perceptions and structural opportunities. Sometimes it is extremely hard to figure out what one's environment encourages and ill-advised decisions are easily made. Nevertheless, as several of our surveys show, a certain pattern of trust and blame attribution has come to be shared among rightful resisters and a significant swath of the rural population. And this set of understandings, mainly about the intentions and capacity of different levels of government, has fostered the conversion of a structural opening into an actionable opportunity to take a chance on rightful resistance.

A Structural Opening

Although it has not been a major theme among researchers who disaggregate political opportunity, there has been some recognition that openings for protest are affected by the actors and institutions that make up a state (Gale, 1986; Goldstone, 2003: 20; Goodwin and Jasper, 1999: 53). McAdam, McCarthy, and Zald (1988: 721), for example, have argued that it is a mistake to imagine that agencies always act in consort to oppose or support popular action, while Klandermans (1997: 193) has suggested that there is also no reason to assume that different levels of government always adopt the same posture toward protesters. Although full-throated opposition by a united state is undoubtedly common, some officials may support certain aims of activists, and the authorities at one level may even encourage challengers to apply pressure on another level (McAdam, McCarthy, and Zald, 1988: 721; Klandermans, 1997: 193–94). Still, to this point, too few researchers have looked at how opportunities are affected by state fragmentation (Zald, 2000: 12); nor has it been widely appreciated that in otherwise strong, authoritarian regimes, allies and even "institutional activists" (Santoro and McGuire, 1997) can sometimes be found within the state (cf. Schock, 1999).

That a layered structure can offer the powerless a chance to make the authorities work for them rather than against them (Klandermans, 1997: 197) accords well with what we have found in rural China. Like many sprawling, multilevel polities, the Chinese state is plagued by monitoring problems and information slippage between policy makers and street-level officials. Central leaders in Beijing often find themselves in the dark when they seek to assess how well their programs have been executed because local power holders block the flow of any information that casts them in an unflattering light. As a result, the Center is often unable to detect breaches of its policies, let alone discipline its disloyal officials.

The problem of misimplementation in rural China has been particularly vexing concerning measures that aim to protect ordinary people (O'Brien and Li, 1999; on tax and fee limits, see Bernstein and Lü, 2003). Since the 1980s, the central government has announced a number of policies designed to limit local extraction, increase the transparency of village finance, introduce villagers' self-government, and prevent local officials from using undue force. On the ground, however, many local officials have ignored these commitments, often with impunity. They have imposed arbitrary fees, diverted public funds, manipulated village elections, expropriated land, and used coercion against reluctant villagers (Bernstein and Lü, 2003; Cai, 2003; Guo, 2001; O'Brien and Li, 1999; Wedeman, 2001). According to two officials in the Ministry of Civil Affairs, policies that instruct local officials to respect villagers' "lawful rights and interests" are typically "hot in the center, warm in the provinces, lukewarm in the cities, cool in the counties, cold in the townships, and frozen in the villages" (Duan Zhiqiang and Tang Jinsu, 1989: 13). Or even more vividly, in the words of a Hebei villager interviewed in 1999, "what the State Council says is completely overwhelmed by local 'countermeasures' [duice]. A force-ten typhoon at the Center fades to a gentle breeze by the time it reaches us ordinary people" (Interview 57).

This divide between the central government and its local representatives creates an opening for rightful resistance – so long as the Center really means what it says. The best evidence suggests that the apparent discord between the Center and local officials is not entirely imaginary. For one, the official news media have repeatedly affirmed Beijing's commitment to control policy violations while criticizing cadres who neglect central policies and infringe on villagers' "lawful rights." *People's Daily*, which is the official mouthpiece of the Central Committee, published, for example, 2,408 articles from the beginning of 1995 to the end of 2003 advocating reductions in "peasant burdens" (*nongmin fudan*), averaging more than 5 articles per week. In the same period, it printed more than 1,000 articles that discussed respecting the "lawful rights and interests" (*hefa quanyi*) of rural people. Outspoken national leaders, moreover, have on more than one occasion lashed out (in public) at wayward local power holders. Premier Zhu Rongji, for instance, at a press conference in 1998, denounced cadres who had created "seething popular discontent" by increasing peasant burdens (Li Ke and Fan Rongjun, 1998, March 19: 1).[1] In March 2004, despite continuing objections from provincial leaders, Premier Wen Jiabao, backed by President Hu Jintao (Interviews 56, 58), vowed to "continue pushing forward reforms on rural tax and fee systems" and announced a surprise decision to rescind all agricultural taxes within five years (Zhengfu gongzuo baogao, 2004, March 17: 1).

The Center has also set up institutions designed to rein in local officials who fail to do its bidding. For many years, the Party leadership has allowed ordinary citizens to report improprieties through "letters and visits offices" (Cai, 2004; X. Chen, 2003; Luehrmann, 2003; Minzner, 2005; Thireau and Hua, 2003), the "reporting" (*jubao*) system, and people's congresses (Cho, 2003; O'Brien, 1994a). Much like the owners of American trucking companies, who print toll-free numbers on their rigs to encourage motorists to report reckless driving, distant policy makers in Beijing have turned to affected third parties to be their watchdogs. By permitting those who have the most information about cadre misbehavior (and the most to lose from misimplementation) to sound "fire alarms" (McCubbins and Schwartz, 1984), central leaders can devote fewer resources to top-down monitoring and bank on other methods to help identify unprincipled agents. Noisy, public defiance is one of the more perilous but effective ways that the leadership learns of official wrongdoing, and it can be particularly valuable when more institutionalized channels of participation are lacking or clogged.

Yet another indicator of the Center's commitment to enforce policies that villagers welcome is that it has made it easier for ordinary Chinese to

---

[1] For similar comments by General Secretary Jiang Zemin, see Bernstein and Lü (2003: 171).

use its measures and official values as weapons against local misconduct. In other words, the structural opening for rightful resistance has expanded since the beginning of the reform era.[2] Since the 1980s, some popular but vague and toothless central commitments have been codified as laws, thus making it easier for villagers to make a case that a violation has occurred. Compared with squishy principles such as "people's democracy" and "rule by law," explicit articles specifying election procedures in the Organic Law of Villagers' Committees (1998) and the right to sue local governments in the Administrative Litigation Law (1991) are much sturdier posts to hang rightful claims on. Measures limiting appropriation, in particular, have become far more detailed and precisely worded. In 1985 the Center first granted villagers the right to reject financial demands that were not authorized by township people's congresses (Yang, 1996: 201–2). By 1991 the Party leadership had reaffirmed their right to reject illegal fees and had provided villagers the information needed to determine the legality of local assessments by capping collections at 5 percent of farmers' per capita net income in the previous year (Nongmin chengdan feiyong, 1991). By 1996 the accounting unit for calculating fee limits was dropped from the township to the village, and regulations prohibited using projected income increases as a basis for determining payments. By the turn of the century, the Center had outlawed dozens of assessments and had demanded revision of many others. It had also established burden-reduction offices down to the county level and had instituted "interim provisions" laying out punishments for officials who violated edicts designed to eliminate unapproved impositions and prevent them from "bouncing back" (fantan) (Bernstein and Lü, 2003: 167–70).

As beneficial policies are turned into laws, they become more accessible to the public. Unlike "red-headed documents" (hongtou wenjian) and most other Party policies, which are transmitted primarily through government channels, laws are widely available through newspapers, journals, books, and radio and television broadcasts. Moreover, the Center has also released some previously secret Party circulars, usually in the wake of periods of heightened unrest. After several riots took place in Sichuan, Jiangxi, and Hunan in the early and mid-1990s, the Center stepped up its efforts to publicize burden-reduction policies through its propaganda apparatus. In 1996

---

[2] The opening for other kinds of popular action (e.g., mobilized rebellion) against local authorities was also wide, at times, in the Maoist era (1949–76), especially during the early stages of the Cultural Revolution and campaigns such as the Four Cleanups.

alone, *People's Daily* published two State Council circulars that demanded reductions in impositions and vowed to punish unresponsive local officials severely (Xinhuashe, 1996, May 7; Xinhuashe, 1996, December 9).

Crosscurrents: Obstacles to Mobilization

As inviting as this structural opening appears, it is not a door that any aggrieved person can dash right through. Viewed from the ground up (rather than from an analyst's perch) and in real time (rather than retrospectively), a set of opportunities can be a very mixed bag.[3] Openings often come accompanied with threats (Goldstone and Tilly, 2002; McAdam, Tarrow, and Tilly, 2001: 47), and promises made by some officials may be broken by others. In rural China, there are two main reasons that the opportunity structure encourages enduring misrule nearly as much as fighting it: first, the Center itself issues a host of contradictory cues; and, second, many local officials are well positioned and ready to proclaim (to anyone who suggests otherwise) that a meaningful gap between higher levels and lower levels does not exist.

Conflicting Cues

Despite its efforts to stop policy violations, the Center has long tried to have it both ways when it comes to permitting popular action against rogue cadres. On the right to expose misdeeds, for instance, two guidelines coexist, which point in different directions. On the one hand, the Constitution (1982) states that Chinese citizens have the right to submit to state organs complaints or charges against, or exposures of, any agency or functionary for violation of the law or dereliction of duty (art. 41). On the other hand, the State Council's Letters and Visits Regulation (1995, revised 2005) instructs villagers to send no more than five representatives when lodging complaints and to pursue charges level by level (art. 12 [1995]; arts. 16, 18, 34, 35 [2005]).[4] Similar ambivalence is evident in the Center's attitude toward

---

[3] And this holds even before the issue of perceptions is introduced.

[4] Uncertainty about the Center's intent has created considerable friction between villagers and local leaders, especially when rightful resisters and their targets disagree on the interpretation of ambiguous regulations (O'Brien and Li, 2004: 88–89). In one Henan episode, after local leaders claimed that skipping levels of government to lodge complaints should be punished, villagers sought clarification from the State Council's Bureau of Letters and Visits, which instructed the officials that this was a misinterpretation of the 1995 regulation (Wang Zirui

rural political organization. On the one hand, the Constitution (art. 111) and Organic Law of Villagers' Committees (1987, revised 1998) establish "autonomous mass organizations" of self-governance at the village level. On the other hand, the Center has regularly refused to allow even government-controlled farmers' associations to be set up (Bernstein and Lü, 2003; Li Xiuyi, 1992; Yu Jianrong, 2003).

Amid all this inconsistency, however, the Center's bottom line has always been clear. Top Party leaders tolerate rightful resistance mainly because it provides them with intelligence about policy violations and helps them break through the "protective umbrellas" (*baohu san*) that local leaders use to fend off oversight. When faced with perceived threats to "stability" (*wending*), higher-level authorities predictably emphasize containing contention rather than disciplining the targets of popular ire. Consider the issue of authorizing villagers to "reject" (*jujue*) illegal fees. Upon inspection, this new right, significant as it is, amounts to an individual, on-the-spot right to dodge excessive extraction if you can. It is not a right to actively "resist" (*dikang*) a tax collector when he or she knocks down your door, let alone a license to engage in proactive prevention.[5] Put another way, by the early 1990s the Center allowed villagers to sound fire alarms; now it permits them to flee a fire that is coming their way. But it still does not condone stomping out fires or preventing them from starting in the first place.

In addition to undercutting popular efforts to call malfeasant officials to account, the Center has also restricted villagers' ability to assert their rights jointly. Top officials may tolerate popular pressure when it suits them, but they remain highly suspicious of organized collective action (Perry and Selden, 2003). Besides discouraging groups from lodging complaints, this attitude is most clearly seen in the Party leadership's approach to "collective

and Wang Songmiao, 2001: 31). That said, bypassing levels is discouraged, and in one study (Zhao Shukai, 2003) of petitioners who reached Beijing in 1998 and 1999, 14 of 15 individuals (or groups) proceeded step-by-step up the hierarchy. Likewise, in our 2003–4 and 2004–5 surveys of 688 complainants who had reached Beijing, only 2 indicated that they skipped all lower levels and went directly to Beijing, 4 bypassed the provincial government, 1 skipped the township, county, and prefecture, and 4 bypassed the township. The remaining 677 respondents had visited all four subnational levels before going to Beijing. For more information on the sampling and administration of this survey, and others discussed in this chapter, see Appendix B.

[5] On the distinction between reactive and proactive claims, see Tilly (1978). In the Chinese context, see Perry (1985) and O'Brien (2002: 142–46). A good discussion of the difficulties Chinese villagers face when mounting "ex ante resistance" to land expropriation and the limited effectiveness of "ex post resistance" can be found in Cai (2003).

incidents" (*quntixing shijian*). Authorities at higher levels typically acknowledge that most group appeals are lawful or at least reasonable. They may even regard such incidents as helpful wake-up calls. At the same time, they frequently insist (often without presenting any evidence) that leaders of collective action are "individuals with ulterior motives" (*bie you yongxin de ren*) (Zhongyang Zhengfawei, 2001) and are quite happy to see them jailed. Given the Center's refusal to permit farmers' associations and its knee-jerk animosity toward "peasant leaders" (*nongmin lingxiu*), it is fair to say that even on an issue as pressing as excessive extraction the Center has only granted the right of rejection to individual villagers, not to farmers as a group. It is no wonder that many protest leaders deny heading any sort of organization, although they are willing to admit privately that they have a "troop of complainants" (*shangfang duiwu*) at their call (Interviews 4, 5, 6, 19, 21, 36, 39).

Mounting rightful resistance always involves passing into a perilous gray zone and being mindful of the fine and shifting line that defines the Center's sufferance.[6] Existing laws, policies, and official values abridge as well as grant rights, and central leaders remain deeply wary of popular action while often siding with local officials who suppress or defame protest leaders. Contradictory cues and uncertain allies limit the opening for rightful resistance and diminish the inclination of aggrieved villagers to take action.

Local Opposition

The state on the ground is represented by its local representatives. The views and actions of these cadres are therefore just as relevant to potential protesters as central cues and policies. Unsurprisingly, because they are the

---

[6] In July 2005 Chen Xiwen, the vice-minister of the Office of the Central Leading Group on Financial and Economic Affairs, stressed that a wave of recent protests demonstrated that local authorities were not doing their job well and that "farmers knew how to protect their rights and interests." He also hailed the media and the Internet for reporting popular contention, thereby enabling the Center to act quickly and to address the problems raised (Wang, 2005, July 4). Several days later, Zhou Yongkang, the nation's public security chief and a member of the State Council, said the protests "had mainly been triggered by domestic economic factors, the behavior of cadres, and by a lack of justice" (Shi, 2005, July 7). Then, just a few weeks later, a *People's Daily* editorial appeared, arguing that "any illegal attempts to disrupt social stability would not be tolerated" (Renmin Ribao Pinglunyuan, 2005, July 28), and the State Bureau of Letters and Visits warned that petitioners should not abuse the system, form "illegal multi-regional unions," or make "unreasonable demands" that disrupt social order (Cui, 2005, August 1).

Figure 1 "Everyone is responsible for upholding traffic safety. Resolutely attack lawless criminals who assemble the masses to make trouble." (Photo by Lianjiang Li, Hunan, 2003)

prime targets of rural contention, local officials typically do what they can to close the structural opening for rightful resistance or to convince aggrieved villagers that it never existed.

Their most common strategy is to conceal beneficial policies and laws. One county leader stood for many others when he said: "As soon as ordinary people learn anything about the law they become impossible to govern" (Chen Lumin, 2001). In places where rural extraction has been heavy, local officials often work hard to keep villagers unaware of the 5 percent cap and, more recently, the tax-for-fee reform (Xi Ling, 1993; Bernstein and Lü, 2003). In Dangshan county, Anhui, for example, when a group of villagers went to a township to request central and provincial circulars about the tax-for-fee reform, township officials claimed they had received no such documents and had only been notified orally. Actually, the Anhui Party committee had instructed that all relevant materials, including a "Letter to Farmers" from the provincial government, a provincial circular, and a tax card, be hand-delivered to every household (Zhang Cuiling, 2002: 6).

Should villagers manage to learn about beneficial laws and policies, local officials often respond to appeals that cite them by misinterpreting

Figure 2 "Resolutely attack lawless people who resist grain requisition, taxes, and reasonable fees!" (Photo by Lianjiang Li, Hunan, 2003)

restrictive clauses as outright prohibitions. In the past few years, cadres in many locations have used a faulty reading of the 1995 Letters and Visits Regulation to deter villagers from lodging collective complaints and bypassing levels. In Dangshan county, grass-roots leaders plastered village walls with posters announcing that "it is illegal to instigate the masses to lodge a complaint" (Zhang Cuiling, 2002: 4–8), while township officials in Henan have tried to impede the search for elite allies by pasting up big-character posters that proclaimed "Skipping levels when lodging complaints is to be severely punished" (Wang Zirui and Wang Songmiao, 2001). (For examples of such posters, see Figures 1, 2, and 3.)

Other than doing what they can to hide their violation of central policies, many local officials have also sought to raise doubts about promising signals emitted by the Center. At every opportunity, they attempt to convince potential activists that the apparent gap between higher levels and themselves is illusory. Township officials and village cadres in particular, often warn disgruntled villagers that they must not take beneficial policies at face value. One township Party secretary in Henan, for example, advised a group of farmers "not to be 'superstitious' [*mixin*] about the Center" (Interview 10), and a township official in Hunan told

Figure 3 "Imperial grain and state taxes cannot be resisted!" (Photo by Lianjiang Li, Hunan, 2003)

a protest organizer not to believe central promises because top leaders did not really mean what they said (Interview 4). Some cadres do not even bother to deny that they have ignored a beneficial policy. They just say that they were following orders, while hinting that the chain of command can be traced straight to the Center (Interviews 12, 53). Although few grass-roots officials dare to express dissatisfaction with higher levels publicly, our 2004 survey in Anhui, Fujian, Guangdong, Hunan, Liaoning, and Shandong provinces produced some evidence about how bitter many of them feel. Among 708 township cadres who were studying at local Party schools, 421 (60 percent) agreed or strongly agreed that "on the issue of peasant burdens, the Center 'sings a beautiful tune' [*chang gao diao*] and then permits township officials to be 'made the scapegoat [*bei hei guo*].'"

Some local leaders go beyond casting aspersions on the Center's sincerity. They also do what they can to shake villagers' confidence in its capacity. Village cadres, in particular, often boast that they have protectors throughout the government. In Shandong, for instance, a village Party secretary taunted angry villagers with the words: "Some of you want to lodge complaints against me. Wherever you go, I have friends. If you want to lodge a complaint at the Party Center, I'll cover your travel expenses" (Liu Weihua, 1999: 22; for a similar story, see Wang Wanfu, 1992: 33). In Sichuan, a villager, when arguing with a county official who had just ordered the appropriation of his land, cited Premier Wen Jiabao's remarks about the need to preserve farmland.[7] The official replied, "Fine, you go bring him here" (Wei shenmo guojia zhengce, 2003, June 22). In Hunan, a township police chief brushed off a protest leader's charge that he abetted township noncompliance with Beijing's fee limits by saying: "Central policies are just dog farts. I have the power to execute you. My father works in the provincial government. Let's see where you can go if you want to lodge a complaint" (Interview 21).

To preempt popular action and prevent "petition chiefs" (*shangfang touzi*) from attaining public office (Li, 2001), some cadres also try to shut down more institutionalized channels of participation and appeal. They, among other things, rig elections of deputies to township and county people's congresses (Cai Dingjian, 2002; J. Chen and Zhong, 2002: 181–82; Li Fan, 2003; Manion, 2000; Shi Weimin and Lei Jingxuan, 1999: 372–407) and order courts to reject lawsuits on matters such as excessive taxation or coercive implementation of birth limits (Interviews 36, 54, 56; O'Brien and Li, 2004; Yang Haikun, 1994: 52–54).

Township officials and village cadres may even use threats or violence against those who object to their actions. In Hunan, for instance, a few days after a farmer asked a village Party secretary to revoke several illegal charges, the secretary ordered him to have his unmarried daughter return immediately from Guangdong for a pregnancy test or to pay a 500 yuan fine. When the villager refused, the secretary had some of his men beat up the villager (Interview 36).

In sum, the opening rightful resisters have to work with is often elusive or narrower than it initially seems. Countermovements may develop within the state (McAdam, McCarthy, and Zald, 1988: 720–21; Zald, 2000: 12)

---

[7] For a Chinese Academy of Social Sciences study on the growing number of disputes related to land appropriation, and a recent shift away from tax and fee protests against grass-roots officials in central China to rights activism directed at realty companies, development zones, and midlevel governments along the Eastern coast, see Zhao Ling (2004). Of course, as in any society, most grievances in China are "lumped"; they are not pursued, let alone escalated. On selection bias in studies of Chinese protest, see Michelson (2005) and Landry and Tong (2005).

(or be there from the outset), and the targets of rightful resistance have extensive resources to head off popular action.

Perceptions of Opportunity

Still, some villagers protest. They break through information blockades and convenient misinterpretations by local officials to gain irrefutable evidence of wrongdoing. They cast aside doubts about the Center's sincerity and capacity and refuse to put up with flagrant policy violations.[8] They read the signals received from the Center and lower levels to mean that they have an option other than withdrawal or violence – rightful resistance. Why is rightful resistance chosen?

The starting point for understanding its appearance is unpacking opportunities and appreciating that openings and threats, honest assistance and hidden hypocrisy, and rights guaranteed but not enforced are all features of the environment that rightful resisters face. But just as vital as any outside factor is how potential activists understand their situation. In the risky, half-opaque world of possibilities and blind alleys found in China, locating vulnerabilities is just as important as their existence. Potential protesters must be aware of an opening and able to tell themselves a story about how rightful resistance offers a way out. Deciding to challenge an abuse of power is never merely "respond[ing] straightforwardly to objective conditions and probabilities of success" (Jasper, 1997: 37; also McAdam, Tarrow, and Tilly, 2001: 46–47). Taking action depends on the "highly selective information" that becomes available and is recognized by protesters in the course of contention (Koopmans, 2005: 27–28). Activists always make choices (Jasper, 1997: 297, 326), and some protest leaders are more entrepreneurial or foresighted (Meyer and Minkoff, 2004: 1464) (or rash!) than others.

Here, we leave the world of structure to explore perceptions of opportunity and how they translate into contention, or at least provide a foundation for action. Two attitudinal factors stand out as facilitators of rightful resistance. For villagers to perceive and exploit openings, they must obtain (and interpret) policy information that reveals misconduct, points to potential allies, and creates a strong sense of injustice. For them to conclude that they do not deserve their lot and can improve it without too much risk, they must

---

[8] Some of these doubts arise from personal experience (see Chapter 4); others are planted by local officials. On what sort of people tend to become rightful resisters, see Appendix A.

deem the Center trustworthy, blame local officials for their plight, and see officials at higher levels as possible champions.

Obtaining Policy Information

Knowledge of beneficial policies comes to Chinese villagers in many ways. Sometimes they learn of protections simply by being attentive in the course of daily life. Without leaving their homes, they hear about useful measures while watching television, listening to the radio, or reading newspapers and magazines (Liebman, 2005; O'Brien and Li, 1995: 763; Tang, 2005: 40; Zhao Shukai, 2003). In Hengyang county, Hunan, for example, protest organizers have long taken note of announcements carried in the mass media. When asked how they knew that photocopies of government documents they had acquired were genuine, several said it was because the papers corresponded so closely with what they had heard on radio and TV (Interviews 4, 17, 21).

Rightful resisters also stumble across beneficial policies during the early stages of contention.[9] In one case from Hebei, a villager who went to a government office to seek the dismissal of several "incompetent" (*bu chenzhi*) cadres noticed while there a copy of the Organic Law of Villagers' Committees. He looked it over, immediately grasped its significance, and showed it to his fellow petitioners. They studied the law together and decided to "lodge complaints against the township government for violating the Organic Law by not holding democratic elections" (Bao Yonghui, 1991). In Sichuan, some villagers started out better informed but did not know precisely what misconduct had occurred nor what they could do about it. After one of them complained to the director of a county agricultural station of high fees, the director told him about the State Council's 5 percent limit, gave him a copy of Sichuan's Regulations Concerning Farmers' Burdens, and advised him that unlawful appropriation could be contested. The villager took his advice. He organized and won a collective lawsuit and then led a group of villagers to lodge a complaint with the provincial people's congress after township officials refused to acknowledge a court order to remit all overcharges (Peng Fangzhi, 1999: 57–61).

Increased mobility has also enhanced policy awareness and increased familiarity with the Center's commitments. Improved roads and inexpensive

---

[9] These policies often reaffirm a prior sense of the Center's intent and replace hazy understandings with specific knowledge.

bus and train tickets have eased travel greatly, allowing villagers to hear (and observe) how policies they like have been carried out elsewhere. Opportunities for work have taken tens of millions far from their homes and have brought knowledge of popular measures to places where officials were holding them back. Migrant workers from Hunan, for instance, learned of central limits on extraction while in neighboring Guangdong province, where local officials had publicized these policies to showcase their achievements in keeping taxation low (Interviews 21, 54).

Some watchful farmers have also found the government's on-again, off-again legal education campaign a good source of information about laws, policies, and central commitments. In one Hebei episode, after a villager heard about the Organic Law of Villagers' Committees, he told a member of legal education work team, "We didn't know there was a law that allowed us to speak out and take charge. Had we known about it, we would have long ago voted out those cadres who do nothing but wine and dine" (Zhengdingxian Minzhengju, 1991: 3). In much the same fashion, a farmer in Hunan obtained a copy of the 1993 Agriculture Law (a number of years after it was passed) during an activity sponsored by the "Third Five-Year Legal Education Campaign" (*san wu pufa*) and was excited to discover that it authorized rejecting illegal fees (Interview 21).

Finally, sympathetic officials and public-spirited intellectuals may supply villagers with materials that embolden them to undertake rightful resistance. In Hunan, for instance, while a farmer was working a short stint as a bricklayer for the Hengyang municipal government, an official walked by and struck up a conversation. During their chat, the cadre inquired about taxation in the countryside, was shocked to learn that fees were nearly 300 yuan (U.S. $35) per person, and asked the villager to bring him evidence that confirmed this amount. After the official reviewed the farmer's payment stubs, he told him that his fees should not be so high and gave the man copies of central and provincial documents limiting peasant burdens (Interview 6).

Through these and other channels many Chinese villagers become aware of policy violations and disloyal officials.[10] Rural researchers have noted that commonly heard remarks in the countryside include "central policies are good, but they are distorted when they reach lower levels" (Cao Jinqing,

---

[10] Zhang (2005: 42) found that protest leaders in three Hunan counties acquired policy documents mainly through native-place ties, classmates, and relatives, especially when these individuals had close connections to the local bureaucracy.

2000: 210), "the scripture is good, but bad monks recite it incorrectly" (Interviews 59, 60, 61; also Lü, 1997: 132), and "policies from higher levels are 'upright' [*zheng*], policies from lower levels are 'crooked' [*wai*]" (Li, 2004: 232). Two of our surveys suggest how widespread such views are. A 1999 survey showed that 73 percent of 1,384 respondents from eighty-seven villages in twenty-five provinces agreed or strongly agreed that "central policies regarding the countryside are good but lower levels do not implement them well." A 1999–2001 survey in four counties in three provinces showed that 82 percent of 1,600 respondents agreed or strongly agreed with this statement.[11]

Interpreting Information

Obtaining information is a start. But information alone is never enough to turn a villager into an activist or to bring on an episode of contention. The structural opening for rightful resistance must be socially and culturally constructed into an opportunity for mobilization (Goodwin and Jasper, 1999: 33; Jasper, 1997: 37; McAdam, Tarrow, and Tilly, 2001: 46). Activists and followers need to connect the dots between their grievances and local misimplementation, and to attribute opportunity in a way that makes sense to themselves and suggests a course of action based on their understanding of reality (McAdam, Tarrow, and Tilly, 2001: 46).

A stark gap between what is promised by the Center and what is delivered below, when perceived, can jump-start this process of attribution. Upon learning about a beneficial policy or "studying" (*xuexi*) government documents that lay it out, many villagers are quick to realize that a large portion of their grievances can be traced to the neglect of policies designed to protect them. Indeed, the contrast between what central measures prescribe and what local officials do is often so great that it propels even not particularly bold people into action. For example, in accord with the 5 percent limit, Hunan's provincial government estimated that fees in 1995 should average around 50–60 yuan (U.S. $6–$7) per person. Yet in Hengyang county, a place whose level of economic development was middling at best, officials in one township demanded 170 yuan (Interview 21), while leaders in another township assessed each person as much as 298 yuan (Interview 6).

---

[11] We are aware that this question is "double-barreled." This is a result of deriving many survey questions from remarks heard during interviews with villagers. Multivariate analysis of some of the survey data is available in Li (2001, 2003, 2004).

Moreover, extraction in Hengyang continued to grow for several years as the local economy stagnated. Many villagers in Hengyang recognized that they had been overtaxed as soon as they learned of the 5 percent cap and saw provincial documents that spelled it out. One activist recalled that he felt like "a fish getting water" (*ru yu de shui*) when, in 1998, he finally obtained copies of central policies limiting extraction (Interview 13). That same year, a young woman was so incensed the day she learned of long-standing fee limits that she challenged her husband to "be a man" and to "struggle against" those "bastards" and "thieves" in the township government (Interview 26).

But the size of the perceived gap between the Center and a lower-level government is not the whole story either. "Cognitive liberation" (McAdam, 1982: 48–51) is not an automatic outgrowth of awareness of the central-local divide, nor is it closely associated with the intensity of one's grievances. It also depends on a pattern of trust that attributes good intentions to the Center and sees (perhaps even assumes) perfidy at lower levels.[12]

Trusting the Center and Blaming Lower Levels

Anyone contemplating collective action must decide whom to mobilize against (Javeline, 2003: 225). Especially where a tiered structure blurs lines of responsibility and policy makers say one thing but tolerate a different situation on the ground, the choice of adversaries is not always obvious and is instead an act of social and cultural construction (see Javeline, 2003: 227; Klandermans, 1997: 191–94). Mobilization depends on identifying targets who resonate with cultural values and also strike a chord in the community. It is unlikely to occur if people "do not know whom to yell at, or they want to yell at everyone" (Javeline, 2003: 21).

Rightful resistance hinges on locating local targets who can be blamed and elite advocates who can be trusted.[13] Our interviews and surveys suggest that many Chinese villagers trust the Center and distrust lower levels in a

---

[12] Of course, not all contemporary villagers hold this view. Some believe the state is united and trustworthy and others that the state is united and untrustworthy. An example of the latter is a former village cadre from Jiangxi who said that "there is a tacit agreement between central leaders and local officials. Local officials bear the blame for violating central policies. In return, the Center turns a blind eye to their corruption" (Interview 62). For an analysis that, however, shows how common high trust for the Center and lower trust for lower levels is (in four counties in three provinces), see Li (2004).

[13] Trust in the Center, accompanied by a belief in the venality of officials at lower levels has been a familiar theme among Chinese rebels for centuries. But compare Michelson

pattern that encourages the transformation of policy violations into opportunities for rightful resistance.[14] Activists, in particular, tend to be highly critical of local leaders and express their feelings openly: "Damn those sons of bitches [township and village cadres]! The Center lets us ordinary people have good lives; all central policies are very good. But these policies are all changed when they reach lower levels. It's entirely their fault. They do nothing good, spending the whole day wining and dining. The only thing they don't forget is to collect money" (Zhu Anshun, 1999: 384).

Such villagers do not believe that grass-roots leaders are looking out for the interests of the populace (cf. Shue, 1988; Thornton, 2004), and they do not trust them to carry out beneficial policies (Li, 2004). They instead find many basic-level cadres to be self-serving, predatory, and high-handed. When choosing targets and searching for possible allies, they blame "lower levels" (*xiaji*) for most of their woes and (at least in public) hold the Center responsible for little of their discontent. As one villager from Hebei put it, "township cadres have all become bloodsuckers and village cadres do their bidding. If the present situation continues, central policies are useless no matter how good they are" (Interview 16).

At the same time, these same villagers tend to idealize top leaders and sometimes explicitly compare them to "wise emperors" (*ming jun*) of old (Interviews 8, 21, 36) A hard-bitten Shandong protest organizer, who had led a four-year battle against a corrupt village Party secretary and his patrons at the township level, expressed this view well. He contended that all high-ranking leaders, including President Hu Jintao, had most likely bought their positions. But he also argued that as soon as he made it to the top, Hu must have undergone a metamorphosis, because he now was the "emperor" (*huangdi*). An emperor, in his view, typically cares more about his "realm" (*tianxia*) than anyone else. In his words, "Emperors of all dynasties wanted the country to be prosperous and strong. Only then could they live in peace and enjoy themselves. If there were crises below, they had no peace.... Central leaders [*Zhongyang lingdao*] are the finest men in all of China, the policies they make ... are very good indeed." For this reason,

---

(2005: 33), who finds "people's trust in the capacity of local, village-level leaders that is no lower than, and perhaps even greater than, higher-level third parties."

[14] Others have noted that measuring perceptions of opportunity is difficult without survey data (Kurzman, 1996: 165) and that favorable opportunities must be defined as such by a large enough segment of the aggrieved population, if they are to facilitate collective action (McAdam, 1982: 48–51). On using surveys of political trust and efficacy in South Africa to assess popular attitudes about opportunities, see Klandermans (1997: 181).

he said, villagers have good reason to trust top officials, who in his words are comparable to "lotus flowers that grow out of the mud without being tainted" (Interview 36).[15]

Reminiscent of the Confucian tradition of ascribing moral virtue to the state (Pye, 1991: 443), such people argue that the Center "truly cares about peasants' interests" and "makes good policies so that peasants can prosper" (Interviews 64, 65). Moreover, these villagers are willing to believe in the Center, or at least give it the benefit of the doubt, even when they know little about what it has done. Many of our survey respondents admitted that they did not know much about how well top leaders had performed but nonetheless insisted that the Center had their interests at heart. For instance, our 2003–4 survey showed that 538 (67 percent) of 809 respondents from two counties (one in Fujian, one in Zhejiang) said that they knew nothing about how well central leaders were doing their jobs, yet 458 (85 percent) of the 538 thought that the Party Center and the State Council "truly care about peasants' welfare."[16]

In dynastic China, the other side of idealizing the emperor was blaming "wicked and shrewd officials" (*jianchen*) for things that went awry. We have observed a similar sentiment in the contemporary countryside (cf. Michelson, 2005: 33). Many villagers seem to assume that the Center has

---

[15] Even when pushed, this man repeatedly dodged questions aimed at discovering if this position was largely strategic, and he said it was his "principle" not to rebel against the Center, adding "if we do that, then we have nothing left." More broadly, our hunch is that a shift often takes place from sincere belief to strategic deployment of official values, especially for protest leaders who have personally brought their complaints to Beijing, typically after suffering much frustration, defeats, or repression. For emphasis on strategic deference to the powerful, see Scott (1985, 1990). On delusional faith in top leaders, see Field (1976). Among Chinese workers interviewed in 2002 and 2003, Lee (2004: 10) notes, "When I talked to them about their faith in the central government, they became ambivalent, admitting that the Center is responsible for appointing these corrupt and irresponsible local cadres. But still, they would insist, the Center is *more* just and righteous because it keeps issuing more regulations favorable to workers' interests. The main problem remains that of local implementation." In another example (Lynch, 2004, September 14), mainly female, mainly retired workers from a liquor factory in periurban Wanli, Fujian, complained to five levels of government and staged a sit-in after losing their homes to make room for new development, and were beaten by more than 100 police officers and hired members of a criminal gang. "Still, the villagers continue to profess faith in the central government," and one protester said he "hoped the real Communist Party can send us a Bao Qingtian [a twelfth-century imperial envoy known for his honesty and integrity]... to give us justice."

[16] The corresponding figures for provincial, city, county, and township leaders "truly caring about peasants' welfare" were 74, 61, 45, and 40 percent, respectively. See Appendix B for information on sampling.

benevolent intentions even though they have yet to enjoy many protections they have been promised. When they sought to explain why misimplementation was widespread, many interviewees expressed doubts about the Center's capacity to monitor and control its officials but still would say the Center "sincerely wants to reduce peasant burdens" or "is determined to uphold justice for peasants" (Interviews 4, 5, 6, 8, 13, 36). They argued that officials could get away with misdeeds because the Center was often unable to see through their schemes or break up their networks of mutual protection (Interviews 4, 21, 36, 62, 63). Activists from Shandong and Fujian, as well as a Hunan villager, each compared today's Center to a man who could think clearly but who had lost control of his limbs (Interviews 36, 37, 46). Our 2003–4 survey produced more evidence of limited confidence in the Center's reach and in its ability to find out what is transpiring in the countryside. Among 809 respondents, more than three-quarters believed that the Center remained unaware of the problems rural complainants sought to bring to its attention and 285 (35 percent) felt that "the Center could not control local officials who protect each other."

Based on their perception that the Center has good intentions but cannot always find out what is happening below, many protest leaders have concluded that Beijing welcomes their offer to check misbehavior by deceptive and disloyal local cadres. As one activist from Shandong put it: "Some wicked officials have sealed off the Center from reality. If peasants do not lodge complaints, the emperor will never know what is going on. If I tell the emperor, he should thank me and take care of me. Anything otherwise and he would be an '*Edou Liu Chan*,'" referring to an emperor notorious for his lack of wisdom (Interview 36). A Hunan protest organizer was equally confident of the Center's willingness (but limited ability) to come to his aid: "Party policies today are good. The Party opposes corruption and wants to prolong its reign so that our country can become prosperous and ordinary people can be well-off. The Party is determined to reverse the trend [of increasing corruption] and to adopt a broad and bright way. An ancient saying tells us that 'commoners bear responsibilities for the rise and fall of the realm.' That's why my fellow protesters and I publicize Party policies" (Interview 8).

Our 2003–4 survey suggests that quite a few villagers share this view. Out of 809 respondents, 627 (78 percent) agreed or strongly agreed that "the Center is willing to listen to peasants who tell the truth and welcomes our complaints," and 702 (87 percent) agreed or strongly agreed that "the Center supports peasants in defending their lawful rights and interests."

It should be noted that although many villagers question the Center's ability to oversee local officialdom in its entirety, they tend to believe that it can call any single official to account, if it decides to. A man from Hunan, for instance, said that if he had the money he would have gone to Beijing to lodge a complaint against cadres who roughed him up, detained him, and confiscated some of his possessions after he publicized central limits on peasant burdens. According to him, if only he managed to get some attention from officials at the Center, then they could easily punish the county and township officials who persecuted him (Interview 19). This view is especially common among petitioners who travel to Beijing. They typically say that persistence is powerful proof that serious improprieties have occurred, and that if they manage to win a hearing, they have a good chance to convince concerned officials that their antagonists are in the wrong and should be disciplined (Interviews 66, 67, 68).

A combination of high trust in the Center's intentions and conditional confidence in its capacity undercuts antisystem protest but promotes rightful resistance.[17] Trust in the willingness of higher levels to back them up sensitizes villagers to the gap between what the Center offers and what local officials deliver; nagging concerns about the Center's competence have convinced many that it is unable to make good on its commitments without help from below; trust in the Center's good intentions leaves villagers hopeful that the Center will be receptive to popular demands;[18] a belief that the Center can call any single cadre to heel suggests that protesters may have a reasonable chance of prevailing. All together, this set of understandings

---

[17] For more on how declining trust in the Center has affected the form that rightful resistance takes, see Chapter 4. Note that our analysis, like many others, questions Gamson's (1968) hypothesis that high political efficacy and low political trust are the ideal combination for popular mobilization. The layered and divided pattern of trust found in rural China instead supports the idea that analysts should examine trust in specific political actors and institutions rather than governments as a whole (Levi and Stoker, 2000: 495–96) and also distinguish between bad faith and ineptitude (Citrin and Muste, 1999; Levi and Stoker, 2000: 476).

[18] Our 2003–4 survey of 809 villagers, for example, showed that 574 (71 percent) agreed or strongly agreed that, "provided that peasants reflect their problems to the Center, the Center will attempt to resolve them." That many villagers seem to have so much faith in the Center's benign intent may well be rooted in China's dynastic past (Bernstein and Lü, 2003: 22; Zelin, 1984). This pattern of trust has certainly been fostered by the current regime. Since 1949 the official media have run a virtually nonstop propaganda campaign that accords the Center credit for most achievements and blames much of what has gone wrong on local officials or "bad elements" in the population.

makes up much of the thinking that lies behind rightful resistance: it is useful, necessary, and feasible to challenge official misconduct on behalf of the Center.

Misperceptions

But is it? Trust in the Center has a foundation, as the presence of an opening makes clear, but that foundation is often not as solid as rightful resisters think. Rural activists in China seldom have full information about the Center's intentions, especially those conveyed in "internal" (*neibu*) directives that are hostile to collective protest. This lack of knowledge often leads villagers to overestimate the size of the structural opening, insofar as their perceptions are skewed by excessive trust in the Center and in its devotion to stamp out local misimplementation. In retrospect, some activists from Hunan admitted that they put far too much faith in the Center's goodwill, while others acknowledged that they had expected too much help from above and underestimated the risks and difficulties they would face (Interviews 4, 5, 6, 21). Although most of these protest organizers said that they still did not regret their decision to act, incomplete information and miscalculations have played a large part in sparking many episodes of rightful resistance.

Overoptimism, it should be pointed out, is not unique to China. It is a common trait of protest leaders everywhere and, if it were not, organizers, quite possibly "would not be doing their job wisely" (Gamson and Meyer, 1996: 285). To decide to proceed, activists must often see a glass as half full when it is far less than that (Gamson and Meyer, 1996: 286). Being overly sanguine about one's prospects can be instrumental in the emergence of popular contention. For one, unrealistic expectations can alter what is possible by enlarging openings. Perceptions, in this way, can be self-fulfilling (Gamson and Meyer, 1996: 287; Goodwin and Jasper, 1999: 52–53; Kurzman, 1996: 165; but cf. Suh, 2001: 443) as activists try different strategies and come across a recipe for action that works (Koopmans, 2005: 28). Second, even rumors and inaccurate or misunderstood information can shift perceptions and promote mobilization (Jasper, 1997: 37; Koopmans, 2005: 28). When the aim is persuading oneself and others to start down an uncertain road, perceptions (justified or not) are as vital as any "objective" opening. Whether activists assess an opportunity structure correctly affects their odds of winning more than their ability to mobilize in the first place.

Conclusion

Rightful resistance becomes possible when local officials violate beneficial policies and other central commitments. A gap between high-level promises and ground-level implementation creates a structural opening that resourceful activists seek to fill. But this opening is often difficult to exploit, because many cadres try to deny the populace access to central measures, and because the Center itself is ambivalent about letting villagers loose on its wayward agents. Only when potential protesters manage to learn about beneficial policies (and other commitments) can they attribute their grievances to local misconduct and conclude that the Center might be an ally. Such villagers may then begin to challenge misrule by mobilizing pressure from above. Even if they are mistaken about the amount of support they enjoy, a combination of trust in the Center and blame for local levels inspires rightful resisters to launch popular action. Rightful resistance begins with a structural opening, but the field of play quickly shifts to obtaining, processing, and deploying information about that opening. Collective action, when it occurs, always emerges out of a brew of structural and perceptual elements.

The appearance of rightful resistance in rural China has several implications for students of contentious politics. First, opportunities and how they are perceived not only affect the volume of mobilization and its timing but also the form it takes (Koopmans, 1999: 105; McAdam, McCarthy, and Zald, 1996: 9–10). Only by getting beyond overaggregated notions of opportunity and exploring perceptions deeply can we see why a certain type of protest (e.g., rightful resistance) has taken off. Unpacking an opportunity structure encourages us to appreciate that opportunities are cross-cutting and evolving rather than one-dimensional and static. Probing perceptions of opportunity brings into focus how disgruntled individuals often grope their way toward figuring out what should and can be done (Koopmans, 2005: 27–28). Respecting the complexity of an opportunity structure and people's perceptions enables us to see how a specific external environment, as it is understood or misunderstood, is conducive to a certain type of contention. The issue is not simply whether doors are opening or closing, but which doors are opening (and are thought to be opening) and which doors are closing (and are thought to be closing).

Second, this chapter also suggests a conceptual point concerning how to understand political opportunities. As efforts to incorporate threats and repression into discussions of opportunity have shown (Brockett, 1991:

Conclusion

262–64; Goldstone and Tilly, 2001; Kurzman, 1996: 155; McAdam, 1996; Meyer and Staggenborg, 1996: 1634; Suh, 2001: 439–41; Tarrow, 1998: 83–87), it is problematic to conceive of opportunities solely as factors conducive to popular action.[19] Opportunities should not be confused with improved opportunities. Openings commonly come packaged with threats, and discussions of an opportunity structure should always incorporate factors that inhibit mobilization (Suh, 2001: 440; Tarrow, 1998). In this chapter, we have used the term "opportunity structure" to refer to the entire external environment, in all its complexity. This formulation encourages researchers to examine contrary trends and to adopt a more rounded view of the context in which contention occurs, similar to what actors on the ground experience. Using this understanding of an opportunity structure, the researcher is led to distinguish, for example, the stance of different parts of the state toward collective action and also to see how protesters' allies among the powerful can give off mixed signals or be hypocritical. Treating an opportunity structure as a bundle of openings and obstacles reminds us that favorable conditions may disappear when allies become gun-shy about what they have unleashed. It also reduces the danger that researchers will ignore factors that hinder mobilization while retrospectively fishing for whatever external factors might have promoted it.

Lastly, this chapter provides some insight into the term "rightful resistance." In China, the Center's ambivalence toward popular action and the mixed opportunity structure that results, makes rightful resistance what it is: rightful, but also resistance. Beneficial policies and official values encourage the disgruntled to challenge disloyal local officials, whereas denying people the protections they are owed turns central commitments into weapons for the powerless and vulnerabilities for local officials. Rights extended but not observed lead enterprising villagers to engage in claims-making performances that are permissible in the eyes of some officials but impermissible in the eyes of others. Rightful resistance is both rightful and resistance – a form of contention based on claims that, as we argue in the next chapter, are neither transgressive nor contained but boundary spanning.

---

[19] We are much less concerned than Gamson and Meyer (1996: 275) that the concept of political opportunity structure "threatens to become an all-encompassing fudge factor for all the conditions and circumstances that form the context for collective action." Our more interpretive inclinations, and our rich data on both structure and perceptions, have led us to opt for an explanation that favors completeness over parsimony.

3

Boundary-Spanning Claims

In studies of popular politics a split exists. Some researchers focus on rather tame and predictable forms of claims making, whereas others become interested mainly when political action spills out onto the streets. For one set of analysts, attention centers on issues related to voting, lobbying, party activity, and various forms of contacting: how, in other words, the popular classes press their demands through approved channels of influence. For the other group, how people react when the authorities are unresponsive and frustration mounts with existing opportunities for expression is of greater concern. Although there are exceptions, insofar as some researchers examine a range of institutionalized and uninstitutionalized acts (Aminzade, 1995; Anderson, 1994; Shi, 1997; Singerman, 1995), the two literatures tend to travel along separate tracks: one spotlighting forms of inclusion and clearly lawful political behavior; the other, consequences of exclusion and actions that are closer to resistance.

In their book *Dynamics of Contention*, McAdam, Tarrow, and Tilly (2001: 4–7, 305) take a dim view of such divisions. They argue that many episodes of contention belong in a single definitional universe and that there is no need for wholly distinct literatures on topics such as revolution, social movements, elections, and interest group politics. For them, so long as popular action entails episodic collective interaction between the makers of claims and their objects, and a government is involved, similar causal processes and mechanisms are at work.

McAdam, Tarrow, and Tilly (2001: 7) of course recognize differences between what they call transgressive and contained contention. These include whether all the parties involved are established political actors and whether innovative means of collective action are employed. But then, in short order, they return to the many links between the two sorts of politics, not the least because it is difficult to locate where the boundary between transgressive and contained contention lies, and because the two kinds of politics "interact incessantly."

After finishing this bout of provocative claims making, "for the sake of clarity" in an analysis that extends from the Mau Mau rebellion to the Montgomery bus boycott, McAdam, Tarrow, and Tilly (2001: 8, 341) choose to concentrate on episodes involving transgressive claims. Although they note that many transgressive episodes grow out of contained contention, little more is heard about the relationship between transgressive demands and demands on the contained side of the line. The reader is left with a stirring charge to breach the boundary between institutionalized and uninstitutionalized politics and to investigate connections that have often been obscured, neglected, or misunderstood (McAdam, Tarrow, and Tilly, 2001: 4–7), but only a sketchy road map for doing so. The relationship of these two types of politics merits further study, and this chapter suggests one way to explore it: namely, by focusing on rightful resistance, and the neither transgressive nor contained claims that characterize it.

Unpacking the State

To examine the links between transgressive and contained forms of contention by looking at episodes that are neither fish nor fowl, some preliminary ground clearing is called for. For a start, much can be gained by joining the growing corps of scholars who eschew the dichotomies of state-versus-society and us-against-them.[1] In particular, it is important to think about "them" more systematically by disaggregating the state. This prescription, uncontroversial though it sounds, goes well beyond the familiar injunction to avoid reifying state power. It involves recognizing that every regime has its own institutional structure and that agents of a government are not always principled agents. Particularly in far-flung, many-layered bureaucracies, officials at different places in the hierarchy often have diverging interests and are subject to different constraints and incentives. From the vantage point of people contemplating collective action, this means that states often present attractive, multidimensional targets. Whether a regime is a democracy or anything short of the most repressive dictatorship,

---

[1] In the Chinese context, see Diamant (2001), Diamant, Lubman, and O'Brien (2005: chap. 1), O'Brien and Li (1995; 2004: 93–94), and Perry (1994). More broadly, see Migdal, Kohli, and Shue (1994).

the segmentation built into a complex system of power cannot help but produce cracks in the facade of unity. And these openings appear not only because there are regime defectors, minority elites, or elites out of power who seize the role of tribune of the people (Tarrow, 1996: 55–60). At a more basic level, as we saw in the preceding chapter, a multilayered structure itself disorganizes the powerful and can provide opportunities for the disaffected "to make authorities work for them rather than against them" (Klandermans, 1997: 194).

Given that states are usually too fragmented to treat as unitary actors, examining which level of government and which specific departments are drawn into popular contention is a must. Once a state is unpacked into institutionally situated officials with their own interests and preferences, it becomes difficult, however, to classify certain claims-making performances as prescribed, tolerated, or forbidden. It also becomes difficult to neatly separate "challengers" and "polity members" (Koopmans and Statham, 1999a: 208, 218; for these terms, see Tilly, 1978). The "rightful" claims we focus on in this book are not prescribed or forbidden, but tolerated (even encouraged) by some officials and denied by others. They sit near the fuzzy boundary between official, prescribed politics and politics by other means, in a middle ground that is neither clearly transgressive nor clearly contained.

While examples of boundary-spanning claims can be found throughout history and around the globe, it is hardly surprising that contemporary China has been a particularly hospitable incubator. Unlike in many industrialized democracies, where the bounds of the permissible tend to be more settled, what is institutionalized and what is not are often hotly contested in newer regimes and those in the midst of rapid change. In contemporary China, contention over what is contentious reaches deep into the state. Lower and midlevel officials, for instance, are often remarkably hazy about precisely which claims are politically acceptable.[2] Much can be learned about the elusive, fluid boundary between unconventional and institutionalized politics in China (and elsewhere) by exploring popular demands that are arguably legal, permissible in some eyes but not in others.[3]

---

[2] In one Hebei village we visited, a former Party secretary (Interview 47) set up a legal advisory office to help cadres who were regularly being tripped up by villagers who knew more about the law than they did.

[3] In Chinese official parlance, this would be called the boundary between "lawful rights" (hefa quanyi) and "unreasonable demands" (wuli yaoqiu). For more on this "fuzzy and permeable boundary," see Goldstone (2003: 2, 11–12).

Unpacking the State

In the remainder of this chapter, we present evidence from our own interviews with Chinese grass-roots cadres and officials at higher levels, as well as from accounts drawn from government publications, other Western scholars, and field reports by Chinese researchers. The episodes of rightful resistance we examine center on clashes involving cadre accountability. Although many other disputes inspire boundary-spanning claims, including conflicts over unapproved fees, contract fulfillment, financial disclosure, land use, and cadre corruption, deploying official discourses and collective action to combat election abuses has become especially common since the late 1980s. One study (Jennings, 1997: 366), for instance, reported that two-fifths of the occasions on which rural residents contacted officials concerned elections; another survey showed that as many as 5 percent of villagers nationwide had lodged complaints concerning election fraud (Shi, 1999a : 403–4).[4] Particularly in regions where basic-level voting is taken seriously, rightful resistance appears to be climbing. Following the 1997 elections in Fujian, a provincial pacesetter, villagers sent more than four thousand letters of complaint about voting irregularities to government offices, ten times the number received after the 1993 balloting (Carter Center Report, 2000).[5] And this upward trend shows no signs of abating, most likely owing to a November 1998 revision of the Organic Law of Villagers' Committees (1987). After a decade as a "trial" (*shixing*) measure, the law was granted permanent status, and local officials everywhere must

---

[4] Five percent seems high. In 1994 the Fujian provincial Bureau of Civil Affairs received 562 election-related complaints and deemed twenty-four elections invalid. (International Republican Institute 1997: 27). Our 1999 survey (see Appendix B) showed that 3 percent of 1,384 respondents from eighty-seven villages in twenty-five provinces said that they had lodged complaints against "unlawful phenomena concerning villagers' committee elections." Our 1999–2001 survey in four counties in three provinces showed that 1 percent of 1,600 respondents had done the same.

[5] According to a Central Committee report on popular protest, more than 70 percent of "collective incidents" (*quntixing shijian*) in rural Shandong during 2000 arose due to "cadre-mass contradictions and conflicts of material interests," and many of these incidents centered on village elections. The main points of conflict reported were: elected cadres who were corrupt, overbearing, or unwilling to open village finances; election manipulation; attempts by lineages or criminal gangs to undermine elections; and county and township officials who did not "work hard to guide elections and correct problems" (Zhongyang Zhengfawei Yanjiushi, 2001: 88). Official statistics show that more than 3 million rural and urban residents took part in 58,000 collective incidents in 2003, a 14 percent increase over 2002, while the number of protesters increased nearly 7 percent (Ma, 2004, June 8). In 2004 the minister of public security reported that the number of collective incidents jumped again, to 74,000, involving 3.76 million people, a dramatic increase from the 10,000 incidents reported in 1994 (Cody, 2005, August 1).

now abide by its provisions. The Organic Law introduces a number of specific requirements concerning nominations, balloting, and vote counting, and it clearly states that no organization or individual is allowed to "appoint, designate, remove, or replace" members of a villagers' committee. It also expressly authorizes voters to contest dishonest elections ("threats, bribes, forged ballots and other improper methods") by lodging reports with local governments, people's congresses, and other departments (e.g., civil affairs offices). In 1998, when the Organic Law only enjoyed trial status, 17 percent of all appeals and letters to the Ministry of Civil Affairs involved elections; in the first half of 1999 this proportion rose to 31 percent (Liu, 2000: 31).

In addition to their significance as everyday events, the following episodes were chosen to shed light on the boundary-spanning quality of many popular demands surrounding grass-roots political reform. For Sinologists who are taken aback by the skill with which rightful resisters work the territory between contained and transgressive contention (and the proportion of happy endings), it should be noted that uncharacteristically successful cases were chosen, not because they are typical, but because they are relatively complete and illustrate how boundary-spanning claims are made and contested.

Pressing for Accountability

How to monitor local officials and to curb cadre misconduct has become an urgent problem in rural China (Bernstein and Lü, 2003; Cai, 2000; Lü, 2000; O'Brien and Li, 1999; Wedeman, 2001; D. Yang, 1996: 202–12; but cf. Edin, 2003; Naughton and Yang, 2004: 11). One way that the central government has tried to rein in arbitrary and self-serving grass-roots leaders has been by rolling out an ambitious program of village elections. By making the lowest-level cadres more accountable to the people they rule, Party leaders in Beijing have sought to shore up the regime and prevent wayward officials from "driving the people to rebellion" (*guan bi min fan*) (Howell, 1998; Kelliher, 1997; O'Brien, 1994b; O'Brien and Li, 2000; Oi, 2004; Shi, 1999a; X. Wang, 1997). But opposition to free and fair elections has, at times, been fierce. Many midlevel leaders argue that empowering villagers in any way will jeopardize public order and make it more difficult for cadres to complete the many tasks (e.g., birth control, revenue collection, land allocation, grain procurement) they are assigned.[6] Some of these officials have acted on their misgivings by blocking or rigging elections, either openly or through subterfuge. Among other tactics, opponents of village self-governance have refused to convene elections, monopolized nominations, held snap elections, required that Party members vote for favored candidates, banned unapproved candidates from making campaign speeches, insisted that voting be conducted by a show of hands, annulled results when the "wrong" candidates won, forced elected committee members from office, and rejected villagers' demands for recalls (Fan Yu, 1998; Ma Changshan, 1994; Li and O'Brien, 1999; Liu, 2000; Peaceful village election, 2004, February 26).[7]

But when local officials frustrate efforts to make grass-roots leaders more accountable, some villagers are far from quiescent; instead they confront those who dare to usurp their right to vote. They assert the right to rid themselves of corrupt, partial, and incompetent cadres by making a host of claims, many of which are boundary spanning.

In one poor Hebei village, for example, a group of farmers lodged a series of complaints requesting the dismissal of several village cadres. After township authorities rejected their appeals, the villagers stationed several rotating teams of petitioners in the township seat to press their case. One day, one of the villagers happened upon a copy of the Organic Law of Villagers' Committees lying on a desk in a township office. He read it, immediately realized its import, and showed it to his fellow complainants. After they studied the law, they decided to "lodge complaints against the township for violating the Organic Law by not holding democratic elections."[8] The activists then devised a plan to increase their leverage and to ensure that their demands would not be brushed aside. They divided

---

[6] A survey of cadres in 120 villages in four counties in Anhui and Heilongjiang (Zweig, 2001: 30) suggests that these concerns may be declining. But see also Bernstein and Lü (2003: 210). Our 2003 survey (see Appendix B) of 708 township officials from six provinces showed that 31 percent agreed or strongly agreed that "holding democratic elections for villagers' committees hinders the township government's efforts to meet its various hard targets."

[7] For a discussion of the "Qianjiang incident" in which 187 popularly elected village leaders were dismissed by township governments, see Li Fan (2003: 374–405).

[8] Studying the Organic Law in order to use it to resist local officials was a recurring theme on a twenty-two-part soap opera shown on China's Central Television Station in the spring of 2001 (Gray, 2001: 77). Villagers, in this series, regarded the law as a "sacred text" and employed it in "extremely creative, clever, and even devious ways in their struggles" (Gray, 2001: 78). Gray argues (p. 75) that this show did "nothing less than teach people how to be *diaomin* [i.e., rightful resisters; see Li and O'Brien, 1996], that is, how to use existing laws to protect themselves from corrupt or incompetent local level officials."

themselves into three groups, two of which went to the township compound and the county civil affairs bureau, while a third composed of village Party members traveled to the county organization department. Facing an angry crowd demanding implementation of a law that had been casually ignored throughout the region, the township caved in and agreed to hold elections. In the subsequent balloting, the man who had originally discovered the Organic Law was elected director of his villagers' committee (Bao Yonghui, 1991). This claim to electoral rights was boundary spanning both because it used a central measure to question the discretion of township officials and to enhance the responsiveness of village cadres, and because it was based on a law that had only trial status, and which township leaders arguably were not obligated to execute. In this case, knowledge followed action and rightful resistance was the result of "contentious conversation" (Tilly, 2002: 111–22) rather than the other way around.[9]

It is not just disregard of the Organic Law that leads rightful resisters to take issue with local officials who try to abridge their rights. Villagers also challenge procedural irregularities that Chinese peasants are often thought to care little about (on rights-conscious peasants, see Bernstein and Lü, 2003; Diamant 2000; Li and O'Brien, 1996; Liebman, 1998; O'Brien, 1996, 2001, 2002; Pei, 1997; Zweig, 2000). Organized election boycotts, for instance, have occurred over relatively technical infractions of the Organic Law.[10] In one case, when residents of a Hunan village found themselves facing an illegal snap election, two young men organized their neighbors to plaster seventy-four posters around the village that called on voters to reject handpicked candidates and "oppose dictatorial elections." The village's walls were literally covered with oversized characters, all written on white paper (a color that is associated with death and ill-fortune). This threatening display drew the attention of county officials, who investigated the charges and ruled that the balloting should be rescheduled and nominations reopened. Although the two organizers were ultimately ordered to cover the posters with new ones written on red paper, their actions delayed an election that violated the Organic Law and other

---

[9] On "fuzzy rights" and their emergence, see Verdery (1999). A special issue of *Conservation & Society*, 2(1) 2004, was devoted to fuzzy property rights in postsocialist societies.

[10] Whether Chinese with a stronger democratic orientation and a keener sense of internal efficacy are more likely to vote is a matter of some controversy (J. Chen and Zhong, 2002; Shi, 1999b). What is not in dispute is that turnout rates are lower than those reported by the government.

local regulations (Zhongguo Nongcun Cunmin Zizhi Zhidu Yanjiu Ketizu, 1994: 119).

In yet another episode of rightful claims making that turned on whether proper procedures had been observed, villagers from Hubei acted as if they had an indisputable right to disrupt an election in which they had been excluded from the nomination process. At the exact moment when the ballots were being distributed, one man jumped up on the stage where the election committee was presiding, grabbed a microphone, and accused the Party-approved candidate of being corrupt and unworthy of election. Immediately, several of his associates stood up and started shouting words of encouragement, affirming his charges. To further dramatize their demands, the protesters then tore up their own ballots as well as those of other villagers who were standing around, waiting to vote. As a result, the election was briefly halted. Although township officials later sought to prosecute the activists for "impeding an election," and the county procurator accepted the case, the provincial people's congress, after consultation with the National People's Congress, decided it was "not appropriate to regard their actions as illegal" because the original nominations had been conducted improperly. The results of the interrupted election were declared null and void and the balloting was rescheduled (Zhongguo Nongcun Cunmin Zizhi Zhidu Yanjiu Ketizu, 1994: 164–65).

Rightful resisters do not only dispute violations of established procedures. They have also drawn on general ideas about the Center's policies to demand, for instance, the right to nominate themselves for villagers' committee posts at a time when self-nomination was permitted only in "demonstration areas" (*shifan diqu*). In one such incident, after a township in Liaoning prohibited several men from putting themselves up for office and did not allow secret balloting, more than a dozen activists traveled at their own expense to the county town, then the provincial capital, and finally to Beijing to file complaints. They knew the Organic Law by heart and, even though none of its clauses spoke directly to the issue of self-nomination,[11] they recited it at every stop along the way while petitioning for a new election (Tian Yuan, 1993).

When they pursue claims that approach the transgressive, protesters often rely on quite assertive tactics. They, for instance, occasionally "skip

---

[11] The trial law only mentions "direct election" (art. 9) and the "principle of self-governance" (art. 1) as plausible grounds for such a claim.

levels" (*yueji*) in the hope that higher-ranking officials will be more sympathetic to their demands (Bernstein and Lü, 2003: 183–84; Fang Guomin, 1993; O'Brien and Li, 1995: 778; Li and O'Brien, 1996, 43; Interview 36; but cf. Wang Zirui and Wang Songmiao, 2001: 31; Zhao Shukai, 2003). In one Hebei case, a group of villagers, after a fruitless trip to the county civil affairs bureau, bypassed the city and province and went directly to Beijing to protest a fraudulent vote. Their main complaint was that the village Party branch had proposed all the candidates in an election.[12] They, on the contrary, demanded that only villagers should have the right to nominate candidates – a right that would not be formally recognized until 1998. This claim, arguably transgressive at the time, was raised in a typically boundary-spanning fashion: the activists maintained that the Party branch should not name the candidates, because villagers then would be voting against the Party leadership if they cast their ballots for anyone other than the branch's nominees. Because they had no desire to challenge Party rule, the branch should refrain from making any nominations. This argument did not go over well at the township and county. But when a Ministry of Civil Affairs official responsible for implementing village self-governance heard their story and learned that a sizable delegation had made its way to Beijing, he was delighted and commented that the activists' demands were "as a matter of fact 'reasonable' [*you daoli*], though strictly speaking not backed up by the law" (Interview 1). Within a matter of days, the official had sent two staff members to look into their claims. In the course of a long investigation that ended with the election being annulled, ministry officials appeared three times on a television show devoted to investigative journalism. Immediately following the evening news, in front of a national audience, they openly supported the activists and warned other local leaders to draw the appropriate lessons (Interviews 1, 2).[13]

Boundary-spanning claims demanding the recall of unpopular cadres have also undermined villagers' committee directors who have engaged in objectionable behavior. In 1996, for example, a township Party secretary outside Harbin barred voters from proposing nominees for village director and instead selected a single candidate himself. A voter who was familiar with the Organic Law put up a poster denouncing this phony "election"

---

[12] On villager dissatisfaction with the electoral process when Party branches or (especially) township governments nominate candidates, see Kennedy (2002).

[13] Media outlets, of course, are often much less accommodating. A 1997 documentary, for example, about villagers petitioning for their electoral rights was abruptly canceled because of fears it would raise unrealistic expectations (Kaye, 1997, November 6).

and demanded a new round of balloting. The poster writer was promptly detained by the township government for twenty-four days, and nothing came of his complaint.

Over the next few years, the village director enriched himself through land speculation that he hid from the public. In late 1998 the real-estate sales were exposed, under pressure from villagers who cited regulations that promised financial transparency. This also happened to be around the time that the revised Organic Law was enacted. When some villagers saw a television program trumpeting the law and learned of their right to recall elected directors, they contacted the original poster writer, went to the township, and purchased two copies of the law and other relevant regulations. The protest leaders then held ten sessions to review the documents, after which they decided to launch a recall drive. In short order, they gathered 746 signatures (more than twice as many as required) calling for the director's removal. After their petition was rebuffed by the village leadership, they proceeded to the township once again and found a new Party secretary who sent a team of investigators to verify the signatures and organize a recall meeting. In the ensuing vote, the village director was ousted by nearly a two-to-one margin. Officials from the National People's Congress and the Party secretary of Harbin (the provincial capital) praised the outcome as evidence of increasing democratic awareness in the countryside and effective use of the Organic Law to supervise grass-roots cadres and protect villagers' rights (Liu, 2000: 32–33).

Another more recent impeachment effort in Zhejiang, however, ended with armed police breaking up a self-organized election and destroying the ballot boxes. After a township leader rejected a request to hold a meeting to dismiss an acting village director, more than half the village's registered voters convened the meeting on their own. The township immediately declared their recall vote invalid, but the villagers went ahead and set up an election committee to nominate a new slate of candidates. They consulted a law professor from a nearby university and a provincial people's congress deputy, and were advised that they were acting within their legal rights. A week later, just after the replacement election began, more than one hundred local officials and police forced two invited observers (a Xinhua journalist and one of the village's legal advisers) to leave the balloting area and then halted the election. Despite this, villagers reportedly remained determined to exercise their right to choose a village chief and said they would reconvene the election at a later date (Peaceful village election, 2004, February 26).

These episodes suggest that rightful resistance is not merely an example of clever but futile claims making, of using the language of power deftly but to no avail. Unlike many disillusioned intellectuals in China's cities, who tend to make sweeping, transgressive demands (such as calling for a reassessment of the 1989 protests), rural rightful resisters usually take issue with more prosaic examples of policy misimplementation and opponents who are within ready reach. They seldom refer to grand constitutional principles to back up their claims and instead cast their charges in the modest language of loyal intentions.[14] They find fault with clear-cut violations of central policies and laws and also subtle instances of manipulation and selective implementation (O'Brien and Li, 1999), while targeting cadres who intentionally misread laws, tailor them, or conform to vague, incomplete clauses while ignoring their spirit. They skillfully "venue shop" (Rochon, 1998: 237) and take advantage of the limited institutionalization of Chinese politics to press their demands wherever their chances look best. Fully aware of the many fissures that crisscross the Chinese state, they make claims that they believe some political elites will find reasonable and well intentioned.

Of course, as we saw in Chapter 1, the odds are stacked against even the most adept rightful resisters, because their targets can almost always point to conflicting norms that make boundary-spanning claims appear extreme. Censorious villagers, for example, may cite specific clauses in the Organic Law or speak of their "democratic rights" but their targets can depict such demands as dangerously transgressive by invoking the principle of "upholding Party leadership" or the need to maintain "stability above all." The specter of populist cadres who ignore state quotas and other assignments is often used by township leaders to delegitimize even well-founded arguments for free and fair elections. Some county and provincial leaders, too, have been slow to throw their support behind villagers' self-governance, on grounds that it would slow economic growth and cripple administrative efficiency. Elections in large parts of Guangdong, Yunnan, Guangxi, and Hainan only began in the late 1990s, a decade or more after the original Organic Law was passed (S. Chan, 1998; Unger, 2000).

[14] Boundary-spanning claims are generally not a symptom of an "alienated legal culture" (Potter, 1994: 357) or of a broader cynicism bred by long experience with arbitrary rule. The goals of rightful resisters do not center on embarrassing a regime that claims to derive its legitimacy partly from adherence to law but that is often unwilling to live with the procedural justice it makes available. Instead, rightful resisters act as if they have a right to due process and strive to make the best of the gap "between professed ideals and lived reality" (Alford, 1993: 58).

Pressing for Accountability

The media are also unlikely to champion boundary-spanning claims unless villagers "try something dramatic or when the tension spirals out of control and attracts the attention of provincial or national leaders" (Liu, 2000: 31). Daring newspapers or television stations that report misconduct by local officials can come under pressure or be subject to editorial reshuffles. Some investigative journalists have been detained, or even roughed up, for championing popular claims (A. Chan, 2002: 20; Interview 43; Lu Yunfei, 1993; Zhu Kexin, 1993). When all is said and done, officials often send in the police to round up rightful resisters who disrupt a rigged election or lodge a complaint (Cai, 2004: 446–47), or they instruct civil affairs bureaus to conduct cursory investigations or spend years gathering evidence. In today's China, making boundary-spanning claims merely helps villagers win a seat at the table; in the "politics of signification" (della Porta, 1999: 69, 92) cadres have many more resources than ordinary villagers to see to it that their understanding of which claims are legitimate comes out on top.[15]

Still, tussles over boundary-spanning claims do not always end in disappointment for rightful resisters. When resourceful villagers cite patently illegal and "undemocratic behavior" or obvious evasion of central intent, their demands can generate considerable pressure on rural cadres and make it difficult to label protest organizers "individuals with ulterior motives" (*bie you yongxin de ren*). And this pressure, like that generated by most nonviolent action, does not hinge on moral authority, "mobilization of shame," or winning over opponents (Schock, 2005: 8). A target's conscience may be pricked, and skillful rhetoric can corner a disloyal official, but more often than not rightful resistance produces concessions through nonviolent coercion: it forces opponents to make changes by undermining their power and legitimacy,[16] while depriving them of resources they use to rule (Schock, 2005: 8, 38). Although large, well-organized protests, for instance, often lead to repression, local officials can also be disciplined for the sheer existence of collective petitions, with penalties growing for the number of complainants, the frequency of incidents, the number of

---

[15] Rural cadres, of course, are not alone in interpreting central documents to their own advantage. Villagers can be just as selective and deceptive as the cadres they challenge in their efforts to bargain out new rights. Rightful resisters may attach exaggerated importance to Party propaganda. Or they may creatively misread laws or vague and ambiguous national policies to push for political changes that even central authorities might not sanction (Li and O'Brien, 1996: 45–46). At a certain point, such claims become transgressive, not boundary spanning.

[16] In particular, it can threaten an official's career by exposing disloyalty to the Center.

injuries or deaths, and the level of government reached (Interviews 56, 58; Minzner, 2005). On the one hand, this encourages local officials to suppress contention at an early stage; on the other hand, it motivates villagers to increase the number, size, organization, and reach of their actions, because this may draw in higher levels after rightful resisters "depict their problems in precisely the form that is necessary to generate elite involvement" (Minzner, 2005).[17] Concessions are particularly likely when activists manage to go a step further and locate champions in the media, who can lift the claims of rightful resisters to the ideological high ground by linking them to the Party's commitment to develop "socialism" and "rule by law."

There is also a progression at work. As the Party leadership experiments with reforms designed to enhance cadre accountability, claims that in the mid-1990s lay near the transgressive end of the spectrum have become more (or even fully) contained. This can be seen in the number of episodes we have recounted that occurred between the passage of the trial Organic Law (1987) and the appearance of the revised law (1998). Many claims about nominations and secret balloting are no longer boundary spanning, and others that were clearly transgressive have now emerged as foci of rightful resistance. Examples of new boundary-spanning claims (Interviews 36, 37; Li, 1999; Li Fan, 2003; Liu Jing and Lin Yanxing, 2003) include such statements as "villagers have the right to choose village Party secretaries," "villagers' committee directors have a right to establish a national association," "directors may sue village accountants who refuse to hand over account books," "villagers' committee candidates have the right to mount public campaigns," "villagers have the right to file administrative lawsuits against township officials who manipulate elections," and "villagers' committee directors have the right to sue townships that dismiss them." None of these issues is dealt with in any detail by the revised Organic Law, the Administrative Litigation Law, or other measures, and their emergence as points of contention is a sign that "contentious conversation" (Tilly, 2002: 111–22) and political change continue to shift the "gray zone" within which rightful resistance flourishes. Every reform or concession, however small,

---

[17] This is one reason that a popular rhyme in the countryside goes "a big disturbance leads to a big solution, a small disturbance leads to a small solution, and no disturbance leads to no solution" (Gonganbu, 2001: 24; Zhonggong Sichuan, 2002: 30). On the "letters and visits" disciplinary system and how it can (perversely) "reward larger and better-organized petition movements directed at progressively higher levels of the Chinese bureaucracy," see Minzner (2005).

opens up space for new boundary-spanning claims to grow. Although the battleground may move on to new frontiers, so long as officials throughout the hierarchy are not fully united, there are weak points in the structure of power – ambiguities in law, policies, and commitments (and in how officials interpret them) that rightful resisters can exploit.

Payoffs

What is to be gained by working at the boundary between official, prescribed politics and politics by other means? What can be learned by looking at claims that are simultaneously normative and nonnormative, in the eyes of some regime members rule conforming, in the eyes of others rule violating?

First, exploring boundary-spanning claims promises a better understanding of the dynamics of contention because it gets us away from the static quality of much research on contentious politics (McAdam, Tarrow, and Tilly, 2001: 18, 43, 73) and draws attention to state and movement trajectories. Perhaps most important in this regard, investigating claims that are neither transgressive nor contained can offer insights into how the very meaning of contained and transgressive shifts over time. Zeroing in on acts that share some of the advantages of transgression (surprise, uncertainty, and novelty) and some of the benefits of contained claims making (accepted, familiar, and easy to employ) (McAdam, Tarrow, and Tilly, 2001: 41) can cast light on those critical moments in the evolution of a repertoire of contention when what is forbidden one year is tolerated the next and is readily accepted the third. Such research may also help clarify why these junctures are sometimes sudden tipping points and sometimes the product of gradual, incremental experimentation (Sewell, 1990; Tilly, 1993).

Moreover, while it is true that, at the extreme, contained contention tends to reproduce a regime (McAdam, Tarrow, and Tilly, 2001: 8), closer to the blurry boundary ambiguity itself can be an engine of change. The actions of rightful resisters may, in other words, exploit existing channels while transforming them at the same time. In systems where the rules themselves are contested, and precious few forms of contained claims making exist,[18]

---

[18] Some examples of contained claims making in China include petitions to people's congress deputies (O'Brien, 1994a; Shi, 1997), lobbying by women's and environmental groups (Jing, 2000; Zheng, 2000), individual visits to protest official misconduct under the Regulation on Letters and Visits (Cai, 2004; X. Chen, 2003; Luehrmann, 2003; Thireau and Hua, 2003),

scrutinizing boundary-spanning claims can provide leverage over questions such as how challengers become polity members and how demands for inclusion come to fruition or not.

In China, people who have become polity members in the eyes of central officials (at least as regards village elections) are fighting to be seen as something more than subjects or challengers by local officials. Certain community members have come to appreciate that unrealized (and often ambiguous) state commitments and "programmatic rights"[19] can be a source of inclusion, and they are busy exploiting the gap between rights promised and rights delivered. To protect themselves and improve their odds of success, these exacting critics tender irreproachable demands and profess little more than a desire to make the system live up to what it is supposed to be. Their claims are usually mindful and circumscribed, local and parochial rather than national and autonomous (Tilly, 1986: 391–93). The regime has promised them a place in the polity, and they expect the system to do justice to its billing.

This finding out what the rules of the game are by probing the limits of the permissible, this renegotiating the terms of citizenship, becomes particularly visible when boundary-spanning claims are examined. For the contained-transgressive border is a key frontier where concessions are extracted, and here it becomes clear whether still-contested demands for inclusion are making headway and citizenship is becoming less partial and incomplete.[20]

Studying boundary-spanning claims also promises to bring the relationship between states and popular contention into clearer focus. Commentators have frequently complained that students of contentious politics overlook the "internal workings of government" (Zald, 1992: 339). McAdam, Tarrow, and Tilly (2001: 74) go so far as to argue that the literature as a whole has been movement-centered: that "to the extent that it enters at all, the state generally acts as a *diabolus ex machina*, producing opportunities, awaiting mobilization, landing heavily on some actors and facilitating

---

class-action lawsuits (Liebman, 1998), and appeals and lawsuits under the 1991 Administrative Litigation Law and various regulations on administrative review (O'Brien and Li, 2004; Pei, 1997; Tang, 2005).

[19] Nathan (1985: 111) notes that all Chinese constitutions have contained some programmatic rights, which were presented as goals to be realized, but which could not be currently enjoyed.

[20] Chapter 6 provides an extended treatment of the implications of rightful resistance for citizenship.

others, but not participating directly in contention."[21] Examining boundary-spanning claims addresses these objections by placing the state at center stage and redirecting our attention away from those contesting power and toward the interplay of popular forces and state actors. By observing how rightful resisters work the territory between different levels of government, for example, we can learn more about why certain sectors of the government accept claims to citizenship while others deny them. Exploring boundary-spanning claims, in other words, requires unpacking the state and at the same time unpacks the state further.

In China, what emerges is a multilayered state that has grand aspirations but formidable principal-agent problems (O'Brien and Li, 1999; Wedeman, 2001; but cf. Edin, 2003; Naughton and Yang, 2004: 11). The Center has structured the implementation environment deftly for some policies, but for others, current methods of cadre monitoring are not working as well as they might. China's street-level bureaucrats have many "resources for resistance" (Lipsky, 1980: 23–25), and on some policies (e.g., increased accountability) many see little reason to accede to central plans.

Peering into the state also clarifies why central officials might promote village elections and condone rightful resistance. In particular, it suggests that empowering ordinary people to serve as watchdogs can make sense even to dyed-in-the-wool Leninists who need on-the-ground sources of information if they are to uncover and stop misconduct by their local agents. Seen in this light, initiating elections and allowing (or even encouraging) boundary-spanning claims are first and foremost solutions to a principal-agent problem: they have less to do with liberal ideology or any newfound affection for pluralism and more to do with preventing local officials from thwarting measures designed to reign them in. Why the Center has risked drawing ordinary people into policy implementation becomes evident only when we steer clear of a society-centered approach to contention and spend time discovering why officials at different points in the hierarchy act as they do.

To do this, an "anthropology of the state" (Migdal, 2001) is needed. This means studying the state from its lowest administrative legs up to its midsection and its head; it also entails examining relations between

---

[21] On the "effort to shift from more static to dynamic analyses of movements and other forms of contentious politics, and the focus on intersections between movements, opponents and authorities [to] broaden the scope beyond a narrower movement-centered analysis," see Andrews (2004: 6).

different levels of government, and identifying a constellation of state-society interactions that occur in the regions as well as at the Center (Diamant, 2001: 453, 473). In the rural Chinese case, this approach leads us to probe various dyads – villagers and village cadres, village cadres and township cadres, township cadres and county officials, villagers and officials at higher levels, midlevel leaders and officials at higher levels – to determine why on certain issues central officials tend to be good listeners, counties are sometimes "paper tigers," and townships are predictably unsympathetic. Like many other states, the Chinese state is less a monolith than a hodge-podge of disparate actors, many of whom have conflicting interests and multiple identities. The same central state that discriminates against villagers when they wish to move to urban areas can be a benefactor that acts on their election complaints. The same village cadres who at times protect villagers from overbearing higher-ups can be antagonists when people lodge complaints about rigged elections. Inspecting dyads and disaggregating the state illuminate the cross pressures under which officials live, and make sense of behavior that otherwise seems inexplicable; they also enable us to see how strategies of contention adapt to the contours of a reforming regime as the popular classes discover which openings can be exploited and where their best opportunities lie.

This research strategy has implications beyond China. Boundary-spanning claims probably emerge everywhere, and examining them across time and territory could enhance our understanding of what is transgressive and contained, and what it means for an act to be transgressive or contained. Although homing in on this type of claims making might complicate efforts to construct airtight categories, it would also provide an opportunity to triangulate between various intrastate and popular perspectives on what is contained and what is transgressive to produce a nuanced, on-the-ground view of the political and discursive opportunity structures (for this latter term, see Koopmans and Statham, 1999b: 228). Much might be learned by examining claims that are normative, nonnormative, or something in between, depending on whose perspective one adopts. Such research can, for a start, help locate a polity across a number of dimensions: what is institutionalized and what is not, what is participation and what is resistance, who is a challenger and who is a polity member, what citizenship entails and who enjoys it.

4

Tactical Escalation

Forms of contention generally have a limited life-span. Even the most creative tactics tend, over time, to lose their power to surprise opponents and stir followers. Tactical escalation offers a means to regain momentum when established techniques of protest no longer create the sense of crises and excitement they once did. As the effectiveness of familiar methods wanes, enterprising activists sometimes turn to even more disruptive acts to demonstrate their commitment, leave their opponents rattled, and mobilize supporters (on the advantages of unruliness, see Andrews, 2001; Gamson, 1990; Guigni, 1999: xvi–xviii; Tarrow, 1998: 91–105, 163). Although confrontational tactics can at times alienate the public and generate a backlash (Rochon, 1988), they can also help draw newcomers to a cause (Jasper, 1997: 248) while offering leverage to actors who have few other resources (Piven and Cloward, 1992).

Tactical escalation typically involves dramatic gestures and provocations that test the vulnerabilities of one's foes. It may appear in the form of a single tactic (e.g., the sit-in, the mock shantytown, the suffrage parade) that vividly symbolizes injustice and is difficult for the authorities and onlookers to ignore. Or it may arise as a cluster of related innovations (Voss and Sherman, 2000) that reflects a fresh approach to protest and signals that a new "tactical grammar" (Ennis, 1987: 531) is at work.

In rural China, much like it did during the American civil rights movement, revitalizing the repertoire of contention has entailed a radicalization of tactics – a move from humble petitioning to the politics of disruption (McAdam, 1983: 738). In places such as Hengyang county, Hunan,[1] rightful

---

[1] Also the Hunan counties of Lianyuan, Ningxiang, and Qidong, as well as Xinyang county, Henan, and Zhangpu county, Fujian. See Duan Xianju et al. (2000), Yu Jianrong (2001), and Interviews 37, 79, 54, 80.

resistance has become far more confrontational since the early 1990s, as the mediated tactics of the past are being demoted or adapted and more direct protest routines have been adopted.

In its basic form, rightful resistance is a rather tame form of contention that makes use of existing (if clogged) channels of participation and relies heavily on the patronage of elite backers. It is mediated in the sense that complainants do not directly confront their opponents, but instead rely on a powerful third party to address their claims. Activists at this point always act under the sufferance of, and energetically seek support from, officials as high as central policy makers, cadres as low as any local official other than the ones they are denouncing, and journalists (or others) who can communicate their grievances to high-ranking authorities. In this basic form, rightful resisters may mobilize popular action, but their main aim is to use the threat of unrest to attract attention from possible mediators and to apply pressure on officeholders at higher levels to rein in their underlings. Protest leaders, in other words, seek to bypass their adversaries rather than to compel them to negotiate.

Direct action is quite different. In Hengyang, for instance, activists increasingly place demands on their targets in person and try to wring concessions from them on the spot. This form of rightful resistance does not depend on high-level intercession but on skilled rabble-rousers and the popular pressure they can muster. Although protest organizers still cite central policies rather than sounding "fire alarms" (McCubbins and Schwarz, 1984), they (and the villagers who join them) try to put out the fires themselves – they enforce rather than inform. In direct rightful resistance, although activists may still view the Center as a source of legitimacy, a symbolic backer, and a guarantor against repression, they no longer genuinely expect higher-ups to intervene on their behalf. Instead, they regard themselves and their supporters to be capable of resolving the problems at hand. Acting as ever in the name of faithful policy implementation, rightful resisters now confront their targets (often face-to-face) and mobilize as much popular action as they can to induce them to halt policy violations. Direct action, in the end, relies on appeals to the community rather than to higher level authorities, and its goal is immediate concessions.

This chapter begins by examining some of the forms that direct rightful resistance takes in rural China. Then we move on to a series of questions suggested by the broader literature on tactical innovation: Are these tactics truly new and how widespread are they? Who is mainly responsible for initiating direct action, newcomers or seasoned complainants? And, most important, why is tactical escalation occurring? Along the way we alight on a number of explanations for tactical change, including ones that underscore the role of prior experiences with contention, resources, and popular support.

It is worth mentioning that studies of tactical innovation usually concentrate on how a repertoire of contention evolves rather than why certain tactics are chosen (Jasper, 1997: 234; Brown, 2003).[2] We tread a middle path here, emphasizing both external forces that structure the options open to rightful resisters and internal factors that sometimes lead them to make tactical decisions that attention to the environment alone would never predict. We derive most of our conclusions from interviews with rural protest organizers about actions they have taken and why they thought certain tactics were effective or not (on the advantages of interviewing versus after-the-fact theorizing, see Brown, 2003). We also draw on government reports that detail episodes of popular unrest, other written accounts, and our own earlier field research.

Three Variants of Direct Action

Mediated contention is a form of seeking grace from intercessors whose characteristic expression is group petitioning. Direct action, on the contrary, rests on a public rallying call and high-pressure methods that are designed to coax local leaders to revoke an improper decision. When employing direct tactics, protesters and their supporters assert a right to resist (not only to expose and denounce) official misconduct.

In contemporary rural China, direct action has three main variants. The least confrontational might be called publicizing a policy. In the course of "studying" (*xue*) or "disseminating documents" (*xuanchuan wenjian*), activists make known or distribute materials that (they contend) show that county, township, or village cadres have violated a central or provincial directive. They do so for the purpose of alerting the public to official misconduct and mobilizing opposition to unapproved "local policies" (*tu zhengce*). The documents they select always relate to issues that concern villagers greatly, be it reducing excessive taxes and fees, decrying the use of violence, or promoting well-run village elections. In Hengyang county alone, activists have publicized the following materials: President Jiang

---

[2] On tactical choices and the development of a student protest repertoire in twentieth-century China, see Wasserstrom (1992) and Esherick and Wasserstrom (1990).

Zemin's 1998 speech on reducing "peasant burdens" (*nongmin fudan*) (Wang Xinqing et al., 1998, January 10: 1), Hunan Provincial Document No. 9 (1996) on the same subject (Interview 7; Yu Jianrong, 2001: 559), and the 1993 Agriculture Law (Interview 6), especially its clauses (arts. 18, 19, 59) that forbid imposing unlawful fees, affirm the right of villagers to "reject" (*jujue*) unsanctioned exactions, and stipulate that higher levels should work to halt such impositions and have them returned to villagers.

Participants in direct action use a variety of methods to make beneficial policies known and to mobilize resistance to their violation. They may begin by showing government papers they have acquired to their neighbors. The most inconspicuous way to do this is in a private home (Interviews 5, 6, 7, 38). A somewhat more overt approach involves photocopying central or provincial documents and then handing or selling them to interested villagers (Interviews 17, 21; also Zhang, 2005: 42). One activist in Hengyang (Interview 17) proudly explained that he charged his neighbors precisely what he paid the copy shop and actually lost a fair sum when some villagers walked off with photocopied documents without reimbursing him.

As their confidence mounts, rightful resisters may turn to more public ways to expose local misconduct. An example of this is playing tape recordings, or even using megaphones or loudspeakers, to inform villagers of beneficial policies. In Henan, for instance, in response to township manipulation of village elections and increasing exactions, a young man from Suiping county used a megaphone to acquaint his fellow villagers with the Organic Law of Villagers' Committees (1998) and central directives prohibiting excessive taxes and fees (Hao Fu and Chen Lei, 2002). In Hengyang county, a middle-aged shopkeeper went a step further and was detained and beaten by township authorities for his cheekiness. He rented some audio equipment, set it up on his roof, and aired central and provincial documents about easing peasant burdens to his entire village (Interview 19).

Disseminating policies need not employ even the simplest technology and can occur at unexpected times, as is seen when resourceful activists appropriate apolitical rituals or celebrations and turn them to their own ends. In rural Hengyang, for instance, rightful resisters hijacked a traditional dragon dance during Spring Festival (for three consecutive years!) to publicize central documents granting villagers a right to reject unreasonable burdens and (on the sly) to solicit donations for their cause. While parading up and down every lane, they summarized the "spirit of central documents" (*zhongyang wenjian jingshen*) in rhymed verse, chanting in unison as they wound their way from home to home (Interviews 21, 39).

Three Variants of Direct Action

Many efforts to make beneficial policies known are limited to a single village; others expand the field of action. An example of the latter is employing "propaganda vehicles" (*xuanchuan che*) or putting up posters throughout a township criticizing excessive fees or rigged elections (Interviews 8, 21, 39). One activist in Hengyang (Interview 5), already famous for organizing a road blockade in 1999, rented a truck and used it as a mobile broadcasting station to transmit provincial directives limiting rural taxation to a number of small hamlets scattered throughout his township (see also Johnson, 2004: 63, 67, 71). Another protest leader, after participating in an expensive and fruitless collective complaint to the Hunan provincial government in 1996, copied excerpts of central documents calling for tax and fee reductions on large posters and had a group of young villagers paste them up around the county (Interview 8).

For many of these tactics, the intended audience does not have to make any special effort. They can stay indoors, open their windows and listen, or simply walk outside and watch what is going on. One variety of dissemination that involves a more direct (if surreptitious) effort to attract a crowd is presenting a movie and then publicizing beneficial policies moments before the show begins. In Henan, as early as 1993, a villager did this with a State Council regulation that limited township and village fees (Yu Xin, 1993). Activists may also inform villagers about poor implementation at rural markets. This again involves taking advantage of a ready-made audience. According to several Hengyang protest organizers, on market days they sometimes simply set up a loudspeaker in the town center and read out documents concerning tax and fee reductions that were issued by the Center, Hunan province, or Hengyang city (Yu Jianrong, 2001: 555; Interviews 4, 13, 40). In such cases, even though rightful resisters may do their best to minimize confrontation, clashes frequently occur after local officials appear. Township cadres, when they heard the Hengyang activists disclosing fee limits on a busy market day in 1998, first cut off electricity to their loudspeaker. But a sympathetic restaurant owner stepped in and supplied the villagers with a generator. Then, a number of officials came out of their offices and ordered the protesters to disperse, only to find themselves upbraided for impeding the lawful dissemination of central policies.

Although they usually shy away from physical confrontation with their adversaries, policy disseminators sometimes publicize policies in ways that cannot help but lead to conflict. One technique sure to produce official ire is distributing documents near a government compound. A Hengyang activist (Interview 6), for example, excerpted central directives limiting peasant burdens on large, red posters and plastered them on several buildings in the township government complex. Protest organizers in Jiangxi have likewise sold pamphlets about Beijing's fee reduction policies directly in front of a Party office building (Ding Guoguang, 2001: 433–34). In both cases, these tactics cornered township officials, heightened their fears that further popular action was imminent, and led to a swift (and negative) response. In Hengyang, township cadres removed the posters; in Jiangxi, the booksellers were arrested.

By far the most assertive form of publicizing policies involves both deliberate confrontation and undisguised mass mobilization. One common tactic employed in Hengyang is to trail behind township tax collectors as they try to collect fees, all the time loudly quoting tax reduction directives (Interviews 13, 21). This practice not only challenges the legality of an exaction; it also often draws scores of onlookers and encourages bolder villagers to withhold their payments. Another highly provocative form of propagating policies involves calling so-called "ten thousand-person meetings" (*wan ren dahui*) in a government compound to study policies that excoriate corruption or limit fees (Duan Xianju et al., 2000). Activists in Xinyang county, Henan, for example, have organized numerous mass meetings (the largest of which township officials estimated drew more than 6,000 participants) to publicize central policies and provincial regulations that call for reducing excessive appropriation (Interview 80). Such gatherings can rapidly turn into melees when township or county officials intervene. In Hengyang, a protest leader organized a mass meeting to force a rollback in taxes and fees. To symbolize the activists' willingness to challenge the township head-on, the speaker's podium was placed just steps away from the main government office building. Hundreds of villagers were invited to attend the rally and the organizers planned to detain and deliver to the city authorities any township official who ventured to interfere (Interview 4). In another widely reported episode in Ningxiang county, Hunan, after a multivillage band of Volunteer Propagandists for the Policy of Reducing Burdens used tape recorders and hired a loudspeaker truck in 1999 to tell villagers about their rights, protest organizers assembled four thousand people outside the town government complex to demand adherence to central and provincial directives that capped taxation and opposed corruption. But before the speakers could broadcast a word, the assembled villagers rushed into the compound. More than one thousand police and five hundred soldiers then dispersed the demonstrators, using clubs and tear gas. Many villagers were arrested or injured, and one man was killed (Bernstein and Lü, 2003: 128–29).

Three Variants of Direct Action

Publicizing documents does not always lead to repression; it can sometimes further protesters' ends. By reading out or distributing central policies, activists expose unauthorized actions, shatter information blockades, and demonstrate (both to officials and interested bystanders) that it may be possible to muster large-scale resistance to local misconduct.[3] In so doing, rightful resisters assert their right to know about beneficial measures and to communicate their knowledge to others. Ordinary villagers may be emboldened to join them, or at least support them, not simply because they have been made aware that central directives have been neglected, but because they have seen fellow community members take the lead in standing up to unsanctioned local acts. As we will see in the next chapter, when a campaign of dissemination unfolds, formerly uninvolved villagers sometimes become much less timid insomuch as they observe new "peasant leaders" (*nongmin lingxiu*) emerging and a weakening of the local government's usual stranglehold over political life.

The second variant of direct action is "demanding a dialogue" (*yaoqiu duihua*). Activists and their supporters, often after collective petitioning or publicizing a policy fails to budge their foes, may insist on face-to-face meetings with local officials (or their proxies) to urge immediate revocation of unlawful local measures. Rightful resisters have used this tactic in Hengyang most notably to fight mounting school fees.[4] Because many townships can no longer collect as much revenue as they used to (owing to both pressure from above and resistance from below), and many poorer districts are financially starved in the wake of the 1994 fiscal reforms, township leaders have frequently allowed local schoolmasters to increase educational fees on their own.[5] Self-styled "burden-reduction representatives" (*jianfu daibiao*), usually after hard-pressed parents come to them for help, may demand that all overcharges be returned. Instead of lodging a collective complaint, which would have been more common in the past, a group of representatives may proceed directly to the school. The arrival of these "peasant heroes" (*nongmin yingxiong*) typically attracts a large crowd, not

[3] For urban workers in China who "are no longer simply presenting their grievances to those in charge, but publicizing them," see Kernen (2003a: 5). On being "not only concerned with handing over a petition to the authorities, but also with inserting their claims into the 'public arena,'" see Kernen (2003b: 9).

[4] On other clashes over school fees in three Hunan counties, see Zhang (2005).

[5] Beginning in 2001, the Center began increasing rural education funding significantly (Bernstein 2003: 31–32). Whether this defuses conflicts between schoolmasters and villagers should become clear soon.

least because the parents who invited them often encourage onlookers to come, support them, and watch the drama unfold. In one such incident in Hengyang, the lead activist requested a face-to-face meeting with the head of a township middle school. In front of a large assembly of local residents, he displayed documents issued by the city and county education bureau that fixed fees at a certain level and told the schoolmaster item by item how much more students had been charged. The presence of nearly twenty hardened "burden reduction representatives," as well as more than one hundred bystanders, led to a round of intense bargaining, after which the schoolmaster agreed to return about 80 percent of the illegal charges (Interview 18).

But events do not always unfold so peacefully. On another occasion also in Hengyang, a schoolmaster postponed a scheduled dialogue so that he would have time to hire a group of local toughs to scare off the "burden reduction representatives." But when the meeting began and the school-master signaled his men to make their move, an elderly bystander came to the defense of the representatives. He said he admired their altruism and would protect them to the end (Interview 18).

"Demanding a dialogue" has also been employed against far more powerful targets than local school heads. In Qidong county, Hunan, a riot occurred in July 1996 in which hundreds of people attacked township and village officials and smashed the signboards of the township government. (Destroying the placards that identify government offices is a symbolic denial of their legitimacy, much like burning a flag or an effigy.) The county Party secretary rushed to the area to look into what had caused the unrest. At the urging of hundreds of villagers, he agreed to have an unlawfully collected education surcharge rescinded. The incident ended, but news of the successful protest spread rapidly. Upon learning of it, villagers in other parts of Qidong county were inspired to rise up and demand dialogues. In early September 1996 three activists arranged a movie presentation in order to read out a Hunan provincial document that reduced peasant burdens, to organize villagers to resist excessive education apportionments, and to gather signatures for a petition to present to the township. After the video ended, just before a group of indignant moviegoers set out for a nearby government compound, a skirmish broke out with township officials who had come to dissuade the protesters from demonstrating. Two days later, more than six hundred villagers, carrying banners and flags, beating drums and gongs, and setting off fireworks, paraded down the busiest street in the township to the main office building to insist on a meeting with the Party secretary and the government head. Over the next three days, hundreds of villagers from four other townships in Qidong marched to their township seats and demanded dialogues with Party and government leaders (Yu Jianrong, 2001: 558–60).

If publicizing a policy aims to remind errant cadres that they are vulnerable to rightful claims, demanding a dialogue is directed at unresponsive targets who refuse to back down. At this stage, negotiation and compromise are still possible, even desired by activists. Cool bargaining and face-saving concessions become distinctly less feasible when protesters turn to the third variant of direct action: face-to-face defiance.

Activists who use this tactic confront local officials on the job and try to halt improper acts. They, for example, flatly reject unauthorized impositions and loudly encourage others to follow suit (Interviews 13, 17). In Hengyang in 1998, one particularly feisty rightful resister followed township tax collectors wherever they went. With two other "burden reduction representatives" at his side, he brandished a copy of a central directive and contested every effort to collect even 1 yuan (U.S. 12¢) too much. The tax collectors dared not challenge him in public, but one of them muttered an insult after he refused to get out of their way and let them do their job. A scuffle broke out, and hundreds of villagers came to defend the fee resister, eventually pinning the beleaguered taxman in his jeep (Interview 17). That same year a similar incident occurred in another township in Hengyang county. Two "burden-reduction representatives" had locked horns with township revenue collectors when they tried to prevent the collection of several unauthorized fees. When the officials struck one of the representatives with a flashlight, a shoving match broke out. Again, angry villagers responded, this time overturning two jeeps the township cadres used for their work (Interviews 13, 41).

Rightful resisters may also rely on face-to-face defiance to challenge rigged elections. In one dramatic episode in the early 1990s, a group of villagers in Hubei successfully disrupted a villagers' committee election in which nominations were not handled according to approved procedures. Just as the ballots were being distributed, one villager leapt to the platform where the election committee was presiding, grabbed a microphone and shouted: "Xiong Dachao is a corrupt cadre. Don't vote for him!" Immediately several of his confederates stood up and started shouting words of support, seconding his charges. To further dramatize their resistance, the assembled protesters then tore up their own ballots as well as those of other villagers who were milling about waiting to vote (Zhongguo Jiceng

Zhengquan Jianshe Yanjiuhui, 1994; on six villagers seizing stuffed ballot boxes, see Agence France Presse, 1999, September 4).

Public-minded intellectuals sometimes urge on direct action. The following episode involved both disseminating policies and face-to-face defiance. In Jiangxi, the deputy editor of a rural affairs journal published 12,000 copies of a *Work Manual on Reducing Farmers' Tax Burdens*. He later said: "I was just carrying out my duty to help farmers personally monitor arbitrary fees," and "at the end of the day, central government policies are not enough to help the farmers. They need to be able to help themselves." The book had a section advising farmers how to seek redress and its subtitle was "The imperial sword is in your hands, farmer friends, hold on tight!" Although the editor ultimately lost his position and the provincial government dispatched the police to confiscate as many copies of the book as they could locate, the story received national attention in the newspaper *Southern Weekend (Nanfang Zhoumo)* (Gilley, 2001, April 5; O'Brien and Li, 2004: 78; Wang Zhiquan, 2002: 6; Yang Xuewu, 2001: 39).

The three variants of direct action described here are interrelated and often appear together. In addition, rightful resisters sometimes employ them in sequence, starting by publicizing policies and then moving on to demanding dialogues or face-to-face defiance. Whatever form it takes, direct action marks a significant break from mediated contention. Its appearance leads local cadres (and protesters themselves) into uncharted territory and introduces new uncertainties, especially when activists lose control of their followers or officials panic. It also opens up the possibility that rightful resisters will continue to escalate their tactics (perhaps toward out-and-out violence) while embracing broader and deeper claims (see Rucht, 1990: 171–72) – claims that are general and ideological rather than concrete and specific (Mueller, 1999: 530–31; Tarrow, 1989), claims that challenge the legitimacy of local government rather than the lawfulness of particular decisions.

How New?

Techniques of protest are seldom invented out of whole cloth. More often, they appear at the edge of an existing repertoire of contention as "creative modifications or extensions of familiar routines" (McAdam, Tarrow, and Tilly, 2001: 49; Tilly, 1993: 265–66; in the Chinese context, see Wasserstrom, 1992: 117, 131–33). Innovations, in this way, signal a broadening of tactics and a growing strategic flexibility by activists who are generating a multipronged strategy that can be deployed on many fronts (Andrews, 2001: 77; McCann, 1994: 86, 145; Rochon, 1998: 202–3; Tarrow, 1998: 37, 104).

This is very much the story in rural China today. Mediated tactics continue to be used while direct, confrontational forms of contention have also been adopted. Especially in locations where the old ways have been found wanting again and again, nearly contained acts are being augmented by decidedly boundary-spanning or even transgressive acts, as protesters begin to enforce central directives themselves and to use policies as a weapon in their battles. As a researcher from the Development Research Center of the State Council put it, "'contention within the system' [*tizhi nei kangzheng*] (such as petitioning) is still the main feature of peasant action, but contention outside the system (such as violence) is also obviously increasing. . . . Peasants start by lodging complaints at the county level or higher, and doing so at the province or in Beijing is also fairly common. . . . If the petitions fail, they often turn to 'direct' [*zhijie*] resistance" (Zhao Shukai, 2004: 213, 221).

The repertoire of contention, in other words, has expanded, and some of the newer tunes are becoming quite popular. Protest leaders in places such as Hengyang are "stretching the boundaries" (Tilly, 1978: 155) of rightful resistance and are trying to breathe life into a form of contention that had been enjoying only limited success. In particular, they have established a "radical flank" (McAdam, McCarthy, and Zald, 1996: 14) at a time when it has become clear that the mediators they put their faith in are often ineffective and local opponents are largely impervious to halfhearted pressure from above.

How Widespread?

We can only speak with confidence, at this point, about tactical escalation in Hengyang and a handful of other counties. Moreover, there are good reasons to believe that protest forms spread slower in China than in more open polities where the media deem dramatic, innovative tactics newsworthy (della Porta and Diani, 1999: 186; Rochon, 1988: 102–4) and rapidly transmits accounts of them nationwide (Soule, 1997: 858). In China, tactical diffusion still depends on word of mouth and informal social networks.[6]

[6] On the limited reach and generality of "diffusion" compared with "brokerage," see McAdam, Tarrow, and Tilly (2001: 335). For a discussion of "relational" and "nonrelational" diffusion,

Complainants, in the course of lodging complaints at higher levels (i.e., using mediated tactics), encounter one another in reception rooms, outside "letters and visits offices," and in "petitioners' camps" (*shangfang cun*) and share stories of their frustration with the old forms and victories with the newer ones.[7] Telephones enable protest organizers in different counties to stay in touch and carry tales of inventive tactics far and wide.[8] Migrant workers bring word of popular action in distant locales. Successful tactics often draw a stream of activists from the surrounding area to confer with "peasant heroes" who have achieved what had seemed impossible (Interview 41). Much as it has in other authoritarian settings, "low-intensity forms of communication . . . enable activists to learn their trade, share experiences, and develop common identities" away from official scrutiny and interference (Euchner, 1996: 150–51).

Direct rightful resistance spreads by imitation; it can also become more common owing to contemporaneous creation. Broadly similar grievances and experiences with contention can help forge a collective identity when limited interpersonal contact establishes minimal identification between transmitters and adopters (McAdam and Rucht, 1993), or even without any direct, relational ties (Soule, 1997: 861; Strang and Meyer, 1993; Tarrow, 2005).[9] And this collective identity can inspire a wave of similar protests when a tactic becomes modular (Tarrow, 1998) and adroit practitioners

---

as well as brokerage, see Tarrow (2005). On "contagion effects" in rural China, see Bernstein (2003: 21).

[7] On finding, at any given time, about fifty thousand aggrieved individuals in a petitioners' camp outside one of the largest of Beijing's complaints' offices, see Beech (2004, March 1). "Training classes" (*peixun ban*) run by some public intellectuals in Beijing have also provided opportunities for rural complainants to meet and discuss their experiences.

[8] According to a Chinese researcher, "some leading figures among the peasantry have close ties with dozens or even a hundred peasant complainants inside and outside the province. Sometimes they even assemble to discuss important matters" (Zhao Shukai, 2004: 222). On the "elaborate organization" of many protests, including the existence of designated leaders, public spokespersons, underground core groups, as well as hired lawyers and invited journalists who cover their events, see Tanner (2004: 141). On the creation of a "basically" national student protest repertoire in China by 1919, see Wasserstrom (1992: 131).

[9] Collective identities can be strengthened on the basis of little more than a snippet of news. After the 1996 protests against education surcharges in Hezhou town, Qidong county, Hunan, news of success spread rapidly and other activists argued that elite solidarity was not as great as it seemed, that villagers elsewhere should not suffer more than those in Hezhou, and that other townships were also vulnerable to direct tactics. One protest leader rallied his followers with the words: "We are all citizens of the People's Republic. We live under the same blue sky. Why do we have to pay this unlawful apportionment if our fellow citizens in Hezhou don't?" (Interview 30; also see Yu Jianrong, 2001: 558–60).

either import it wholesale or reinvent it (with perhaps a local twist) to fit their particular situation (Scalmer, 2002: 2).[10]

To this point, Chinese researchers have uncovered evidence of what we call direct rightful resistance in the provinces of Sichuan, Anhui, Hunan, Jiangxi, Henan, Shaanxi, and Hebei (Yang Hao, 1999; Jiang Zuoping and Yang Sanjun, 1999; Duan Xianju et al., 2000; Yu Jianrong, 2001; Liu Shuyun and Bai Lin, 2001; Jiang Zuoping et al., 2001; Ding Guoguang, 2001; Hao Fu and Chen Lei, 2002; Xiao Tangbiao, 2002; Zhao Shukai, 2004).[11] Our 2003–4 and 2004–5 surveys (see Appendix B) showed that direct action occurs throughout rural China. Among 1,314 respondents from twenty-eight provinces who had lodged complaints since 1980, 786 from twenty-six provinces had also led or taken part in "publicizing central policies and laws"; 829 from twenty-seven provinces had led or taken part in "demanding dialogues with local government leaders"; and 280 from fourteen provinces had led or joined other villagers in "rejecting unreasonable burdens."

Origins of Direct Tactics

It is only a start to say that tactics wear out "in the same way that rote speech falls flat" (McAdam, Tarrow, and Tilly, 2001: 138). New tactics are not a "blind reflex" (della Porta and Diani, 1999: 185) or an automatic response to anything. They must be created through an interactive process (Jasper, 1997: 295; Tarrow, 1998: 102) that entails "incessant improvisation on the part of all participants" (McAdam, Tarrow, and Tilly, 2001: 138) and "a series of reciprocal adjustments" (della Porta and Diani, 1999: 186–87). This process depends on strategic decisions by protest leaders and their foes, as well as newly available resources and changes in the external environment. Most of all, in rural China, it hinges on activists who reflect on their earlier experiences with mediated tactics, learn from their successes and failures, and come up with perhaps brilliant, perhaps ill-advised ways

---

[10] On "improvisations upon familiar scripts" in the Shanghai student movement of the 1920s and the protest movement of 1989, see Wasserstrom (1992: 133) and Esherick and Wasserstrom (1990).

[11] Our interviews suggest that direct rightful resistance may be particularly well developed in Dangshan county, Anhui, Gushi county, Henan, and Fengcheng county, Jiangxi. Furthermore, direct tactics in Hunan have appeared not only in Hengyang, but also in the counties of Lianyuan, Ningxiang, Qidong, Taoyuan, Xiangyin, and Yizhang (Duan Xianju et al., 2000).

to pursue their ends the next time around (on tactical virtuosi, see Jasper, 1997: 301, 319–20).

In the following sections, we discuss four factors that have contributed to tactical escalation in the Chinese countryside: defeats, information about government policies and assurances obtained during mediated contention, advances in communications and information technology, and popular support for disruptive protests.

Defeats

Defeat sometimes drives protest leaders underground or spurs them to give up. It may also, however, motivate them to up the ante and touch off a round of tactical escalation. Recurring failures can trigger thoughts about jettisoning ineffective tactics (Beckwith, 2000; McCammon, 2003), while the harsh policing often associated with defeat may usher moderates into private life, leaving the stage to those with more militant inclinations (Tarrow, 1998: 84–85, 150, 158, 201; see also della Porta, 1999: 89–90; della Porta and Diani, 1999: 211).[12] In rural China, a growing realization of the inadequacy[13] and riskiness of mediated tactics has undermined the faith some activists had in lodging complaints and has induced them to take direct action.

For many longtime complainants, the bitter truth is that protectors at higher levels have too often shown themselves to be all talk and little action. Anticipated backers frequently turn out to be little more than a symbolic source of legitimacy, who intervene only when egregious wrongs threaten political stability (such as after village cadres in Henan killed a villager who persisted in pursuing complaints) (Zhang Sutang and Xie Guoji, 1995, March 29: 4). In less incendiary circumstances, rightful resisters who employ mediated tactics are commonly ignored, given the runaround, or harassed. Even if they do receive a favorable response from someone in

---

[12] In Hengyang in 1998, thirteen "burden-reduction representatives" were whittled down to six by threats leveled by a township government. Backed into a corner, the remaining activists felt they either had to accept defeat or change their course of action. They decided to press on and engage in direct action by publicizing the Center's effort to reduce farmers' burdens to every household in the township (Yu Jianrong, 2001: 555).

[13] Our 1999 survey of 1,384 villagers in twenty-five provinces included 190 participants in collective complaints. Of these 190, 3 percent were very satisfied with the outcome of their action, 18 percent relatively satisfied, 24 percent neither satisfied nor dissatisfied, 31 percent dissatisfied, and 23 percent very dissatisfied. For more on this survey, see Appendix B and Li (2001: 1).

power, their antagonists at lower levels often ignore "soft" instructions from above or delay endlessly in implementing them (O'Brien and Li, 1999; Wedeman, 2001; but cf. Edin, 2003; Whiting, 2004: 119).

Defeats arise first and foremost because mediators do not mediate. Delegations languish for weeks waiting for an appointment with leaders who never emerge. Sympathetic words are not backed up with written instructions (Interview 4). Complainants are treated politely in person and then undercut behind their backs (Interview 5). The appearance of many open doors in Beijing (e.g., letters and visits offices at the Central Committee, the Party Discipline Inspection Commission, the National People's Congress, various ministries, *People's Daily*, *Farmer's Daily*) and at lower levels can keep hopes of rightful resisters alive for a while, but only intensifies their resentment when they receive no response, are referred to yet another office, or a complaint ends up in the hands of the official charged with misconduct (on letters and visits, see Bernstein and Lü, 2003: 177–90; Cai, 2004; X. Chen, 2003; Luehrmann, 2003; Minzner, 2005; Thireau and Hua, 2003).[14] According to a researcher from the Hunan Organization Department, "People who visit higher levels to lodge complaints very rarely obtain justice. Justice for them is like a carrot dangling in front of a donkey. The donkey walks for many kilometers but can never eat the carrot" (Zhang Yinghong, 2002; also Cai, 2003: 664, 679).

In the end, many veteran activists have come to doubt the capacity of the Center to ensure faithful policy implementation, and some even think of it as a "clay Buddha" (*ni pusa*) that local officials must bow to but can ignore with impunity (Li, 2004; Interview 10). All this has led to growing frustration among protesters who had relied on mediated tactics and has encouraged some of them to find new ways to pursue their goals.

Information and Assurances

Despite its frequent failure to produce much redress, mediated contention can generate resources and create openings that promote direct contention.

---

[14] Complainants are often rounded up and sent home during annual people's congress sessions and at other times when officials are busy announcing their achievements or showing off their city (see Beech, 2004, March 1). Before the 2004 National People's Congress, for example, the Ministry of Land and Resources issued an urgent circular instructing local officials to use "firm and effective" measures to handle longtime complainants who were disputing land requisitions and to "do everything possible to stabilize the masses in their locality" (*jinliang ba qunzhong wending zai dangdi*) (Guo Tu Ziyuanbu, 2004, February 1).

Activists, most notably, have obtained copies of authoritative "red-headed documents" via mediated contention that confirmed policy violations were taking place. In Hengyang, for instance, Hunan Provincial Regulation No. 9 (1996) on limiting exactions has played a large part in helping activists pinpoint misconduct by local officials. Such documents can be shown to potential supporters to prove, in detailed and clearly worded language, that township and county cadres have betrayed their superiors.

Some of these measures even authorize direct action when central directives are ignored. A 1991 State Council regulation, for example, states: "It is the obligation of farmers to remit taxes to the state, to fulfill the state's procurement quotas for agricultural products, and to be responsible for the various fees and services stipulated in these regulations. Any other demands on farmers to provide financial, material, or labor contributions gratis are illegal and farmers have the right to reject them" (cited in Bernstein and Lü, 2003: 48). Even more authoritatively, the 1993 Agriculture Law (art. 18) explicitly grants villagers the right to refuse to pay illegal impositions. It is true that these acts offer little protection if rejecting a demand leads to detention, a beating, having one's home torn down, or having one's valuables or livestock confiscated. Nor do they spell out punishments for cadres who flout the limits. But this incompleteness has only stimulated some protest leaders to devise their own ways to make these rights real. Among other initiatives, activists in various provinces have organized mass meetings to study and publicize the Agriculture Law and provincial caps on taxation, and they have openly challenged officials who fail to comply with them (Interviews 6, 7; Duan Xianju et al., 2000; Ma Zhongdong, 2000).

Participants in mediated contention also sometimes obtain oral or written assurances that disseminating beneficial policies is legally protected. When several farmers in Hunan asked whether they could publicize documents concerning excessive fees, officials at the provincial Letters and Visits Office encouraged them to do so, so that villagers knew what was forbidden and what was not. On one occasion, the office director also reassured them that such actions were lawful and jotted some supportive remarks on the cover of a provincial regulation he gave to the lead complainant (Interview 5). Another Hengyang protest leader received similar words of encouragement when he visited the Ministry of Agriculture in Beijing (Interview 6). More remarkably, when several farmers lodged a complaint at the Fujian provincial government concerning a township's illegal sale of their contracted farmland, the staff member who received them at the Letters and Visits Office reassured them that they had the right to block the purchaser from taking over the land (Interview 37). Acting on a belief that they had located a "guarantor against repression" (Tarrow, 1998: 79), each of these protest leaders then transformed a few kind words (in fact, the only politically correct response) into permission to pursue a broad-based campaign of publicizing policies. In the Fujian case, villagers also went a step further: they took the official's advice literally and physically blocked the land buyer's men when they came to claim the property (Interview 37).

Strictly speaking, there is no law that allows Chinese citizens to publicize Party policies and state laws. But this is an act whose correctness no one can legitimately challenge. While an official who scrawls on a letter of complaint "disseminating policies is protected by law" may be seeking mainly to get a group of activists out of his or her office and to discourage them from returning (see Guo, 2001: 434), enterprising activists often waste little time expanding this discursive crack into a window of opportunity. They interpret official "instructions" (*pishi*), as informal and offhand as they usually are, to be evidence that a large gap exists between authorities at higher and lower levels. What might have been little more than a brush-off, in other words, can easily justify upgrading a general license to publicize policies into an explicit go-ahead to challenge abusive local officials and mobilize opposition to improper decisions in one's own village.

In sum, even though mediated contention usually fails to generate the hoped-for relief, it can provide activists with crucial information about official misconduct, suggest political openings (that may or may not exist), and (by changing protest leaders' expectations and their store of resources) set the stage for direct rightful resistance.

Communications and Information Technologies

Some activists in rural China use remarkably low-tech (or no-tech) means to mobilize and coordinate direct action. In Jize county, Hebei, for example, protest leaders set off firecrackers to assemble villagers in front of a general store before leading them to demand a dialogue with township leaders (Yang Shouyong and Wang Jintao, 2001: 40–42), while in Hunan village lookouts used gongs to summon community members to defend protest organizers who were about to be arrested (Duan Xianju et al., 2000; Interview 6).

But some newer technologies (which have only recently reached the countryside) have played an even bigger role in facilitating direct rightful resistance. We have already seen how audio equipment such as tape recorders, loudspeakers, and mobile broadcasting stations can help publicize policies and rally supporters. Insomuch as direct action requires considerable coordination and planning, telephones have also become an important tool for protest leaders. More and more activists these days use mobile phones to arrange multivillage or even multitownship actions. In Hengyang, for instance, one farmer (Interview 4) set up a telephone tree that connected hundreds of activists in nearly a dozen townships. Many of his fellow organizers now have cell phones or land lines at home; those who do not can rely on neighbors who are willing to pass on messages about the time and place of meetings, upcoming actions, the number of protesters to turn out, and so on. In Hunan, villagers have even used mobile phones to protect investigators who have come to do research on rural contention. One protest leader called two journalists sent by the magazine *Window on the Southern Wind* (*Nanfeng Chuang*) to warn them (three times!) to change taxis after his followers discovered that county officials had learned the license plate number of their vehicle; later, after the reporters stayed in one location too long and were detained, another activist phoned to offer to mobilize hundreds of villagers to free them (Interview 43; on other rescues, see Bernstein, 2003: 15; Johnson, 2004: 69).

Personal computers are another breakthrough that has promoted the use of direct tactics. Computer printing, in particular, can aid both in publicizing policies and reproducing letters of complaints. Activists in Anhui province, for instance, painstakingly entered a beneficial tax policy on a computer, character by character, and then distributed printouts to stir up resistance to unlawful taxation (Zhang Cuiling, 2002). Shortly before a number of "burden reduction representatives" in Hengyang demanded a dialogue with a school head concerning tuition and fee increases, they circulated printouts of their letter of complaint to parents of local schoolchildren (Interview 18).

Most of these newer technologies are no longer forbiddingly expensive. Mobile phones can be bought for 200 to 300 yuan (approximately U.S. $25–$40) and calls run about 60 fen (U.S. 7¢) or less per minute. Shops that provide word-processing and computer printing can be found in virtually all county towns and many townships.

The technology that has transformed protest the most is also one of the most widely available: photocopying. In Hunan, it costs 30 fen (U.S. 4¢) to reproduce a page, and copy shops can be found in most township seats. Photocopying not only eases duplication of central, provincial, and city regulations; it also lends a patina of authenticity and legitimacy to those documents and impedes crackdowns by officials who previously would have claimed they were bogus (Interviews 4, 6, 7). In Hengyang, when a deputy township head and the chair of the township people's congress attempted to shut down a group of activists who were reading copied regulations over a loudspeaker and alleged that they were publicizing phony "black documents" (*hei wenjian*), several activists challenged them to produce the real or "red" (*hong*) versions. Rebuffed, the officials had nothing more to say. The protest leaders then immediately announced to the surrounding crowd that these officials were "active counterrevolutionaries" (*xianxing fan geming*) because they had "defiled" (*wumie*) central policies (Interview 44).

All these technologies enable adept rightful resisters to reach out to (and fire up) a mass constituency in a way that was less critical when they were simply lodging complaints and depending largely on elite allies rather than disgruntled, agitated villagers. Advances in duplication and communication (with faxes, e-mail, text messaging, and the Internet not far behind)[15] (Tarrow, 1998: 132) also help organizers mount popular action and gauge how disruptive they can be without crossing into "forbidden zones" (*jinqu*).

Popular Support

In rural China today, there is not much evidence of a "strategic dilemma" where disruption is necessary to draw attention but militancy reliably alienates the public (cf. Jasper, 2004: 9, 13; Rochon, 1988). So long as rightful resisters refrain from demanding excessive donations or harassing free-riders, tactical escalation usually generates more community approval than disapproval. Particularly in locations where villagers have become exasperated with the Center's failure to rectify long-standing wrongs, unconventional tactics do not undermine the legitimacy of protest and drive away supporters but more often lead to comments such as "when officials push people to rebel, people have to resist" (Interview 45).

Direct tactics can help a group of activists expand their base by creating solidarity, forging a collective identity, and strengthening trust. It is often the case that the more assertive and enterprising protest leaders are, the more their stature rises – though popular acclaim does not always translate

---

[15] On the use of mobile phones, text messaging, e-mail, and Internet bulletin boards to coordinate anti-Japanese protests in urban China, see Yardley (2005, April 25). For a discussion of Falun Gong and other Chinese "cybersects," see Thornton (2002, 2003).

into active participation in the next round of contention. As discussed in Chapter 5, interested onlookers sometimes join protests or become leaders themselves; more frequently, they offer financial support or applaud the actions of activists whom they have come to respect or even admire. In this way, although direct tactics establish a "radical flank," they do not redound chiefly to the benefit of those who employ moderate, mediated tactics. Instead, they often set in motion a sequence of events where wary but hopeful spectators (and some new participants) are delighted to see imperious, corrupt, and abusive officials get their comeuppance and even privately egg rightful resisters on to ratchet the level of confrontation up a notch.

The following episode illustrates how the back-and-forth between protest leaders and their followers can lead to tactical escalation. In Shandong, an elected village director lodged numerous complaints and even filed a lawsuit against an accountant who was the front man for a corrupt village Party secretary. But the director could not secure access to the accounts that confirmed the financial shenanigans of the two men. (To shield their underlings and themselves, township officials had spirited away the account books to their office and locked them up.) In 2002, with a new election approaching, the director realized that he might lose, largely because he had been so ineffective in bringing the Party secretary and the accountant to justice. His supporters were concerned and urged him to use bolder, direct tactics. The director demanded a meeting with the township head, during which he threatened, if he was again prevented from seeing the accounts, to mobilize his followers to occupy the township office building. The township head relented but only granted permission to review the books for a single day. The director agreed but decided to spring a surprise. At the end of the appointed time, nearly sixty of his supporters suddenly appeared, seized the accounts, and ran off with them. This incident led the township leadership and the village Party secretary to cancel the upcoming election, thereby allowing the village director to retain his position. It also helped the director win back many of his former backers who had been disappointed with his lack of resolve (Interview 36).

Popular support for direct tactics arises for a number of reasons. Above all, it derives from widespread frustration with the ineffectiveness of mediated contention (Interviews 4, 5, 6). Of nearly equal importance, participating in direct rightful resistance, or offering financial or moral support to those who do so, is often not perceived to be as risky as it might seem. Unless atypically heavy-handed county leaders authorize the use of violence against rightful resisters, such as occurred in Hengyang in 1999 and Yiyang, Henan, in 2002 (Interviews 4, 7, 79), township officials are often hamstrung, not least because the township police are responsible to the county public security bureau, not the township. Although township leaders may seek to get around this by fabricating "riots" (*sao luan*), their case for repression is sometimes belied by the facts. In 2003, for instance, a township Party secretary in Xinyang county, Henan, phoned the county leadership to report that thousands of villagers were about to start a riot near the government compound. When hundreds of county policemen arrived to restore order, they found a peaceful mass meeting underway, at which a well-known activist was doing nothing more than reading a central document about peasant burdens through a loudspeaker. The county police left without taking any action, and the head policeman complained that the township Party secretary should be sacked for making a false report (Interview 80).[16]

More broadly, since their ham-fisted involvement in suppressing the 1989 protest movement, China's security forces have become much more concerned with the misuse of force. The police increasingly seek "to minimize popular anger through more moderate policing of protests" (Tanner, 2004: 148) and rely on containment and management rather than deterrence and quick suppression. This shift has meant that many low-key protests are permitted to continue (and crowds allowed to disperse), with little danger to most participants (Tanner, 2004: 148). Moreover, from imperial days to the present, protest leaders have always paid the highest price when collective action backfired, while followers have been protected by their numbers, their relative anonymity, and the authorities' fear of alienating a broad swath of the population. In fact, a common outcome has been arrest and imprisonment of ringleaders followed by concessions on the subject of the protesters' demands (Bianco, 2001; Bernstein and Lü, 2003; O'Brien, 2002: 150).[17] In some senses, taking part in a demonstration is even less dangerous than participating in typical mediated tactics, such as

---

[16] Of course, alarming the county leadership sometimes succeeds, and villagers underestimate the risks of direct action. In the Daolin incident of 1999, hundreds of People's Armed Police were sent in after township officials reported that a peasant leader and his associates planned to organize an attack on the township government compound, while (according to one of the protest leaders) they were only calling a mass meeting to "study the Center's burden-reduction policies." In the ensuing confrontation, a villager was injured by a tear-gas canister and subsequently died under mysterious circumstances in the county hospital. One key organizer was later arrested and sentenced to seven years in prison; another organizer went into hiding and dared not return home until September 2004 (Interview 54).

[17] On the high risks leaders of collective appeals typically face, see Cai (2004: 447–48).

openly identifying oneself by signing or thumb printing a collective letter of complaint. While direct tactics require considerable planning and coordination, and place protest leaders in no small jeopardy, they also often ease the job of amassing and retaining popular support.

Who Innovates?

In many countries, new tactics are associated with new activists (della Porta and Diani, 1999: 189; Jasper, 1997: 231, 241) – with successive "micro-cohorts" (Whittier, 1995: 56) who enter a movement often after working in another movement (Meyer and Whittier, 1994; Voss and Sherman, 2000: 328).[18] Although in rural China we see some of this, particularly among new recruits who took part in mass campaigns during the waning days of the Maoist era, our limited evidence suggests that tactical escalation is mainly the handiwork of seasoned complainants who have learned new tricks as their abilities, resources, and commitment have grown. In Hengyang, for instance, *all* thirty-two protest leaders on whom we have information had been involved in collective action for at least eight years, and *all* of them employed mediated tactics before moving on to direct action (on protest in Hengyang in the late 1980s and early 1990s, see Bernstein and Lü, 2003: 187–89; Yu Jianrong, 2003).

Of course, long-time complainants do not always graduate to direct rightful resistance.[19] Those who do, in Hengyang, have typically been middle-aged or slightly older men who say they feel boxed in, in that they have few other options to improve their economic, social, or political position. A number of Hengyang protest leaders who were under thirty-five years of age simply left the countryside and became migrant workers after a multivillage, collective complaint in 1996 failed to produce any relief. Older complainants (like interviewees 4, 5, and 6), however, could not easily do the same, not least because they often had elderly parents and teenage children to look after. Some of these men had also been migrant workers themselves for a time but were unwilling to relive the discrimination and exploitation they had experienced (Interview 5). Others had served in the army and found themselves locked out of the village leadership when they returned home (on veterans and rural protest, see O'Brien and Li, 1995:

---

[18] A younger, more militant generation of activists often appears at the peak of a protest cycle, in the midst of escalating violence and repression (Zwerman and Steinhoff, 2005: 89).

[19] On "lumping" claims, see Michelson (2005) and Landry and Tong (2005).

758; Bernstein and Lü, 2003: 148–49; Yu Jianrong, 2003: 1).[20] After years of fruitless mediated contention, most felt they had no alternative to escalation, unless they were willing to discard their ambitions, their self-respect, and their hopes for a better life (Interviews 4, 5, 6, 8, 19).

Personal, psychological factors also help explain why some veteran complainants have adopted direct tactics.[21] Most of the innovators we have encountered are unusually assertive and self-confident characters, who, for example, enjoyed telling anyone who would listen how much pride they took in fighting wrongdoing.[22] Along these lines, one activist in Hengyang said, "I have been combative since I was young and have no tolerance for injustice and evil" (Interview 8). Another protest leader from Hengyang was proud to announce that he "had been rebelling against abusive cadres since Mao Zedong was still ruling China" (Interview 6).[23] Indeed, several rural organizers even compared themselves with vaunted Party martyrs and vowed that they would rather die than knuckle under to unjust and corrupt local officials (Interviews 13, 19, 21; also Interview 36; Duan Xianju et al., 2000). One activist from Lianyuan county, Hunan went so far as to allude to the famous Qin Dynasty rebels Chen Sheng and Wu Guang by claiming that "kings and generals are not born to be kings and generals" (Duan Xianju et al., 2000). These diehards not only refuse to retreat, they also have no use for tactics that have repeatedly shown themselves to be inadequate. For protest leaders with such hard-charging personalities, disenchantment with mediated contention only feeds their indignation, brinksmanship, and

---

[20] Our 1999–2001 survey of 1,600 villagers in four counties (two in Jiangxi, one in Jiangsu, and one in Fujian) (Li, 2004: 244) showed that both men and army veterans were considerably overrepresented among rightful resisters. This survey did not distinguish between mediated and direct forms of rightful resistance. For some tentative thoughts on the broader question – "who tends to lead rightful resistance?" – see Appendix A.

[21] For survey data on personality traits shared by many protest leaders, see Appendix A. For a psychological explanation of worker-rebel defiance in Cultural Revolution Shanghai, which focuses on personal inclinations, ambitions, and audacity, arising from factors such as alien native place of origin, difficult family circumstances, participation in youth gangs, and military service, see Perry and Li (1997: 66–69, 190–91).

[22] Wood (2003: 234–37) highlights the "pleasures in agency" experienced by many participants in collective action. Her study of insurgency in El Salvador showed that feelings of increased autonomy, self-esteem, and pride came about "in the course of making history, and not just any history but a history they perceived as more just" (p. 235).

[23] On "insolent" protest leaders, see Guo (2001: 432). On their persistence and reputation for courage, see Bernstein (2003: 13). On the "forceful personalities" and "common feistiness" of worker-rebels during the Cultural Revolution, see Perry and Li (1997: 67, 69). On the assertiveness of leaders of rightful resistance, see Appendix A.

dreams of grandeur while boosting their commitment to find a way to do whatever it takes to prevail.

That many rightful resisters possess strong personalities and no lack of self-esteem also means that they are likely to find it humiliating to let their supporters down. Tactical innovators in rural China are typically highly attuned to questions of dignity and "face" and believe (often correctly) that they will be mocked as cowards if they back down after a few setbacks (Yu Jianrong, 2001: 568).[24] This is especially true when protest leaders have openly vowed to defend their neighbors to the end and have repeatedly solicited contributions from the public to lodge complaints. As time goes by, they often feel growing pressure to find a way, any way, to deliver at least a portion of what they have promised. They wish to show that they have the mettle to stand up to the authorities for as long as it takes and to demonstrate that their acts of defiance will ultimately have a payoff.

Lastly, architects of direct rightful resistance seem to possess an abiding faith in the Center's desire (if not capacity) to halt policy violations. They appreciate better than most that officials up to the province level are unlikely to redress popular grievances (Interviews 4, 21, 36), yet they continue to say that some leaders at the Center truly wish to end misimplementation of beneficial measures (see Guo, 2001: 435–37; Li, 2004). In the words of a protest leader from Fujian, "central leaders share a common interest with people like me, at least to the extent that they agree that what I'm struggling against also undermines Party rule" (Interview 37). Similarly, although an activist from Shandong repeatedly dodged questions about whether he genuinely trusted the Center,[25] he insisted that so long as China's president wished to stay in power, he would need people like him to help control wayward local officials (Interview 36; also Interviews 46, 79). For such individuals, declining trust in the Center's capacity does not cause a lapse into passivity; instead, it strengthens their resolve and encourages them to step up their efforts to assist a besieged and weakened Center.

---

[24] Rumors that he had been bribed by a county government spurred an activist to begin a campaign of publicizing fee-reduction policies; see Johnson (2004: 57–58).

[25] To what extent rightful resisters use central policies as an instrument and to what extent they actually have faith in such policies is difficult to assess. It is always problematic to gain access to a protester's true motivations (Hollander and Einwohner, 2004: 542), and there are dangers in inferring intent from actions. We suggest a hypothesis: some degree of sincere belief in the Center is critical at first, in order to become a rightful resister. But declared trust in the Center may become more strategic with time, as rightful resisters scale the official hierarchy, allies prove unreliable, and defeats often mount.

Some Implications

Rightful resistance in rural China has evolved since the 1980s. Some long-time activists, seeing few alternatives and too proud to accept defeat, have turned to more confrontational forms of contention. Instead of counting on higher-level patrons to address their claims, these rightful resisters and their followers have increasingly come to demand justice on the spot. In an attempt to halt policy violations, they have transformed tiny openings into opportunities to deploy new, more disruptive tactics, such as publicizing policies, demanding dialogues, and defying officials face-to-face. In the course of doing so, they have exploited the spread of communications and information technologies, including mobile phones, photocopying, and computerized printing. Direct tactics, to this point, have generally not overstepped the Center's sufferance (so long as protest leaders and their followers stop short of violence and clearly illegal acts), and they almost always meet with popular acclaim, as rightful resisters persist, win occasional victories, and keep trumpeting their willingness to sacrifice all for the interests of the Party and the people.

These developments have several broader implications for research on contentious politics. Tactical escalation, it should be noted, has brought about what McAdam, Tarrow, and Tilly (2001: 144–58) call "object shift," in two different senses. On the one hand, the focus of rightful resistance has shifted downward, because direct contention is usually aimed at lower-level officials than mediated contention. Local adversaries are confronted, not bypassed. Protesters give up on high-level patrons and take matters into their own hands. On the other hand, rightful resisters sometimes turn on their ineffectual (or two-faced) advocates at higher levels and attack them. Consider this example from Hengyang: after a protest organizer's wife (Interview 38) was beaten by township cadres and several hired toughs, another activist (Interview 5) led a delegation of villagers to the county to insist that the perpetrators be punished. At this point, the protesters were employing mediated tactics because they treated the county as a potential ally against their township foes. But when the county head summarily rejected their demands, the activists decided that the county was in truth a backstage supporter of their antagonists. Instead of proceeding up a level to the city government (which they still considered an ally), they decided they would challenge the county itself by setting up a human blockade on a county highway. As their perception of the county's stance changed, their tactics had morphed from mediated contention (aimed at the county, by appealing to it for help) to direct action (against the county, by blocking the county road). So far, direct contention has mostly targeted township and village cadres; this episode shows it can move up the hierarchy, with potentially explosive consequences (for another example, see Li, 2001: 1–2).

Much more research is needed on which tactics tend to be used at which levels in the hierarchy. Are protesters less confrontational at lower levels and more confrontational at higher levels? Or does a progression toward transgression occur at each level, before they move up the hierarchy? Most rightful resisters, to this point, seem to "take strong measures only after courteous ones fail" (*xian li hou bing*) at each level (Interviews 5, 36, 37). At the county, for instance, protesters usually begin by lodging complaints and then move on to staging demonstrations, sit-ins, and traffic blockades only if their demands are rebuffed. Direct rightful resistance remains uncommon at the municipal or provincial level. Still, confrontational tactics are showing signs of reaching upward. Complainants in Beijing, for instance, have applied for permission to hold demonstrations in Tiananmen Square, knelt down en masse at the Monument of People's Heroes, and carried mourning wreaths to the gate of the Zhongnanhai compound where top leaders reside (Interviews 56, 58, 66). In March 2005, just days before the annual session of the National People's Congress, more than three thousand complainants in Beijing signed a collective petition that demanded an overhaul of the letters and visits system and judicial review of the constitutionality of the newly promulgated Regulation on Letters and Visits (2005) (Interview 58).[26]

The "addressees" (Szabo, 1996) of contention have changed in another important way. In rural China, the audience for collective action is broadening well beyond fair-weather friends in officialdom. Rightful resisters now regularly turn to another third party – the public. The strategic dilemma that researchers have observed in the West (della Porta and Diani, 1999: 182–83; Jasper, 2004: 9, 13; Rochon, 1988) can easily be overstated in the Chinese countryside, where radicalism typically attracts support rather than chases it away. Many of our interviewees in fact believe that protest

---

[26] More ominously, in a letter posted on the Internet, a protest leader from Fujian wrote that petitioners from Hunan and Sichuan he encountered in the "complainants' village" in Beijing wished they had explosives so that they could imitate Iraqi suicide bombers and blow up county government buildings. He called for an overhaul of the letters and visits system to restore people's trust in the Party (Zhongyang: Shangfang, 2005). On rightful resistance evolving into full-fledged dissent, see Chapter 6 and Li (2004).

organizers should have acted earlier and even more dramatically (e.g., Interviews 25, 45). This is a good reminder that tactical escalation is often as much about building a protest subculture as winning specific battles (see Jasper, 1997: 237) and that we need to look deep inside protest groups to understand how internal solidarity is built and collective identities form (see della Porta and Diani, 1999: 181–82). This implies more attention to recruitment and leader-group dynamics, and further consideration of the ways in which tactical choices can "widen the circle of those psychologically prepared for mobilization" (see Rochon, 1998: 162), play a role in knitting a group together, and "reinforce affective ties among protesters" (Jasper, 1997: 237).

The evolution of rightful resistance also suggests how political opportunities can figure in tactical escalation. Yes, some sympathetic officials have provided rightful resisters information about beneficial policies and assurances that it is safe and advisable to go beyond group petitions (on expanding opportunities and tactical innovation, see McAdam, 1983: 737; Minkoff, 1999; Szabo, 1996). But the inability of protesters to locate allies who will stick with them to the end has often been more significant than new openings. Journalists may promise to expose official wrongdoing but then disappear after blackmailing wrongdoers. Backers in weaker bureaus, such as Civil Affairs and Agriculture, may be overpowered by representatives from the Organization Department or the Public Security Bureau. Letters and Visits officials and staff and deputies of peoples' congresses may wish to help petitioners, but lack the resources and clout to do so. Ranking officials at higher levels may be willing to scrawl a few words of support on a complaint but unwilling to offer any follow-up when their "instructions" are ignored. Activists have learned that they must rely on themselves and their constituency more, both for protection and to prevail. Their advocates at higher levels have often shown themselves to be virtual allies at best, and this has altered the costs and benefits of different forms of contention. Seen in this light, whether opportunities have expanded or contracted hinges on the tactics under consideration. Tactical escalation in rural China thus depends less on whether the system is open or closed (cf. Kitschelt, 1986: 66) than on which doors are opening and closing. The key question, as we saw in Chapter 2, is "opportunity for what?" (Meyer and Minkoff, 2004: 1461–63, 1484). A shifting opportunity structure (not an improving one) has undermined mediated rightful resistance and promoted direct action.

At the same time, tactical innovation requires that skillful activists seize available opportunities (Jasper, 1997; McAdam, 1983: 737).[27] Protest leaders may understand or misunderstand their situation, and then devise brilliant or foolish moves.[28] In the Chinese countryside, a growing realization that most of their anticipated allies are missing in action has demoralized less committed activists and encouraged protesters who are more assertive to search for new, more effective tactics. After repeated failures, some rightful resisters have developed a new (perhaps more realistic) appreciation of the openings and threats they face, and have adjusted their tactics accordingly. Crises, turbulence, and shocks (brought on mainly by defeats), and the response of activists to them, have precipitated tactical escalation (see Beckwith, 2000; Voss and Sherman, 2000: 341). Through a long and bumpy process of experimentation, protesters in different locations have groped their way from mediated to direct contention.

[27] On political opportunity structures as "a system of permissive incentives rather than of firm constraints," see Rochon (1998: 203).

[28] Tactics are also chosen partly for psychological, cultural, and biographical reasons. They express moral visions and identities. Activists may find some certain tactics enjoyable and others dull. Protest leaders may have their self-image tied up in being at the cutting edge. For these and other reasons, tactical choices can diverge from what an opportunity structure would predict. See Jasper (1997: 244–45, 301, 320).

5

Outcomes

Concepts may not be about outcomes, but politics is. In the final analysis, the significance of any form of popular contention depends on its effects. What consequences does rightful resistance have for those who wage it, for villagers who observe it, and for policy implementation? And what can we learn about how the outcomes of contention arise by exploring rightful resistance in the Chinese countryside?

Thinking about Consequences

Gauging the impact of popular protest is notoriously difficult. Questions of causality and definition dog even the most careful attempts to link an episode or cycle of contention to a specific outcome (Amenta, Carruthers, and Zylan, 1992: 310; della Porta and Diani, 1999: 231–33; Giugni, 1998, 1999; Kriesi et al., 1995: 207–8). Grappling with all the factors that come together to produce social, political, or personal change becomes only more complicated when the indirect and unintended effects of collective action are taken into account (Linders, 2004; Tilly, 1999). Given the many obstacles researchers face, it is no wonder that studies of both resistance and social movements have traditionally paid more attention to the origins and dynamics of contention than to its consequences (Burstein, Einwohner, and Hollander, 1995: 276; Cress and Snow, 2000: 1094; Kriesi et al., 1995: 208; McAdam, McCarthy, and Zald, 1988; Scott, 1985).

But this is changing. After years of fitful progress, research on the impact of contentious politics is taking off. A number of important books, articles, and edited volumes have appeared over the past decade, many by scholars who study the effects of social movements (for reviews, see della Porta and Diani, 1999: chap. 9; Giugni, 1998; Tarrow, 1998: chap. 10; also Andrews,

2004, chap. 2). As the field matures, efforts have been made to identify a wide range of policy, procedural, cultural, and biographical impacts and to separate out short-term versus long-term consequences, direct versus indirect results, and intended versus unintended outcomes (Gamson, 1990; Kitschelt, 1986; Kriesi et al., 1995; McAdam, 1989, 1999; Tarrow, 1998; Zolberg, 1972). Some thought has also gone into strategies for teasing out cause and effect, often through the use of counterfactuals and cross-national comparisons (Banaszak, 1996; Giugni, 1999; Kitschelt, 1986; Kriesi et al., 1995; Linders, 2004).

One feature of the field has not changed much, however. To this point, most studies of the impact of contention have focused on advanced industrialized countries (della Porta, 2002: 288, 296; Giugni, McAdam, and Tilly, 1999). This is not surprising insofar as protesters often find a reasonably hospitable climate in democratic or democratizing societies. Compared with authoritarian settings, it is easier for the disgruntled to mobilize and express their grievances, and it is more likely that the authorities will offer a favorable response. Unlike closed polities, the right to protest also receives at least some protection in liberal democracies, and changes in policy often occur for which a case can be made that public pressure played a significant role.

But does this mean that contention (short of revolution) has little effect outside the democratic world? That hardly seems likely. In authoritarian countries such as China, where popular input in policy making is limited and organized movements are typically crushed or pushed underground, we need to follow the lead of analysts (della Porta, 1999: 66; della Porta and Diani, 1999; Kriesi et al., 1995; McAdam, 1999) who look beyond quick policy or procedural victories and eschew simple notions of success and failure (Andrews, 2001, 2004; Amenta and Young, 1999; Einwohner, 1999: 59; Giugni, 1999; Tilly, 1999) while scanning for a range of possible impacts. These "secondary outcomes" (Linders, 2004: 374) are usually unforeseen and appear after the peak of protest activity (Andrews, 2004: 4, 19; Tarrow, 1998). And they may be more associated with policy implementation, personal change, and an evolving political culture than with dramatic policy reversals or institutional breakthroughs.

A number of studies of protest in the West have already examined how popular contention can affect implementation (Andrews, 2001, 2004; Giugni and Passy, 1998: 82; Linders, 2004; Rochon and Mazmanian, 1993), the values of activists (Banaczak, 1996; McAdam, 1999; McCann, 1994; Mansbridge, 1986; Rochon and Mazmanian, 1993), and the wider public (della Porta, 1999; Gamson, 1998; Koopmans and Statham, 1999; Kriesi et al., 1995: 211; McAdam and Su, 2002; Mansbridge, 1986; Tarrow, 1998; Zolberg, 1972).[1] There are particular advantages, however, of exploring these effects in contemporary rural China. For one, these are arguably the most prominent consequences of collective action in the Chinese country-side, not a sideshow to the main event. Second, they offer an opportunity to determine whether current understandings, largely derived from research in pluralist systems, carries over to a nondemocratic context. Third, they promise a fresh perspective on two issues that have long troubled students of contentious politics: how to get a grip on indirect outcomes, and how to think about causality when change is a result both of popular action and openings provided by elites.

An Interactive Approach to Outcomes

Explaining the consequences of contention entails an effort to ascribe cause and effect. But when events are intertwined and many parties are involved, causal attribution becomes difficult. Among the methodological problems raised most often in the literature on protest outcomes, one pertaining to attribution stands out as especially nettlesome: if social forces and state actors both contribute to a result, how can we tell who is responsible for what (della Porta and Diani, 1999: 232–33; Giugni, 1999: xxiv; Kriesi et al., 1995: 207–8)?

The most common advice offered is to head in two directions at once. On the one hand, efforts must be made to isolate the independent effects of contention (Andrews, 2004: 20–21; Amenta, Carruthers, and Zylan, 1992: 312; Giugni, 1999: xxiv; McAdam, McCarthy, and Zald, 1988: 727). We should try, in other words, to figure out what might have happened in the absence of popular pressure in order to disentangle the role of societal and state actors (della Porta and Diani, 1999: 231–33; Giugni, 1999: xxiv; Kriesi et al., 1995: 207–8). To exclude the possibility that a change would have occurred anyway, and to avoid exaggerating the consequences of protest, it

---

[1] Until recently, however, researchers have focused on whether contention has such consequences, rather than how it produces them (McAdam and Su, 2002: 700). On paths to local, nonpolicy outcomes, involving six causal conditions, see Cress and Snow (2000). On using historical comparisons to show how movements interact with contexts to generate different implementation outcomes, see Linders (2004: 394). For attention to "contexts within which movements are influential, and the mechanisms through which they shape processes of change," see Andrews (2004: 199).

is necessary to control for other variables and to determine precisely what caused what.

A second thread in the literature, often present in the same studies that draw attention to independent effects, reflects a more interactive approach to attribution. Here, attention centers on the interplay between forces of change both inside and outside the state. Outcomes are understood to be the result of some combination of disruption, persuasion, and bargaining in the course of interaction between protesters, targets, and third parties (Amenta, Halfmann, and Young, 1999; Andrews, 2004: 2–3, 6; Burstein, Einwohner, and Hollander, 1995; Einwohner, 1999: 58; Giugni, 1998: 389; Jenkins and Perrow, 1977; Linders, 2004: 395; Lipsky, 1968; Markoff, 1996: 36; Soule and Olzak, 2004). Causal mechanisms are recognized to be inherently complex, and effects arise from a swirl of activity as officials, the media, and other interested onlookers respond to popular agitation, while also acting on their own. Multiple causal chains are at work simultaneously (Tilly, 1999: 268), and "no particular strategic element can be evaluated in isolation" (Burstein, Einwohner, and Hollander, 1995; quoted text in della Porta and Diani, 1999: 229). This conjunctural approach to attribution (Ragin, 1987) suggests that the task of the analyst is not so much to untangle the role of protesters and elites as to trace how a confluence of mass and state actors join to produce a result (Giugni, 1998: 14; Tarrow, 1998: 162).

An interactive understanding of outcomes reflects the simple truth that most consequences of contention are the result of an ongoing give-and-take between forces in society and forces in the state. Collective action is typically but one factor in a long chain of events – a factor that at times can play a crucial role as initiative shifts back and forth between those inside and outside government. Either-or questions about the impetus behind change thus spring from an unrealistic vision of what protest can accomplish directly (how often are consequences unmediated by the powers-that-be?) and threaten to impoverish our understanding of outcomes.[2] Too much interest in apportioning credit inevitably lends a defensive cast to analysis of the effects of protest, as attention falls on whether contention has an impact rather than how it has an impact (for this distinction, see Andrews, 2001: 73; also McAdam and Su, 2002: 700).[3]

---

[2] Even the consequences of direct tactics hinge on government policies, absent allies, and rightful resisters perceiving and acting on shifting opportunities. See Chapters 2 and 4.

[3] Linders (2004: 376) writes: "From this perspective, then, the primary analytical task is not to identify which of a series of possible causal features have the greatest influence on a particular

Consequences of Contention

A nuanced appreciation of the interplay of societal and state actors has long been present in research that uses the concept of "political opportunity structure" to examine the origins and dynamics of collective action. Studies of both the American civil rights movement (McAdam, 1982; McAdam, McCarthy, and Zald, 1988: 721) and women's movement (McCann, 1994), for instance, have been highly attuned to divisions within the elite and to the importance of allies within officialdom. This attention to institutional activists, ideological allies, fair-weather friends, pragmatic intermediaries, and insiders who pursue outside goals is no less appropriate when studying outcomes (Amenta, Halfmann, and Young, 1999; Jenkins and Perrow, 1977; Lipsky, 1968; McCammon et al., 2001; Markoff, 1996; Santoro and McGuire, 1997; Soule and Olzak, 2004; Tarrow, 1998: 163), where it is even more important to set aside overly society-focused predilections and to redirect our gaze away from those contesting power to their relationships with the powerful.

Consequences of Contention

Improved Policy Implementation

Much of the pioneering research on the impact of contentious politics focused on policy or institutional change (della Porta, 1999: 66; Giugni, 1999: xxi–xxiii; McAdam, 1999: 119). Although some studies have delved into the relationship between protest and policy implementation (Andrews, 2001, 2004; Giugni and Passy, 1999; Linders, 2004; Rochon and Mazmanian, 1993), this has scarcely been a prominent theme, not least because agitating for scrupulous enforcement of existing commitments rarely possesses the drama associated with struggles to influence policy making, bring about structural reform, or topple a regime. Still, in China, where direct impact on high-level politics is so difficult, most popular contention (as we have seen throughout this book) surrounds misimplementation of beneficial measures that already exist but which local officials have chosen to ignore.[4]

outcome but instead to identify and specify the mechanisms through which movements and institutions collaborate, wittingly or unwittingly, to produce social change."

[4] Studies of political participation (what McAdam, Tarrow, and Tilly, 2001, call "contained contention"), have identified this same pattern in both Maoist (Burns, 1988; Falkenheim, 1978; Townsend, 1967) and post-Mao China (Bernstein and Lü, 2003, chap. 6; Cai, 2004; Jennings, 1997; Luehrmann, 2003; Minzner, 2005; Shi, 1997).

Rightful resistance in rural China affects implementation in a number of ways. Above all, it draws the attention of the Center to insubordination by local leaders and prompts them to take corrective steps. Clashes between villagers and local officials over the past two decades have alerted Chinese leaders to a number of areas in which misimplementation is endemic, most notably unwillingness of local cadres to revoke unapproved taxes and fees, disregard of measures that bar corruption and use of excessive force, manipulation of village elections, unlawful requisition of farmland, and distortion of popular central policies (such as economic development) into harmful "local policies" that justify wasted investment and unauthorized extraction (Bernstein and Lü, 2003; Guo, 2001; Li and O'Brien, 1996; O'Brien and Li, 1999; Zhongyang Zhengfawei, 2001).

In addition to shining a spotlight on official misdeeds, rightful resistance sometimes spurs the Center to intervene in the implementation process. A massive series of demonstrations in Sichuan in 1993, for instance, led the Central Committee and the State Council to issue an emergency notice that banned forty-three fees that had been illegally levied by local governments (Bernstein and Lü, 2003: 130–37).[5] Likewise, after several highly confrontational protests in 2000 in Jiangxi, the central government quickly sent in a team of investigators, which instructed county officials to slash unapproved fees by 24 million yuan (approximately U.S. $3 million) (Ding Guoguang, 2001: 433–34). In the wake of popular complaints, Beijing has also stepped in to ensure the conduct of honest grass-roots elections. The Ministry of Civil Affairs, as we saw in Chapter 3, has been drawn into dozens of disputes over mishandled balloting and its involvement has led to numerous elections being annulled (Howell, 1997; Li and O'Brien, 1996, 1999; Liu, 2000; O'Brien, 2003; O'Brien and Li, 2000; Shi, 1999a). In one 1995 case, for example, after a county government turned a deaf ear to their complaints, a group of angry farmers from Hebei traveled to the capital to protest a fraudulent vote. When a ministry official responsible for carrying out the self-government program heard that the delegation was in his outer office, he shouted "bravo" (*tai haole*). Upon hearing their tale of local chicanery, he immediately dispatched two staff members to look into their charges. In the course of an extended inquiry that ended with the election being overturned, ministry officials went on the well-known, muckraking television program *Focus* (*Jiaodian Fangtan*) (three times!) to

---

[5] This episode in Renshou county also involved violence and rioting, and to that extent went beyond rightful resistance.

back the farmers and to caution local officials nationwide to draw the appropriate conclusions (Interviews 1, 2).

Rightful resistance is most likely to improve policy implementation when activists force concessions on-the-spot (via direct tactics) or when they mobilize sympathetic and powerful advocates who have a stake in seeing a policy upheld. (Crusading reporters can be crucial allies, too, as increased editorial freedom and competitive pressures have given rise to more market-oriented media, and exposés of official wrongdoing can generate huge audiences.) At the same time, rightful resistance may also rouse midlevel officials to act on their own. In recent years, collective action has led township and county leaders in some locations to discipline corrupt, derelict, and abusive subordinates. For instance, after hundreds of villagers staged a boisterous demonstration at a county compound in Sichuan in 1998, county authorities promptly ordered the removal of nine corrupt village cadres, who were also made to return the funds they had misappropriated (Jiang Zuoping and Yang Sanjun, 1999).

Many of the effects of rightful resistance are mediated (see Amenta, Halfmann, and Young, 1999; Tarrow, 1998: 174), in that villagers rely on others to do their bidding and because the specter of further unrest can provide ammunition for elites in their bureaucratic battles. In China's cities, on several occasions (e.g., the protest movements of 1986 and 1989), civil disorder has weakened the position of high-level backers, or even contributed to their downfall. In the countryside, however, contention has more often provided leverage for reform-minded elites to outmaneuver their rivals when drawing up regulations that specify how laws should be implemented. Reformers in the Ministry of Civil Affairs, for instance, repeatedly invoked the threat of rural unrest in their dispute with opponents in the Party's Organization Department over enforcement of the Organic Law of Villagers' Committees. For more than a decade, the Organization Department had insisted that elected villagers' committees had to be placed under the leadership of appointed Party branches (Interview 3; Liu, 2000; O'Brien and Li, 2000). It was only an upturn in popular resistance directed at abusive village Party secretaries that tipped the balance in favor of the ministry's view. In 2002 the reformers finally persuaded the Organization Department to stop opposing a guideline that required that all future village Party secretaries demonstrate their popularity by putting themselves up before the citizenry in a village-wide election (Zhonggong Zhongyang Bangongting and Guowuyuan Bangongting, 2002, July 18).

Partly by drawing on the power of the central government, partly by generating pressure on their own, rightful resisters strive to ensure that popular policies are carried out. And sometimes they succeed. Illegal levies are rescinded, manipulated elections are overturned, land seizures are reversed (or paid for), diverted funds are returned, victims of official violence are compensated, and rogue officials are brought to heel. When mediated forms of rightful resistance work, it is usually not a question of insiders coming to accept outsider goals (Lipsky, 1968; Santoro and McGuire, 1997) or outsiders becoming insiders. Instead, we see reformist senior officials who, for their own bureaucratic and personal reasons, share the goals of protesters from the outset (Tarrow, 1998: 88).[6] These high-level advocates are not regime defectors, minority elites, or elites out of power who seize the role of tribune of the people (Tarrow, 1998: 79), but ranking members of the government who are disposed to champion popular demands, so long as they do not target certain off-limit central priorities (e.g., birth control). As part of a "sandwich strategy" (Fox, 1993; O'Brien and Li, 1999) intended to hold their subordinates in line, they countenance certain kinds of protest and provide ad hoc entry to the implementation arena.[7]

Effects on Activists

Beyond its impact on policy implementation, taking part in collective action may also be a life-altering event (McAdam, 1989; McCann, 1994: 271; Tilly, 1999: 268; Zolberg, 1972). It can affect the "hearts, minds, and social identities" of participants by transforming their "understandings, commitments, and affiliations" (McCann, 1994: 230; Mansbridge, 1986: 188–91). For those who become leaders, protest can serve as a learning experience that makes them aware of new possibilities and often leaves them more inclined to take part in other popular action. In this way, contention is sometimes a "watershed" in the life of activists, "a point in time around which their biographies can be seen in 'before' and 'after' terms" (McAdam, 1989: 758).[8]

---

[6] The calculations of officials may also evolve in the course of watching challenges unfold. See Amenta, Halfmann, and Young (1999: 2).

[7] When mediated forms of contention fail and protesters turn to direct tactics, rightful resisters must rely on themselves and the public more. But they still depend on their fair-weather friends in government to offer rhetorical support, to refrain from repression, and to punish cadres who suppress lawful efforts to publicize and enforce central policies.

[8] For data on the demographic background of protest leaders, see Appendix A.

Consequences of Contention

In China, rightful resistance has started to affect what protest leaders think and do. Activism has led many of them to reconsider their relationship to authority, while posing new questions, encouraging innovative tactics, and spurring thoughts about political change. In some cases this has led to feelings of empowerment and a greater readiness to participate in more disruptive (and more direct) action, as "activism begets future activism" (Tarrow, 1998: 165). In other cases it has led to disillusionment and despair, especially when official procrastination, neglect, or repression saps the confidence of protesters that the Center will make good on its promises. In either situation, one of the more striking (and largely unexamined) consequences of collective action in China has been its spillover effects on the attitudes and life course of activists.

Whereas merely participating in rightful resistance with like-minded persons can certainly have an impact, many individual-level consequences depend on how an episode turns out. Contention perceived to be successful has perhaps the most straightforward effects. Victories can take many forms and protesters often interpret success liberally. Popular action, ideally, may lead to an official investigation and speedy redress of villagers' grievances. Far more likely, activists may have to settle for prompting officials to "instruct" (*zhishi*) their underlings to acknowledge a problem and do their best to address it (Interviews 4, 5, 6). Rightful resisters may even judge their efforts effective if they simply gain access to documents that detail a beneficial measure and win permission to distribute them (Interviews 4, 6, 7, 8). When outcomes such as these materialize, participants tend to feel that the justness of their contention has been confirmed. For some, this may end their activism, and its main personal effect may be on the perceived legitimacy of the regime, as they conclude "the Center is on our side and can still control its officials" (Interview 9; also Interview 10).

For many others, however, limited successes may instead increase their sensitivity to social injustice and inspire them to mount further challenges. Even tiny gains or small gestures (such as being told by a senior official that "publicizing Party policies is protected by law") (Interview 4; also Interviews 6, 7, 8) can be remarkably empowering. A few kind words may convince rightful resisters of the vulnerability of their targets and lead them to conclude that the Center truly means what it says and is willing to act as a "guarantor against repression" (Tarrow, 1998: 88). Protesters may then decide (rightly or wrongly) that the risks of contention are not overly high and the payoffs are likely to be large. Even if they are mistaken about their role in bringing about a change, such as villagers who were certain that their agitation led directly to the tax-for-fee reform (Interviews 8, 11, 12), activism can enhance a person's willingness to question authority and enter into conflicts with the powerful. It can signal a growing assertiveness and cement a rightful resister's identity as a dedicated and confident activist.

In addition to boosting a person's sense of efficacy, rightful resistance sometimes enhances the self-esteem of protesters and affects their goals in life. Provocative actions, such as holding a string of public meetings to publicize documents, may leave activists feeling proud, even like a "hero" (Duan Xianju et al., 2000), because they enjoy being looked up to and take satisfaction in having conveyed the people's voice to higher levels (Interviews 4, 5, 6, 13, 41; Li, 2000).[9] One such man, who was leading an effort to reduce exorbitant school fees and was mobilizing his neighbors to challenge excessive irrigation charges, said he would stop organizing protests only if township authorities draped him in a garland of flowers, put him in an open truck, and gave him a parade through every village in the township – only this would restore his reputation after having been jailed for three years for spearheading resistance to illegal fees (Interview 13). Some devoted rightful resisters have publicly announced that what they now sought was not wealth but rather dignity, honor, and posthumous fame (Duan Xianju et al., 2000; Interviews 4, 13). Quite a few "peasant leaders" in Hengyang claimed (rather grandiosely) that they had come to consider it their mission in life to defend the interests of the Party and the people (Interviews 4, 5, 6, 7, 13, 14).

The effects of less than successful rightful resistance on the attitudes and behavior of activists is even more varied. For some, frustration diminishes their trust in the Center, or at least in its capacity to ensure that popular policies are carried out (Li, 2004). More than a few interviewees said that the Center was a "clay Buddha" that was unable to respond to the prayers of the faithful (Interviews 14, 15). Thoughts like this can lead to disenchantment and cynicism, and discourage activism when formerly feisty villagers conclude it is unwise to go looking for trouble. An activist from Hebei, for example, was treated rudely at the State Council's Letters and Visits Office in Beijing, and then saw seven of his fellow complainants detained when they returned home. After this dispiriting turn of events, he said he would never again rely on lodging complaints to oust corrupt officials, because

---

[9] Especially for those who have never participated in protests, simply taking action in public rather than achieving a desired result can produce a feeling of satisfaction.

the Center was too distant and the protective network of local officials was too strong (Interview 16).

Defeat does not, however, cause all rightful resisters to lapse into despair and passivity. Some become disposed to pursue highly disruptive acts either to prompt concessions on the spot or to be noticed by officials at higher levels.[10] Protest leaders may conclude that because polite forms of contention, such as lodging complaints, are ineffective, forceful and attention-grabbing tactics (like blocking a road or organizing a sit-in) are needed to heighten the pressure on higher levels to intercede (Gonganbu, 2001; Zhonggong Hebei, 1999: 28; Zhonggong Sichuan, 2002; Zhongyang Zhengfawei, 2001). These people often are unwilling to negotiate with targets who they believe "should not share the same sky" (Interview 7; on contention leading to polarized attitudes, see Tarrow, 1998: 165), and are less tolerant of protesters who are less ardent than themselves. In popular action directed at overtaxation in Hengyang, as time went by and positions hardened, moderates who were ready to cooperate with local officials were mocked as traitors and ostracized (Interviews 17, 18).

Following high-level neglect or local repression, some particularly tenacious activists have become what officials sometimes call "professional complainants" (*shangfang zhuanyehu*) who visit higher-level governments again and again, or even station themselves permanently in Beijing (or provincial capitals).[11] Often months or even years into an "activist career" (McAdam, 1989: 753), they camp out in what have come to be called "complainants' villages" (*shangfang cun*) and scratch out a living by helping newcomers find inexpensive lodging or by directing them to relevant ministries. Not a few have abandoned their regular jobs, used up all their savings, and stand near the brink of financial ruin. A number of "old-hand complainants" (*shangfang laohu*) from Hunan said that although it was their destiny to "bankrupt their family" (*baijia*), they did not regret their actions. On the contrary, they felt that neglect and repeated setbacks only confirmed how unworthy their

---

[10] Based on interviews with "over ten" complainants who reached Beijing in 1999, Zhao Shukai (2003) found four common responses to failure: continue petitioning; give up on petitioning and shift to head-on confrontation; move, despite problems this might cause with one's household registration and schooling for one's children; and accept defeat.

[11] "Petitioning can lead to petitioning at higher levels. After the initial petition, if the problem it stemmed from is not only unresolved but also produces new conflicts, this can lead to further petitions. For example, if a villager is detained, or a group of complainants is violently dispersed, or reprisals emerge, this can increase peasant dissatisfaction and lead to additional complaints" (Zhao Shukai, 2003).

lives had been before they stood up for their rights, and they vowed they would continue their struggle for a life with dignity (Interviews 4, 5, 6).

A decline (rather than total loss) of confidence in the Center's ability to enforce its wishes has also encouraged some rightful resisters to develop a new understanding of what they can expect from the Center, what the Center needs from them, and what they can do to help the Center. They have decided that whereas they must continue to act in the name of the Party, they should not expect immediate intervention from high-ranking officials, and instead must take matters into their own hands (with whatever public support they can muster). This realization often signals a growing sense of agency and self-worth, insofar as such people feel that the Center not only welcomes their assistance but is in dire need of it. This transformation is also commonly accompanied by a heightening of emotions and a willingness to take greater risks or even consider martyrdom. Protest leaders, at this stage, may know full well that open confrontation with local officialdom increases the likelihood of repression, and that the odds of success are poor, but they still say things like "I will struggle on so long as the Communist Party is still in power and I am alive" (Interview 19) or "I am prepared to die for the glorious cause of defending the Party's leadership and the peoples' interests" (Interview 13).[12]

When rightful resisters reach this point, many no longer limit their contestation to mediated tactics such as collective petitioning and demonstrating; instead they sometimes adopt the more direct tactics discussed in Chapter 4 and take on the proactive role of guardian or even self-implementer of central policies. Typical acts include publicizing central policies to mobilize popular resistance to local officials who violate them, demanding face-to-face meetings with local leaders to urge immediate reversal of unlawful decisions, and confronting township staff who come to collect illegal fees and attempting to drive them off (Duan Xianju et al., 2000; Interviews 13, 17, 18; Yang Hao, 1999: 79; Yu Jianrong, 2001: 548–49).

Less than successful rightful resistance can also give activists a new appreciation of the benefits of organization, while also contributing to the formation of a collective identity. Activists in Hunan increasingly speak of a common cause and identify themselves as members of a larger community of aggrieved rural folk (Interviews 5, 8, 19, 20, 21; Duan Xianju et al., 2000). Mainly as a result of trading stories and getting to know each other

---

[12] On the move toward martyrdom during the student uprising in 1989, see Calhoun (1994).

while lodging complaints at the municipal or provincial level, they have once again punctured the "cellularization" (Shue, 1988)[13] characteristic of rural society in the Maoist era. In so doing, they have sometimes come to recognize that they must join forces and organize for self-protection.[14] In August 1999, for example, eighty-seven peasant leaders from more than a dozen townships in Hengyang gathered in the provincial capital to lodge a massive collective complaint (Interviews 4, 5, 6, 7, 20, 22). Activists from this county often travel to neighboring villages to publicize central documents and leadership speeches concerning overtaxation, and by 2002 they had coordinated their effort to overturn excessive school fees by adopting a uniform letter of complaint (Duan Xianju et al., 2000; Interviews 4, 13; Yang Hao, 1999: 79; Yu Jianrong, 2001: 548–49; Yu Jianrong, 2003).

With the creation of informal networks, and even multitownship alliances, popular unrest in some places (e.g., rural Hunan, Sichuan, and Jiangxi; on regional variation, see Bernstein and Lü, 2003; Thornton, 2004) has begun to outgrow the boundaries of individual villages, and some activists have become committed movement entrepreneurs who organize one action after another. With a corps of "comrades" (*tongzhi*) to fall back on, these protest leaders have developed a sense of solidarity and an appetite for contention. Their actions may signal the stirrings of a subculture of frustrated, assertive risk takers who are capable of sustaining opposition (Bernstein and Lü, 2003: 155–57; O'Brien, 2002; in another context, see McCann, 1994: 261) and enjoy what they are doing (on the pleasures of protest, see Jasper, 1997: 220). Many of these organizers take great pride in acting as the guardian of the Center's interests and in representing fellow villagers whom they deem to be of "lower quality" (*suzhi bijiao di*), and they enjoy being looked up to as fighters for justice and equality (Interviews 8, 36, 37, 79).[15]

Finally, disillusionment with the Center can generate demands for far-reaching change. In the 1980s and early 1990s, rightful resisters tended to focus on concrete issues such as excessive fees and rigged elections in their

---

[13] For Shue (1988), the first wave of post-Mao reforms was the decisive occurrence that broke down the cellularization of rural society.

[14] On the increasing size and organization of protests, see Bernstein and Lü (2003: 116–20), O'Brien (2002: 140–42), Tanner (2004: 141–42), Zhonggong Zhongyang Zuzhibu Ketizu (2001).

[15] On insurgents in El Salvador who took "pleasure in agency," attached value to making history, and expressed pride in being the author of their successes, see Wood (2003: 18, 234–35).

own village. Although this local and parochial focus by and large persists, more recently, the language of dissent is showing signs of becoming broader and more charged, with seasoned activists in Hengyang, for instance, saying to fellow protesters from nearby villages: "We must stop being slaves! We must become masters! We must resist local officials who deprive us of our legal rights and ride roughshod over us" (Interview 4).[16] To encourage the authorities to respect their demands, some rural people have called for "peasant associations" (*nonghui*) to be set up, and villagers in Hebei and Anhui have drawn up their own versions of a Law of Peasant Associations, with the two Hebei men submitting their draft and a petition to former Premier Zhu Rongji.

The most dramatic effect of total disenchantment with the Center is exemplified by the story of a young activist, named Zhou Decai, from Henan. After leading a number of unsuccessful protests against excessive levies, he left his village and became a migrant worker in Guangdong. But he spent most of his time courting media attention and overseas support for a "democratic revolution," while writing essays explaining why China needs multiparty democracy. In November 2002, when the Sixteenth Party Congress was in session, Zhou attempted to organize a demonstration in Tiananmen Square opposing excessive taxation and lack of democracy (personal communication, 2002; Zhou Decai, 2002: 2). A rural researcher based in Beijing wrote that villagers like Zhou were not as exceptional as they might seem (Dang Guoying, 2002).

Rather than advocating the end of one-party rule, it is certainly more common for rightful resisters to be drawn into conventional politics, as yesterday's "peasant hero" becomes today's elected cadre or local people's congress deputy (in another context, see Marwell, Aiken, and Derath, 1987). Even after this occurs, however, they may not stop organizing popular action, and instead may continue to act as "complaint representatives" (*shangfang daibiao*) or "burden-reduction representatives" who use their status and institutionalized authority to "broker" (McAdam, Tarrow, and Tilly, 2001) community complaints or even lead village-wide resistance to unlawful policies concocted at higher levels (Interview 23; Li, 2001).

---

[16] The language of no longer being slaves was a staple of popular protest during the Republican period. See, for example, Smith (2002), on this imagery during the Shanghai labor movement, 1895–1927. The idea of "slaves arising" also figures in the *Internationale*, which has been sung in Chinese protests from the Republican era to the present. On collective singing of the *Internationale* during the student protests of 1989, see Calhoun (1994).

Consequences of Contention

Impacts on the Community

Collective action can also produce ripple effects in the community, especially on spectators who have direct contact with activists (Rochon, 1998: 150–51). It can alter the perceptions of mass publics and may lead to increased engagement in politics (Mansbridge, 1986: 188–91). As ideas formulated among a small coterie of activists emerge as widely held beliefs in larger populations, it can put new issues on the agenda and affect public opinion as a portion of the early risers' message "is distilled into common sense" (Tarrow, 1998: 174–75; also Rochon, 1998; Zolberg, 1972: 206). Contention, in this manner, can make the unthinkable thinkable (Gamson, 1998: 57) and create social and political pressure for change.

In China, rightful resistance has "sensitized" (Kriesi et al., 1995: 211) interested onlookers to new goals and possibilities. It has done this both by intensifying the sentiments of certain villagers on the periphery of popular action and by influencing the thinking and conduct of uninvolved community members whose interests protest leaders claim to champion. The main evidence that some rural people are being politicized by contention is that some villagers have come to admire and even share the moral courage of activists, and they are increasingly willing to participate in fund raising or daring acts of defense when rightful resisters are detained or face repression.

Popular challenges, above all, alert the public to beneficial policies and to discord that exists between the Center and local governments (Interview 24; Li, 2004; O'Brien and Li, 1995; Yu Jianrong, 2001: 548). This often makes outside observers more aware of the vulnerability of local officials and lifts their hopes that the problem of misimplementation can be resolved with the Center's help and through activists who will not give up (Interviews 24, 25). That some protest organizers endanger themselves by taking the lead in opposing unlawful "local policies" also sends out a clear message that villagers must help themselves and cannot simply wait for the Center to fix their problems. Contention thus affects shared notions about how to protest (della Porta, 1999: 66–67) and brings a portion of the "cognitive liberation" (McAdam, 1982: 48–51) that activists have experienced to a wider audience (Interviews 24, 25, 26).

Changes in attitude are also accompanied by changes in behavior when anxious but positively inclined bystanders edge closer to the action. As their confidence in the activists' intentions and skill grows, members of the public sometimes begin by coming forward with donations. To lodge complaints at higher levels and publicize central policies, rightful resisters need money for expenses. According to a number of interviewees (Interviews 4, 5, 13), fund raising is most difficult at the outset, when many villagers doubt whether popular action will accomplish anything or fear that the activists will simply pocket their contributions. But as contention continues and the activists prove themselves, public confidence and donations often grow. In Hengyang, for instance, when township officials switched off the electricity to stop protesters from using a makeshift loudspeaker to publicize central policies in a crowded market, a villager who ran a nearby restaurant supplied the silenced activists with his diesel generator free of charge. Concerned community members also sometimes visit injured activists in the hospital and give them money for medicine or food. They also aid families of jailed protesters, either with direct financial support (Interviews 4, 13, 17, 28) or by doing work for them, such as repairing a roof (Interview 27).

Success (or more often a harsh crackdown) can bring in new recruits, too. In Hengyang, for instance, a villager was so furious when he witnessed township officials beating up an activist's wife that he helped organize subsequent protests. In his words: "I could not stand such brutality against good people who were trying to help people like me. I also knew that the township was doing something that would not be tolerated by the Center" (Interview 29). Since the early 1990s, a number of riots have taken place in Hunan and Sichuan after county police or township officials sought to arrest well-liked peasant leaders by spiriting them out of their homes in the middle of the night (Duan Xianju et al., 2000; Jiang Zuoping and Yang Sanjun, 1999; Xiang Wen, 2000; Yu Jianrong, 2001). In Yizhang county, Hunan, for instance, a squad of policemen was sent to arrest a protest leader late one night. As soon as the police entered the village, however, a lookout spotted them and beat his gong to wake up his neighbors. In a matter of minutes, the police found themselves besieged by hundreds of angry villagers and were later driven away empty-handed (Duan Xianju et al., 2000).

Besides riots or sieges, previously uninvolved villagers sometimes take part in dramatic rescues after local officials detain or harm protest leaders. In an incident in Hengyang in 2002, several activists drew a big crowd when they went to press a township schoolmaster to reduce fees. When the cornered principal gave a signal to his hired muscle to beat up the chief activist, an elderly bystander stood up and shielded him. He announced that he had no children or grandchildren who had to pay the fees, but that in listening to the debate between the chief activist and the schoolmaster he had become convinced that the protesters were right and he would not stand to see the man hurt. He then turned to the school head and said: "If you want to have your men hit this man, they'll have to do it over my dead body!" (Interview 18; also Interview 7). Other onlookers became equally agitated and threw their support behind the activists, and the schoolmaster quickly backed off and agreed to reduce the fees.

At a minimum, members of the public often offer moral support to able activists and treat them like heroes. Instead of shying away from peasant leaders who have spent time in prison, for example, villagers may praise them and call for verdicts against wrongly convicted "good men" (da haoren) to be reversed. In a central Hunan township, a throng of villagers, from teenagers to eighty-year-olds, presented a paroled peasant leader eggs, meat, and fish as a sign of respect. Several called him "chairman" (zhuxi) and compared him with Chairman Mao, because, as one put it, "Like Mao Zedong, he led peasants, lowered our burdens, and brought real benefits to us" (Zhang, 2005: 29–30). In Ningxiang county, Hunan, villagers gave a leader of the 1998–99 Daolin demonstrations (Bernstein and Lü, 2003: 128–29, 148–49) a hero's welcome when his prison term ended in December 2003. They dispatched seven vehicles to pick him up in Changsha and set off fireworks when he and his entourage reached his hometown (Interviews 50, 51). In other parts of Hunan, villagers now often extol activists as their protectors and offer them free meals when they stop by (Duan Xianju et al., 2000). One protest leader in Hengyang, who had enjoyed this largess, said that villagers treated him better than they treated the township head – a man to whom villagers would no longer offer a cup of tea or even a seat (Interview 5).

Where rightful resisters have a continuing presence, some people have begun to view them as community leaders. Villagers go to them, for instance, rather than village cadres or township officials, when they have conflicts with local bullies (Interviews 4, 5, 6, 13). They also may vote for protest leaders in village elections, despite efforts by local officials to prevent such "scoundrels" (lan zai) from becoming candidates (Interviews 6, 17, 23). In places such as Hengyang, a long-standing, local tradition of peasant activism has been revived[17] and protest leaders have become recognized

---

[17] Hunan was, of course, the very place where Mao Zedong was so impressed with peasant activism in the 1920s. Hengyang county, at that time, however, was notably quieter than neighboring Hengshan county and the other four counties that Mao (1971) surveyed before writing his "Report on an Investigation of the Peasant Movement in Hunan" (Interview 58; Yu Jianrong, 2001: 142–70). Some students of the Republican-era peasantry (Bianco, 2001: 42–43; Yu Jianrong, 2001) emphasize the aloofness of the peasantry outside the "liberated regions," and the degree to which peasant involvement was instigated by the Party. Bianco

public figures who derive their power from acting in the name of the Center and their moral authority from taking personal risks for the benefit of other villagers.

Understanding Outcomes

More than a generation ago, Michael Lipsky (1968: 1146, 1153) pointed out that protest is a "highly indirect process" in which people other than activists and targets play crucial roles. He highlighted, in particular, the importance of reference publics and of drawing third parties into controversies in ways that served protesters' goals. More recently, Sidney Tarrow (1998: 164, 171, 174) has also stressed that contention does not produce its major effects immediately or directly, but through ongoing interaction of protesters, conventional political forces, public opinion, and elites (also Amenta, Halfmann, and Young, 1999; Linders, 2004: 395; McAdam and Su, 2002: 697; Soule and Olzak, 2004).

This chapter has shown that protest outcomes in rural China, when they arise, are a product of sustained interaction among activists, targets, elites, and the wider public. Popular agitation first alerts concerned officials to poor policy implementation and sometimes prompts them to take corrective steps. As a consequence of participating in contention, some activists feel empowered and become more likely to take part in future challenges, whereas others feel disillusioned and lapse into passivity. In the course of witnessing or hearing about collective action, some interested onlookers are sensitized to protester's concerns and public opinion is affected. Ideas about what is possible and how to protest evolve, and bystanders may become more likely to help with fund raising, to rescue activists in trouble, or to join demonstrations when their champions are detained.

All of these outcomes are mediated (to varying degrees) by the powers-that-be, and none arrives in the teeth of unified elite opposition; each is an outgrowth of a process in which social and state forces feel each other out and arrive at new understandings. Even for the most personal of consequences, such as those pertaining to self-change (Kiecolt, 2000), the state's hand in shaping the opportunity structure is evident, whether it be through instituting grass-roots elections, tightening control over the

(2001: 43), for example, writes: "Wherever it was not enrolled by an elite of professional revolutionaries, the Chinese peasantry did not join in the battle that was being waged in its name."

requisition of farmland, or drawing on villagers to help monitor and stop local corruption. Sometimes the Center intentionally provides openings, for instance, by granting rural people the right to reject unwarranted fees in the 1993 Agriculture Law (art. 18); more often it sets the stage for contention by tolerating what it formerly refused to abide. Without collective action, better implementation, changes in activists' outlook and conduct, and effects on the wider public would not emerge; nor would they appear without involvement from above.[18] In each instance, popular pressure is one factor among many, and outcomes arise from a confluence of mass and elite forces. In such circumstances, it is unwise to fix on isolating the independent effects of contention or disentangling the role of societal and state actors. For none of these effects does it pay to ask, where does the initiative lie?

In rural China, a realistic account of protest consequences accords villagers a critical role, but acknowledges that it is highly circumscribed. Results of contention are the result of a continuing back-and-forth between many parties and the interplay of forces both inside and outside the state. This interaction is not so much the explicit bargaining that Burstein, Einwohner, and Hollander (1995) emphasize, as a testing process to see if certain gray zones can now be traversed. And whether they can or not, learning occurs and the next round of contention starts from a slightly different place.

In the end, to do justice to protest outcomes it pays to steer clear of simple dichotomies like state versus society or us versus them, and to examine how specific parts of a state interact with (and provide opportunities for) particular social forces in a given location.[19] This involves finding out why, for example, sympathetic officials sometimes choose to champion protesters' demands and sometimes fail them utterly, and investigating institutional pressure points where elite unity crumbles or is exposed as a facade. Even authoritarian regimes are composed of far-flung bureaucracies, and their multilayered structure cannot help but disorganize the powerful and present opportunities for the disgruntled "to make the authorities work for them rather than against them." (Klandermans, 1997: 194). To detect some of

[18] Involvement can range from energetic advocacy backed up with real follow through to rhetorical support backed by very little.

[19] Despite the national focus of much scholarship on outcomes, proximate, local impacts on the immediate circumstances are what many protesters seek and what they achieve (Andrews, 2004: 4, 191; Cress and Snow, 2000: 1095–96). On the "local character of most contentious politics," see McAdam et al. (2005: 11).

the more significant consequences of protest, we need, once and for all, to jettison a movement-centered approach to contention that has been much criticized (Andrews, 2004: 21; Jenkins and Klandermans, 1995: 3; McAdam, 1996: 355; McAdam, Tarrow, and Tilly, 2001: 74) but still persists, and to engage explanations of change from literatures as far away as policy implementation and public opinion (Andrews, 2004: 21–22; McAdam and Su, 2002; Soule and Olzak, 2004). To understand how top-down openings and bottom-up pressure work together to produce change, we should pay more attention to the inner workings of government and seemingly small changes in state-society relations. In particular, we need to explore the fissures that divide every state and the way that popular forces exploit them.

A Note on Variation

In this chapter, to underscore outcomes of contention that have emerged despite a generally unwelcoming opportunity structure, we have "selected on extreme cases of the dependent variable" (for a defense of this practice, see Collier and Mahoney, 1996: 72). To find out if our findings are representative of broader trends in rural China would require a different research strategy that systematically explored rightful resistance that also led to repression (or, more benignly, lack of implementation or any response).[20] A next step, of particular import to scholars curious about how generalizable our findings are, would be to give more attention to sources of variation. Researchers would need to speak with protest leaders and villagers in a wider range of locations to discover the extent to which rightful resistance has affected implementation, activists, and the wider public elsewhere. They would want to investigate if the consequences of rightful resistance depend on the specific political tradition, history, and culture of a locality and, if so, in what ways? Do regional differences exist,[21] and are the protest consequences we have discussed more pronounced, for example, in China's central grain belt, where Bernstein and Lü (2003) have argued cadre-peasant tensions are most acute? Is a similar dynamic

[20] On strategies for choosing "negative cases" wisely, see Mahoney and Goertz (2004).
[21] Uighur protests in Xinjiang, for example, often diverge from rightful resistance because protesters see little difference between the Center and the local state and because many of the grievances in play are not seen to be legitimate by the Center (Hastings, 2005). Chinese Academy of Social Science researcher Yu Jianrong (Zhao Ling, 2004) has argued that since 2001 the focus of rural activism has shifted from tax to land disputes and from central China to more developed coastal areas.

at work in urban areas? Do tactics (mediated versus direct) or the size of a protest matter?[22] Does violence deliver the goods more reliably than rightful resistance, insofar as it "shocks" central authorities into responding and redefining their own interests? More broadly, how do the many potential intercessors at higher levels view rightful resistance in various policy areas, and why do some choose to respond while others fail to? And, finally, which community members are most amenable to the call of rightful resistance, and under what circumstances do villagers lend their support to (or reject) protest leaders?

---

[22] Cai (2004: 441), relying on 1999 data from eleven provinces, found that "the average number of participants involved in collective appeals ranges from seventeen to thirty-one – far more than the regulated five" – and that "these numbers reflect citizens' belief that a large turnout exerts more pressure on the local government."

6

Implications for China

Although the previous chapter emphasized relatively small-scale changes rather than dramatic policy effects or institutional breakthroughs, rightful resistance may also have larger implications for state-society relations and political change. First, insofar as rightful resistance creates hardened activists and affects the way Chinese villagers think about the responsibilities of the powerful, microlevel shifts in values may presage a transformation in political identities. Second, the rising number of otherwise unrelated episodes of rightful resistance may together inspire power holders to consider policy innovations and institutional reforms. Third, if rightful resistance continues to spread and escalate, it could have implications for the regime's durability, as activists begin to insist that central policy makers apply their own rules to themselves and abide by principles they have established.

Citizenship

Consider the following story: More than five months had passed, but the oversized characters scrawled on a storefront in the center of a Hebei village were still legible. "We're citizens. Return us our citizenship rights. We're not rural labor power, even less are we slaves. Former village cadres must confess their corruption" (see Figures 4 and 5). The village leaders had little doubt who was behind this infuriating graffiti – namely, several of the twenty rightful resisters who had tried to topple the village Party secretary and his predecessor for practicing graft – but they felt it was unwise to take any action. The corrupt cadres were said to be afraid that whitewashing the wall would only add fuel to the complaint and confirm their guilt. Instead, they would tough it out: refuse to turn over the accounts, stick with their

Figure 4 "We're citizens. Return us our citizenship rights. We're not rural labor power, even less are we slaves." (Photo by Lianjiang Li, Hebei, 1995)

story that the books had been destroyed in a fire, and wait for the summer rains to weather the charges away. But in the meantime the allegations would stand unrebutted, there for all to see (authors' observations, July and December, 1995; also Interviews 72, 73).

Claims to citizenship have been a rallying cry for the excluded in many times and many places. In this one north China village, a group of enterprising rightful resisters framed their critique of power in terms of citizenship rights and, in so doing, hamstrung a team of extremely hard-nosed cadres.[1] Couching a long-standing grievance in the language of community membership, the protesters' claim to inclusion had become unassailable. By reworking official "rights talk,"[2] they had turned a contested demand for

---

[1] For more on this village, and the unfolding of a bitter, collective complaint there, see O'Brien and Li (1995). This is the village, discussed in the Preface, that provided us with our first full episode of rural contention.

[2] Although "rights talk" always implies a certain assertiveness, in contemporary American discourse, for example, it tends toward the absolute, individualistic, and ontological in that individuals possess rights by virtue of being human beings. In contrast, Chinese rights talk tends to be relative, social, and phenomenological in that subjects-citizens of a given state only have rights defined in relation to obligations to each other and their relationship to rulers. Put differently, in Chinese rights talk, rights are not what human beings possess

117

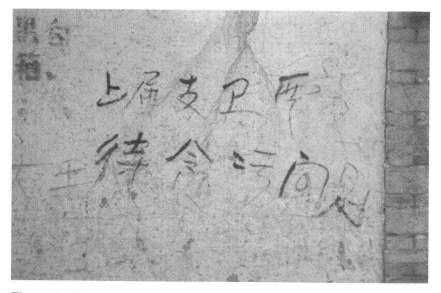

Figure 5 "Former village cadres must confess their corruption." (Photo by Lian-jiang Li, Hebei, 1995)

accountability into a simple plea for respect. Decollectivization had freed them. New political reforms had promised financial openness. As citizens, they had a right to inspect the village accounts and, as citizens, they had a right not to be treated as slaves.

In this one Hebei village claims to citizenship have begun to affect how villagers and cadres interact. Hundreds of miles away, in Hengyang county, Hunan, rightful resisters now commonly refer to each other as "citizens" (*gongmin*) and one of their chief claims is that they are undertaking "to defend the citizenship rights" (*baohu gongmin quan*) of all villagers (Interviews 4, 6, 17, 20, 22, 27, 39, 74, 75).[3] The activists in these two locations

simply for being what they are; rights are what socially defined persons have by being what they are defined to be. This difference has many ramifications. In many Western theories of democracy, for example, the equality of rulers and the ruled is a given; in current Chinese rights talk, it is something to strive for. On the emergence during the 1990s of a small but significant group of Chinese thinkers who, to varying degrees, view human rights as universal, individual, and grounded in common humanity, see Weatherley (1999: 132–41) and Svensson (2002: 276–80).

[3] Typical statements by protest leaders from Hengyang included: "Since I saw too large a gap between social reality and the state's policies concerning peasant burdens, as a citizen I felt obliged to stand up for the poor peasants and the Party" (Interview 4); and "I lodged

may be "pioneers of rights consciousness" (*quanli yishi de xianjuezhe*) (Zhou Qingyin and Wang Xinya, 2000a: 19), but they are not alone. Evidence abounds that the language of citizenship is alive in the Chinese countryside today (Huang Haiyan, 2004; Li Changping, 2003, March 1; Ma Zhongdong, 2000; Xiao Han, 2002, January 1). The notion of being a citizen is seeping into popular discourse at many points, but are Chinese villagers citizens in anything other than the narrowest juridical sense?

In its most general definition, citizenship refers to a privileged legal status. A citizen is a full member of a community (Marshall, 1976: 84; Barbalet, 1988: 18). As citizens, categorically defined persons perform duties and possess rights, the most basic of which is the right to have rights (Kymlicka and Norman, 1995: 310). In nearly all communities, some residents are complete citizens and others fall short. Citizenship, in other words, excludes at the same time that it includes; it draws boundaries and ranks the populace (Riesenberg, 1992: xvii; Kerber, 1997; Shafir, 1998: 24). Citizens are in a privileged position vis-à-vis other community members (e.g., children, criminals, foreigners, guest workers) because they possess rights that noncitizens and incomplete citizens lack.

By this measure, villagers in contemporary China have certain rights, but theirs is a partial, local citizenship. Rural people have few opportunities to participate in the exercise of power outside the village, and their inclusion in the wider polity is not well established. Although villagers have obtained a foothold in grass-roots politics,[4] and some resources to fight the misuse of power, their ability to rein in state sovereignty is slight. The state has yet to recognize certain citizenship rights (e.g., the right to elect top leaders, the right to organize), and it has not taken the steps needed to ensure that all the rights it recognizes are honored. The inclusion that rural people have been offered is piecemeal and incomplete.

If citizenship were solely a status awarded by the state, this would be the end of our story about changing identities. But citizenship is more than

---

complaints not for myself, but on behalf of the masses, who are citizens of our country, but have been deprived of their right to autonomy by those corrupt Communist Party members. I lodged complaints to secure justice for peasants who do not realize that these policies exist" (Interview 27).

[4] On village elections, see Kennedy (2002), Li (1999, 2003), Liu (2000), O'Brien (2001), O'Brien and Li (2000), Pastor and Tan (2000), and X. Wang (1997). On villagers, particularly migrant workers, not being treated as full-fledged citizens outside their home villages, see Solinger (1999). On the notion of village (rather than national) citizenship in China, see He (2005).

a collection of rights bestowed on passive recipients (Turner, 1992: 2). It is also an outcome of historical processes that emerges as members of the popular classes seek to improve their lot by confronting the powers-that-be. Citizenship, in other words, arises out of negotiation between representatives of the state and social groups, and all initiative does not lie with the state. In fact, in many places, enlarging the scope of citizenship requires prolonged struggle (Giddens, 1982: 165, 171–72; Tilly, 1995: 230), and new rights are acquired only through bottom-up pressure and the painstaking extraction of concessions. Citizenship, in this sense, is less granted than won, less accorded than made.

Understood this way, citizenship is a "way of life growing within" (Marshall, 1976: 70) that reflects new aspirations and expectations. Its spread depends on changes in people's hearts and minds, and it leads to changes in behavior. As seen with the Hebei rightful resisters who denounced corruption using the soothing language of community membership, the rise of citizenship implies new identities and a growing fluency in "rights talk." To understand how citizenship develops, tallying up what the central state recognizes and what the local state enforces is important, but tracing changes in claims making, popular consciousness, and expectations is just as critical. In this regard, becoming a citizen involves adjustments in psychological orientation: in particular, changes in one's awareness of politics, sense of efficacy, and feelings toward government. It implies a willingness to question authority and suggests that people view their relationship with the state as reciprocal. It entails a readiness to enter into conflicts with the powerful and a certain assertiveness in articulating one's interests (Shi, 2000).

When the spotlight shifts to how citizenship rights emerge, the growth of rightful resistance takes on a new meaning. It becomes a sign that some ordinary people are speaking the language of power with real skill: that they are making officials prisoners of their rhetoric by advancing claims in an especially effective way. It is evidence of villagers increasingly identifying, interpreting, and challenging official misbehavior using the vocabulary of rights[5] and "naming, blaming, and claiming" (Felstiner, Abel, and Sarat, 1980–81; Diamant, Lubman, and O'Brien, 2005: 7–8) based on a

---

[5] This should not be exaggerated or understood too literally, particularly because the Chinese words for power or authority (*quanli*) and rights (*quanli*) are homonyms. That said, even in eighteenth-century Europe, "food rioters did sometimes appeal to justice (or 'fair' prices) and they certainly protested against unfair practices; but the language of 'duties,' 'obligations,' 'reciprocity,' and even of 'rights' is mostly our own" (Thompson, 1991: 350).

contractual understanding of their relations with the powerful. It indicates that a growing number of rural people expect local officials, in some small way, to be "public servants" (*gongpu*)[6] and that they believe that every person should enjoy equal standing before the law.[7]

When villagers come to view the Center's promises as a source of inclusion and entitlement, they are acting like citizens before they are citizens. Certain citizenship practices, in other words, are preceding the appearance of full citizenship as a secure, universally recognized status. In fact, practice may be creating status, as local struggles begin in enclaves of tolerance, spread when conditions are auspicious, and possibly evolve into inclusion in the broader polity.[8]

---

[6] Interviewee 8 used the term "public servant" particularly often. An elderly activist who had only four years of formal education, he wrote: "'Cadres are public officials of the government in charge of law enforcement and administration. They are paid with public funds, so they are public servants. Cadres should have an upright character, a strong sense of justice, and a spirit of 'worrying before others and enjoying after others.' ... They should understand where their power comes from and why it goes away." In another of his unpublished essays, he raised thirty-six questions, one of which was: "Why don't the people have the right to elect and recall so-called 'public servants' who engage in misconduct and neglect their duties?" Another protest leader (Interview 4), in his application to establish a farmers' association, pleaded: "Please, [cadres of] the public security bureau, the procurator, and the courts, you should put the interests of the Party and the people above everything else, understand and sympathize with the people, stop serving as protective umbrellas of corrupt elements, come to the countryside, and truly serve the people and the Party."

[7] In our 1999 survey, when asked "On whom do you think the law should be binding?" 93 percent of 1,384 respondents chose "everyone should be equal before the law, the laws should be binding on everyone." But when answering the follow-up question: "On whom do you think the laws are in reality binding?" only 36 percent chose the same answer, while 50 percent chose: "The laws are binding only on ordinary people and not on the powerful and rich." For information on survey sampling, see Appendix B.

[8] On urban workers in China "strugg[ling] to perform and thus realize a legal status, bestowed by the central government's law and regulations but denied them by local state agents," see Lee (2001: 218). In his study of the origins of citizenship rights in Europe, Tilly (1998: 56), also stresses bargaining and struggle, albeit on a national scale. The early history of citizenship in ancient Greece and medieval Europe, in other accounts (Riesenberg, 1992: xv, 5), is often depicted as local and parochial as much as national and universal. Somers (1993: 594–98; 1994: 83), for example, traces the origins of citizenship in England to pastoral regions in the fourteenth century rather than to the industrializing cities of the nineteenth century. It was in distant woodlands, where certain rural dwellers translated community autonomy and solidarity into a capacity for association and participation, that English peasants first appropriated labor laws and interpreted them as conferring citizenship rights. This suggests that citizenship may emerge deep in "the local node of a national legal structure" (Steinberg, 1995: 22) – in small communities, where power is unfragmented, and manageable size encourages participation and makes it easy to observe one's rulers in action (Dagger, 1981).

For now, however, despite occasional instances of something more,[9] the claims rightful resisters put forward mainly demand entry into the realm of policy implementation. They seldom press for wider civil and political rights to association, expression, and unlicensed participation; nor do they often question the legitimacy of existing laws and policies, not to mention the right of unaccountable leaders at higher levels to make laws and policies. Even the most assertive rightful resisters rarely demand provincial or national elections, wisely avoiding an issue that might alienate the allies they need to enforce their claims against local officialdom.

Rightful resisters know that they exist at the sufferance of higher levels and that the "rights" they act on are conditional. Unlike the rights discourse employed by some liberal intellectuals, there is little evidence that most rightful resisters consider rights to be inherent, natural, or inalienable; nor do most of them break with the common Chinese practice of viewing rights as granted by the state mainly for societal purposes rather than to protect an individual's autonomous being (Edwards, Henkin, and Nathan, 1986). Demanding citizenship is therefore more a claim to community membership than a claim to negative freedoms vis-à-vis the state. Rightful resisters seldom contend that rights flow from human personhood,[10] but rather that the government's right to loyalty depends on ensuring that its officials fulfill their obligations. They typically argue, as some Chinese have for centuries (G. Wang, 1991), that the duties of those below must be reciprocated by the duties of those above. As a number of protest leaders in Hengyang insisted, in return for their compliance with the many strictures under which they live, the Center owes them unflinching execution of beneficial policies and, in particular, protection from unlawful extraction (Interviews 4, 5, 6, 8, 13, 19, 21, 22).

Rightful resisters (and other villagers), accordingly, are best thought of as occupying a position between subjects and citizens. When they use unenforced citizenship rights as a weapon, they are demanding that the representatives of state power treat them equitably, respect their claims, and deliver

---

[9] On a trend, since the early 1990s, toward more general, less particularistic claims in Hunan, see X. Chen (2003) and Yu Jianrong (2003). For more on claims radicalization, see Chapters 3 and 4.

[10] The increasingly common use of the words "slave" (*nuli*), "serf" (*nongnu*), and "second-class citizen" (*erdeng gongmin*) by rightful resisters to describe their status and how they are mistreated suggests this may be changing. Claims based on human personhood also appeared in earlier times. On labor protesters in the first part of the twentieth century who complained about being treated like "cattle and horses," see Smith (2002).

on promises made by officials at higher levels (Bernstein and Lü, 2000: 756–59; Li, 2004; Yu Jianrong, 2003; Zweig, 2000). Theirs is an effort to use "the resources that are at hand, the very same aspects of social structure that support power and domination" (Ewick and Silbey, 2003: 1336) to open clogged channels of participation and to make still-contested rights real. The huge disparity between what is promised and what villagers experience creates openings daily for them to challenge blatant misconduct, obvious evasion of central intent, and flagrant violations of announced rights. In this sense, Chinese rightful resisters may be more like American civil rights activists of the early 1960s than like the pay equity activists of the 1980s who were discussed in Chapter 1. Speaking both as and for people who are still closer to subjects than citizens, they risk repression at every turn, but are reasonably well positioned to "win big" (i.e., to shake up power relations), provided they do not "lose big" (i.e., end up being crushed by their local opponents) first. In the long term, their ad hoc entry to the implementation arena may prepare the way for more permanent access to political power. Although Chinese villagers are only partial citizens in the local polity, we may be witnessing the process by which a more complete citizenship comes about.

Political Change

Beyond fostering changes in political identities, rightful resistance can also alter routine politics and generate new loci of decision making. In the course of taking advantage of existing channels of participation, rightful resisters may simultaneously broaden them. They can help place new issues on the agenda in a forceful and suggestive way (in another context, see Tarrow, 1998: 175) and foster an environment that facilitates policy innovations, institutional change, and readjustments in state-society relations.

How might these changes come to pass? First, by amplifying the voice of the rural population and affecting the Center's priorities. When protest impinges on "social stability" (*wending*) and threatens to undermine the legitimacy of the regime, it encourages top leaders to pay more attention to the demands of villagers than they would have otherwise (Cai, 2004; Edin, 2004; Kennedy, 2004; O'Brien and Li, 1999; Yep, 2004). Over the past two decades, for instance, as rightful resistance concerning fees mounted and became more confrontational, particularly after a number of episodes led to "significant collective incidents" (*zhongda quntixing shijian*) and local crackdowns, Beijing stepped up its efforts to reduce excessive extraction.[11] In this way – gradually, indirectly, but surely – rightful resistance spurred a policy change. Escalating contention led the leadership to lose faith in past approaches and to craft new methods to contain appropriation: reliance on top-down discipline (1980s) was followed by permitting villagers to reject illegal impositions (1990, 1993), the tax-for-fee reform (ca. 2000–2), and, most recently (2004), a decision that agricultural taxes would be reduced by 1 percent per year and abolished within five years (Bernstein and Lü, 2003; Interviews 7, 56, 58, 71; Wen Jiabao, 2004, March 17; Yep, 2004).

In addition to inspiring concessions on rural taxation, rightful resistance has also prompted Chinese leaders to introduce institutional reforms that could meaningfully recast state-society relations. The number of complaints lodged at letters and visits bureaus and elsewhere skyrocketed in the decade leading up to the Sixteenth Party Congress (2003) (Cai, 2004: 433–35; Michelson, 2004: 6; Minzner, 2005; Yu Jianrong, 2004, October 19; Zhou Zhanshun, 1999).[12] Chinese journalists went so far as to describe it

[11] The noted Chinese rural investigator Yu Jianrong (2004) has traced the Center's growing concern. In 1985 Beijing deemed peasant burdens "a prominent negative factor that damages party-mass relations, worker-peasant relations and further implementation of rural economic policies." By 1990, as the number of incidents of rightful resistance was taking off, unlawful appropriation was said to "seriously harm farmers' initiative to develop production and to damage Party-mass and cadre-mass relations. Should it continue to worsen, it will inevitably affect rural economic development and social stability." Three years later, after an instance of rightful resistance against illegal apportionments in Renshou county, Sichuan evolved into a riot, Beijing acknowledged that "reducing peasant burdens is not merely an economic problem, but a political problem. It affects the development of the national economy and political stability in the countryside and even nationwide." By 1996, after large-scale protests occurred in Hunan, Jiangxi, Henan, Hubei, Sichuan, and Anhui, the Center warned that "heavy peasant burdens have become a very prominent problem that affects rural reforms, development and stability.... Reducing peasant burdens is an extremely urgent political task." Finally, by 2004, resistance to extraction had become such a challenge that Premier Wen Jiabao (2004, March 17) called the reduction of peasant burdens "the emphasis of emphases in all our work." See also Cai (2004: 449) on the tax-for-fee reform as "an attempt by the central government to resolve a source of conflict after peasants persistently put up resistance, including collective action," and Yep (2004: 42, 48) on how "the rising threat of rural instability explains the urgency and enthusiasm" for tax-for-fee reform in Anhui province and, more generally, how "growing regime receptivity to peasant frustration has led to policy change."

[12] Relying on data from the State Letters and Visits Bureau, Lee (2004: 4) reports, "in 2000, there were a total of 10.2 million cases of petitions to their provincial, county and municipal offices nationwide, an increase of 115% over 1995. 76.5% of the petitioners were involved in 'collective petitions,' defined as those involving five people or more. The total numbers of collective cases and collective petitioners in 2000 saw a 280% and 260% rate of increase respectively over those of 1995." In the first three months of 2005, the State Council's

as a "torrent of complaints" (*xinfang hongliu*) (Hu Kui and Jiang Shu, 2003, December 11). Partly in response, Party leaders began to consider reforms that would enhance the likelihood that collective petitions were addressed. President Hu Jintao, among others, proposed instituting a system by which letters and visits offices would convene all concerned departments to deal with complex disputes that had, in many cases, dragged on for years (Zhao Ling, 2004, November 4: 12). Meanwhile, the State Council revised the 1995 Letters and Visits Regulations in order to streamline the complaint process and make buck-passing more difficult (Interview 58). The new regulation (effective May 1, 2005) incorporated Hu's proposal (art. 5) and forbade any organization or individual from retaliating against petitioners (art. 3). It also requires that materials submitted by petitioners not be passed on to accused individuals or departments (art. 23) and calls for those with a conflict of interest to recuse themselves from handling a petition (art. 30). The measure further stipulates that public hearings may be held to resolve important, complicated, and difficult cases (art. 31) and requires that all counties and townships institute "letters and visits leadership days" on which responsible officials can be directly approached (art. 10).[13]

Still, policy and institutional changes usually come slowly if at all, and rightful resisters often feel betrayed when their efforts to ensure faithful implementation come to naught. As we have seen throughout this book, failure frequently has even more profound long-term consequences than success. If the Center does not deliver on enough of its promises, this could give rise to further protest and more use of direct tactics and ultimately violence, as the spearhead is pushed up and rightful resisters mobilize to protest the disparity between what the Center says and what the Center does or fails to do (Interview 30; Yu Jianrong, 2003; Zhao Shukai, 2003; on increasingly violent resistance, see Tanner, 2004: 142–43). There is evidence of this already insomuch as some rightful resisters say that "water far away cannot quench thirst nearby" (Interview 31) or, more ominously, "all crows

Letters and Visits Bureau noted that letters and visits had increased more than 90 percent compared with the number of petitions in the same period in 2004 (Davis, 2005, August 27). Minzner (2005) reports that about 11.5 million petitions are received each year by county-level and higher government and Party organs, or nearly twice the number of cases handled by the formal court system.

13 At the same time, the new measure continues to limit to five the number of complainants' representatives who may appear to present a petition, and, in effect, bars petitioners from revisiting any department for sixty days once a complaint is accepted (arts. 16, 33). The regulation also explicitly bans inciting others to engage in petitioning (art. 20). For a thorough consideration of the 2005 regulation, see Minzner (2005).

under heaven are equally black" (Interviews 32, 33). That many rural people still extend the benefit of the doubt to central authorities suggests that the regime retains a reserve of legitimacy. But popular faith in the beneficence of the Center will weaken if aggrieved villagers repeatedly fail to receive the protection and assistance they expect (Li, 2004). At a certain point, the Center's good intentions will no longer matter unless they are backed up by a capacity to right wrongs.

The spread of direct tactics that has become apparent since the mid-1990s[14] suggests that trust in the Center is indeed waning. When rightful resisters turn to higher levels, what awaits them more often than not is disappointment. They may hope to find kindly representatives of a concerned Center, but instead are often received by long-faced, ill-tempered bureaucrats who brush them off, give them empty promises, or pass them off to others (Interviews 14, 15, 34; Zhang Yinghong, 2002). Complainants usually must spend considerable time and money making appeals, and they may be turned away if the injustice or social impact is not deemed sufficient or if the agency lacks the resources or clout to address a problem (Cai, 2004: 444–46). If more and more villagers lose confidence in the state's capacity to control its agents, or come to doubt that central authorities truly want beneficial policies to be executed, this could engender cynicism and political passivity (Interview 16). But it could also generate even more reliance on direct tactics (or violence) and pressure for sweeping reforms, such as popular election of national leaders or even the end of one-party rule (Zhou Decai, 2002). Longtime activists in parts of Hunan, for instance, continue to frame their claims in terms of policy implementation, but by "policy" they sometimes now mean constitutional principles, such as popular sovereignty and rule by law (Interviews 5, 35; on the "generalization" of claims, see Rucht, 1990: 171).[15]

Today's rightful resistance could thus evolve into a more far-reaching counterhegemonic project, particularly if rightful resisters come to doubt not only the Center's ability to deliver on its promises but also its desire to do so. Acting at the edge of prevailing rules, in other words, does not commit rightful resisters to existing arrangements or the broader system. Although successful rightful resistance probably enhances regime legitimacy in the

[14] See Chapter 4.

[15] "The gradual 'nationalization' of reciprocity, solidarity, trust and moral duty may soon result in the constitution of a peasant citizen who is still predominantly oriented towards the collective good in the village, but at the same time 'generalizes' it by thinking (and acting) beyond the village boundaries" (Brandstädter and Schubert, 2005: 17).

short term, some groups of activists may graduate from combating illegal mistreatment alone (and occasionally) to combating legal mistreatment together (and regularly).[16] As we saw in Chapter 5, rightful resistance has already begun to generate homegrown networks of activists, which could serve as the local nexus of a wider rights movement. Large-scale petitions in 2004, partly organized by outside lawyers and journalists, have demanded the recall of county and municipal leaders in Fujian, Hebei, and Sichuan (Interviews 58, 69, 70). Recent reports suggest that intermingling of veteran protesters from various parts of the country and nearly all walks of life is turning the "complainants' village" in Beijing into a hotbed for coordinating cross-class and cross-regional popular action (Interviews 58, 66; Zhao Ling, 2004, November 4: 12; Su Yongtong, 2004, November 4: 13). Members of the banned Chinese Democratic Party (Wright, 2002) reportedly even had some success in recruiting disillusioned activists there in 2004. Although most of the petitioners turned down this invitation, others reportedly joined the party (and were subsequently jailed), and still others contemplated organizing their own party (Interviews 56, 66). Although it remains far too early to draw any conclusions, such developments suggest that a corps of willing recruits may be available to be mobilized by social movement entrepreneurs, should they appear.

But even if most rightful resisters continue to embrace established values and even if nothing approaching a large-scale movement appears, we should not underestimate the implications of rising rights consciousness and a growing fluency in "rights talk" in a nation where rights have traditionally been weakly protected. Thanks in part to the spread of rightful resistance, terms such as "rights defense" (*weiquan*) have gained acceptance in reform-minded journals and adventurous newspapers and, more gradually, in the mainstream press, including *People's Daily*.[17] As these ideas work their way

---

[16] Examples include efforts in the early 1990s to overturn household registration policies (Li Kang, 1994: 267), and more recent attempts to establish a countywide farmers' association (Interview 4).

[17] Early advocates of the term "rights defense" published in *Strategy and Management*, *Window on the Southern Wind*, *Southern Weekend*, and *Southern Metropolitan Daily*. The first article in *People's Daily* that mentioned both "peasants" (*nongmin*) and "rights defense" was written by Wu Xinghua (1997, February 15), a New China News Agency reporter known for his frank reporting of protests against excessive extraction in Hunan. From February 15, 1997, to November 11, 2004, 177 articles containing the words "peasant" and "rights defense" appeared in *People's Daily*. For Web sites that include the term "rights defense" in their name and that collect Chinese articles on the topic, see: http://www.weiquan.org.cn/ and http://www.weiquancn.com/ and http://www.wq-investigation.com/.

into public consciousness, and as activists use the media to advance and publicize their cause, ordinary people may become increasingly skilled at "rights talk" and this could promote more assertive efforts to defend and extend villagers' rights.

Rightful resisters, in the end, are subalterns, but they are not as constrained in thought as Gramsci (1971) suggests or as constrained in action as Scott (1990: 90–91) suggests.[18] As villagers creatively appropriate and refashion official rights' discourses and exploit new opportunities to press fresh claims, their contention tiptoes beyond the strict constructionism that normally constrains them. Think of the Hebei graffiti artists mentioned at the beginning of this chapter: in one sense they were using a familiar tactic (writing a wall poster) and seeking a "return" (*huan*) of their rights. In another sense, they were cloaking a daring proactive claim in reactive terms, demanding citizenship rights they had never enjoyed, while making it appear they had just been deprived of them.[19] Or, when rightful resisters cite people's congresses as a model for turning villagers' representative assemblies into policy-making bodies (Interviews 48, 49), or claim that the principle of people's democracy entitles them to vote in Party primaries (Li and O'Brien, 1999; Li Jingyi, 1992), or use vague clauses calling for direct elections to demand open nomination procedures (Interviews 1, 2; Tian Yuan, 1993), their resistance is both loyal and proactive.[20] These actions, like other "not always pure" forms of contention (Hollander and Einwohner, 2004: 549) possess elements both of accommodation *and* resistance. They are a means to advance interests within existing limits and a way to assert new rights and pry open channels of participation that few power holders at any level could have foreseen.

In the end, how episodes of rightful resistance play out nationwide will have a bearing on where China is heading, at least if there is a bottom-up element to the ongoing transition and not everything originates in the Party leadership compound in Beijing. Among other issues, how countless

---

[18] Scott's (1990: 94–107) position is complex, and some of the evidence he considers suggests less constraint in action than his turning of Gramsci upside down implies.

[19] Some midlevel officials use the phrase "'return' [*huan*] power to the people" analogously when promoting village elections, even though the people have never had the power that is being returned to them (Interviews 76, 77, 78).

[20] On proactive claims in rural China, see Gilley, 2001; Li and O'Brien, 1996; O'Brien, 2001, 2002: 142–46; Yu Jianrong, 2003. On competitive, reactive, and proactive claims in rural Europe, see Tilly, 1976. Tilly has moved away from this typology, but others (Perry, 1985; Sewell, 1990: 529–30) continue to find it useful.

Political Change

incidents of rightful resistance unfold should offer clues to how resilient the regime is and how likely it is to crumble when faced with future challenges. China watchers and Chinese villagers alike would then be better placed to address questions of whether reform and "quiet revolution" still have some way to go, or whether the engine for change is becoming conventional forms of transgressive contention, like riots, illegal protests, and ultimately revolution.

Interviewee List

1. Official at the Ministry of Civil Affairs, Beijing, July 1995
2. Official at the Ministry of Civil Affairs, Beijing, July 1995
3. Researcher, Beijing, October 1997
4. Activist, Hengyang, Hunan, January–March 2003
5. Activist, Hengyang, Hunan, January–March 2003
6. Activist, Hengyang, Hunan, January–March 2003
7. Activist, Hengyang, Hunan, January–March 2003
8. Activist, Hengyang, Hunan, January–March 2003
9. Villager, Jiangxi, July 1997*
10. Protest leader, Henan, Beijing, September 1999
11. Activist, Hengyang, Hunan, January–March 2003
12. Township government head, Hengyang, Hunan, March 2003
13. Activist, Hengyang, Hunan, January–March 2003
14. Former activist, Hebei, July 1994, August 1997, July 1997
15. Protest leader, Henan, Beijing, September 1999
16. Former activist, Hebei, July 1997*
17. Activist, Hengyang, Hunan, January–March 2003
18. Activist, Hengyang, Hunan, January–March 2003
19. Activist, Hengyang, Hunan, January–March 2003
20. Activist, Hengyang, Hunan, January–March 2003
21. Activist, Hengyang, Hunan, January–March 2003
22. Activist, Hengyang, Hunan, January–March 2003
23. Activist, Hengyang, Hunan, January–March 2003
24. Villager, Hengyang, Hunan, January 2003
25. Villager, Hengyang, Hunan, January 2003
26. Activist's spouse, Hengyang, Hunan, January–March 2003

27. Activist, Hengyang, Hunan, January–March 2003
28. Activist's spouse, Hunan, January 2003
29. Former activist, Hengyang, Hunan, March 2003
30. Villager, Chenzhou, Hunan, April 2000
31. Villager, Shandong, July 1997*
32. Villager, Hebei, July 1999*
33. Villager, Jiangxi, October 2000*
34. Villager, Jiangsu, October 2000*
35. Activist, Hengyang, Hunan, January–March 2003
36. Activist, Shandong, November 2003
37. Activist, Fujian, April 2004
38. Activist, Hengyang, Hunan, January 2003
39. Activist, Hengyang, Hunan, March 2003
40. Activist, Hengyang, Hunan, January–March 2003
41. Activist, Hengyang, Hunan, March 2003
42. Rural Researcher, Wuhan, Hubei, August 1994
43. Rural Researcher, Guangdong, October 2003
44. Activist, Hengyang, Hunan, January 2003
45. Former village Party secretary, Hengyang, Hunan, January 2003
46. Villager, Hengyang, Hunan, March 2003
47. Village Party secretary, Tianjin, August 1998
48. Village Party secretary, Hebei, October 1993
49. Villagers' committee director, Hebei, October 1993
50. Activist, Ningxiang, Hunan, June 2004
51. Villager, Ningxiang, Hunan, June 2004
52. Rural researcher, Anhui, October 1999
53. Township Party secretary, Hebei, September 1993
54. Rural researcher, Hunan, May 2004
55. Rural researcher, Guangdong, November 2003
56. Rural researcher, Beijing, September 1999
57. Villager, Hebei, October 1999*
58. Rural researcher, Beijing, August 2004, March 2005
59. Villager, Anhui, September 1997*
60. Villager, Jiangxi, September 1997*
61. Villager, Hebei, December 1997*
62. Villager, Jiangxi, July 1998
63. Villager, Anhui, October 1997*
64. Villager, Hebei, July 1999*

65. Villager, Shandong, July 1998*
66. Complainant, Hunan, Beijing, August 2004
67. Protest leader, Henan, Beijing, September 1999
68. Protest leader, Shandong, Beijing, July 2004
69. Lawyer, Beijing, August 2004
70. Rural researcher, Fujian, May 2004
71. Rural Researcher, Beijing, August 2004
72. Former village Party secretary, Hebei, December 1995
73. Former member of a village Party branch, Hebei, December 1995
74. Activist, Hengyang, Hunan, March 2003
75. Activist, Hengyang, Hunan, March 2003
76. Official of a county organization department, Shanxi, July 1997
77. Official of a county organization department, Shanxi, July 1997
78. Official of a county bureau of civil affairs, Shanxi, July 1997
79. Activist, Henan, Beijing, February 2005
80. Former reporter and editor of a legal journal, February 2005

* Indicates survey respondents who either wrote comments in the margins of a questionnaire or answered open-ended questions.

APPENDIX A

Who Leads Rightful Resistance?

Who tends to lead rightful resistance? This question cannot be answered directly or with confidence, although it has been noted that organizers of rural protests are often male and demobilized soldiers (O'Brien and Li, 1995: 768; Bernstein and Lü, 2003: 143; Yu Jianrong, 2001: 565). Based on his fieldwork in Hunan, Yu Jianrong (2000; 2001: 565; 2003: 2) also found that "spokesmen for peasant interests" (*nongmin liyi daiyanren*) were typically thirty to forty-five years of age, former migrant workers, neither Party members nor village cadres, who had lower middle school education or more and enjoyed an upper middle level of family income. Others have presented evidence that, among the aggrieved, men, older people, and those with higher incomes and/or a cadre in the household are most likely to appeal to higher authorities (Michelson, 2004). Minzner (2005), citing a study by Zhao Shukai (2003) of nearly two hundred petitioners who registered their complaints with *Farmer's Daily* in 1998 and 1999, notes that visitors to letters and visits offices in Beijing tended "to be men, 35–60 years old, often with a middle-school (junior high school) degree." Zhang's (2005: 44) research on peasant leaders in three Hunan counties emphasizes older men in their sixties and seventies or middle-aged peasants in their thirties and forties, all of whom had worked for the government previously but who were not presently employed in the state apparatus.

Our recent fieldwork suggests that villagers who were targets (or the children of targets) of political campaigns such as land reform and the Cultural Revolution, and those who were punished for breaking the one-child policy were more likely to organize or take part in collective protests. Partly corroborating this, our 1997–98 survey (see Appendix B) showed that respondents who were male, demobilized soldiers and/or Party members, current or former village cadres, whose pre-1978 family class labels were "rich peasant" or "landlord," and who had been migrant workers were significantly more likely to have been "complainants' representatives" (*shangfang daibiao*). In this survey, however, age, education, and household income were not significant predictors.

In more recent 2003–4 and 2004–5 surveys (see Appendix B) that included 650 villagers who had lodged complaints since 1980 (and who were interviewed in their homes), we used two sets of indicators to identify leaders of rightful resistance. First, we asked respondents whether they considered themselves to be "complainants' representatives." Then we asked if they had ever led the following three forms of rightful resistance: publicizing central policies and laws, demanding dialogues with local leaders, and rejecting "unreasonable" (*bu heli*) peasant burdens. It turns out that complainants' representatives and leaders of these three types of rightful resistance had about 70 percent overlap. So instead of treating them separately, we defined leaders of rightful resistance to be individuals who either called themselves "complainants' representatives" or said they had led one or more of the three forms of protest. Then we compared protest leaders with villagers (from the full sample) who had not lodged any complaints, to discover who tends to lead rightful resistance.

Multivariate logistic regression showed that males, the older, the better-educated, PLA veterans, and non-Party members were significantly more likely to lead rightful resistance. Incumbent or former village cadres were less likely to be leaders of rightful resistance, whereas respondents who personally or whose family members had been targeted in Maoist political campaigns, and those who personally or whose family members had been punished in the past ten years (by the time of the survey) for violating the birth control policy were more likely to be leaders, but the impact of these variables was statistically insignificant when the effects of other variables in the model were controlled. Respondents who personally or whose family members had been punished for failing to pay taxes, fees, and apportionments were significantly more likely to lead rightful resistance.

Respondents who considered themselves more assertive vis-à-vis the powerful and more courageous in standing up to injustice were also significantly more likely to be leaders of rightful resistance, after controlling for the predictors mentioned previously. We used six indicators to measure personal characteristics of respondents, all of which were drawn from interviews with rural activists:

1. "I'm not fearful of officials and I don't hesitate to object to any official who has done something wrong."
2. "I'm competitive and eager to win and I'm not fearful of strong and bullheaded people [*bu wei qiang bao*]."
3. "I can't stand the powerful and influential bullying the powerless and weak and I like to stand up for the weak."
4. "I'm not afraid of suffering a beating, arrest, or death in the course of upholding justice."
5. "I can't stand unfairness in society and I 'like to poke into it' [*ai guan xian shi*] even when it is not my own business."
6. "I've been relatively strongly influenced by Mao Zedong Thought and can't stand corruption and inequality."

Respondents were asked if they felt that these descriptions fit themselves. Because many of these traits are arguably desirable, it is possible that respondents claimed to have them even though they did not. Still, our survey showed that respondents who scored higher on a simple summation scale constructed from these six indicators (Cronbach's alpha = 0.81) were significantly more likely to be leaders of rightful resistance. More specifically, 409 leaders of rightful resistance had an average score of 4.33 on the scale (range, 0–6), while 713 nonparticipants averaged 3.47.

APPENDIX B

Sources

Survey Samplings

Our 1999 survey was administered by eighty-seven university students in their home villages, which were located in eighty-two counties, twenty-five provinces. In each village, the interviewer drew a simple random sample of 10 percent of adults between eighteen and seventy years of age from the "village small group" (*cunmin xiaozu*) that his or her family belonged to. Altogether 1,384 villagers were interviewed.

The 1999–2001 survey was conducted in two counties in Jiangxi province, one county in Jiangsu province, and one county in Fujian province. The four counties were selected because our associates had good working relations with local leaders and could sample and interview rural residents without restriction. Sampling in each county was conducted in three stages. First, five townships were selected. Second, four administrative villages were selected from each township. Samples of townships and villages were based on the principle of probabilities proportionate to size such that all townships in a county and all villages in a township had equal probability of being chosen regardless of population. Within each village, a simple random sample of 40 individuals older than the age of eighteen was drawn based on household registration records. The sample was then randomly divided into a base group and a backup group. If a selected villager in the base group was not available or turned down a request to be interviewed, then a villager with a similar demographic background in the backup group was approached. Interviewing took place in respondents' homes, and 20 individuals from each village were interviewed, regardless of the village's population. Altogether, 1,600 villagers were interviewed.

The 2003–4 survey was conducted in one county in Fujian province and one county in Zhejiang province. We adopted the same sampling procedure used in the 1999–2001 survey, except that nine protest leaders (who were not selected randomly into the sample) were included. Altogether 809 respondents were interviewed, 45 of whom had lodged complaints by the time of the interview.

The 2003 survey of township officials was conducted in Anhui, Fujian, Guangdong, Hunan, Liaoning, and Shandong provinces. Primary survey sites were provincial and city Party schools, where the respondents were undergoing political training. Altogether, 844 questionnaires were distributed and collected, 136 of which were dropped from the analysis because respondents skipped more than a quarter of the questions. Owing to political constraints, the survey was conducted in an opportunistic manner. The requirements of probability sampling were compromised to avoid attracting unwanted attention.

The 2004–5 survey of rural complainants had two phases. First, 605 villagers who had lodged complaints since 1980 were interviewed, using the 2003–4 survey instrument from Fujian and Zhejiang. This survey was conducted in fifteen provinces, with oversampling in Anhui, Fujian, Henan, and Liaoning. Then, 664 villagers who came to Beijing to lodge complaints were interviewed in Beijing, using a significantly shortened version of the 2003–4 questionnaire. No probability sampling procedures were employed.

Written Materials and Interviews

In addition to the surveys, this book is also based on archival sources and interviews. Key written resources we relied on include government reports on peasant burdens, villagers' self-government, social stability, and political reform; central circulars that detail how to handle popular protest and rural unrest; accounts and analyses of "collective incidents" and "peasant leaders" written by journalists, policy researchers, and scholars based in China; letters of complaint and essays penned by aggrieved villagers and protest leaders; and Western studies, including our own, of collective action in the Chinese countryside.

Over the past decade we have, jointly or individually, conducted hundreds of interviews. Our interviewees (eighty of whom are cited in the book) included officials and researchers in Beijing, provincial, municipality, county, and township officials, village cadres, ordinary villagers, and protest leaders and participants in the provinces of Anhui, Fujian, Guangdong, Hebei, Henan, Hunan, Jiangsu, Jiangxi, Liaoning, Shandong, Shanxi, Sichuan, Tianjin, and Yunnan. Interviews sometimes occurred in informal settings (e.g., at banquets, on trains) and sometimes were semistructured. The more structured interviews with villagers typically began with a set of questions about a person's age, education, Party membership, political positions held (if any), family background, and out-of-the-ordinary experiences (e.g., having been in the army or an urban wage worker). Afterward, respondents were usually guided to recount, in detail: what problems they had encountered (if any) with village cadres and higher-ranking local officials; if (and how) they thought problems, such as overtaxation, corruption, and violation of central policies should be addressed; what they thought about the letters and visits system and village elections; what they had seen or heard about village elections and various types of contention, including administrative litigation, lodging complaints, and tax resistance; whether they had engaged in any form of contention (contained or transgressive), and if yes, how did each episode unfold and what were the outcomes for them and others involved; and how they felt about such actions now.

Our most detailed source on protest leaders was a series of in-depth interviews with "complainants' representatives" in Hengyang county, Hunan, most of which were conducted in January and March of 2003 by Dr. Yu Jianrong of the Chinese Academy of Social Sciences. Hunan, along with a number of other provinces in China's central agricultural belt (see Bernstein and Lü, 2003), has been a hotbed of popular contention since the late 1980s. Dr. Yu enjoyed exceptionally good access to protest organizers in Hengyang, and he invited Lianjiang Li to conduct joint fieldwork with him to explore the causes, dynamics, and consequences of a decade-long cycle of protest in Hengyang. All the interviews in Hengyang were recorded and transcribed. Some were also videotaped.

Bibliography

Abel, Richard L. (1995). *Politics by other means: Law in the struggle against apartheid, 1980–1994*. New York: Routledge.

Agence France Presse. (1999, September 4). Six Chinese farmers jailed for denouncing fixed elections.

Alford, William. (1993). Double-edged swords cut both ways: Law and legitimacy in the People's Republic of China. *Daedelus*, 122(2), 45–69.

Amenta, Edwin, Bruce G. Carruthers, and Yvonne Zylan. (1992). A hero for the aged? The Townsend movement, the political mediation model and U.S. old-age policy, 1934–1950. *American Journal of Sociology*, 98(2), 308–39.

Amenta, Edwin, Drew Halfmann, and Michael P. Young. (1999). The strategies and contexts of social protest: Political mediation and the impact of the Townsend movement in California. *Mobilization*, 4(1), 1–23.

Amenta, Edwin, and Michael P. Young. (1999). Making an impact: Conceptual and methodological implications of the collective goods criterion. In Marco Giugni, Doug McAdam, and Charles Tilly (Eds.), *How social movements matter* (pp. 22–41). Minneapolis: University of Minnesota Press.

Aminzade, Ronald. (1995). Between movement and party: The transformation of mid-nineteenth century French republicanism. In J. Craig Jenkins and Bert Klandermans (Eds.), *The politics of social protest: Comparative perspectives on states and social movements* (pp. 39–62). Minneapolis: University of Minnesota Press.

Anagnost, Ann. (1992). Socialist ethics and the legal system. In Jeffrey N. Wasserstrom and Elizabeth J. Perry (Eds.), *Popular protest and political culture in modern China* (pp. 177–205). Boulder, CO: Westview Press.

Anderson, Leslie E. (1994). *The political ecology of the modern peasant: Calculation and community*. Baltimore: Johns Hopkins University Press.

Andrews, Kenneth. (2001). Social movements and policy implementation: The Mississippi civil rights movement and the war on poverty, 1965 to 1971. *American Sociological Review*, 66(1), 71–95.

Andrews, Kenneth. (2004). *Freedom is a constant struggle: The Mississippi civil rights movement and its legacy*. Chicago: University of Chicago Press.

Bai Yihua. (2002). Peng Zhen yu ba yi nongmin de minzhu (Peng Zhen and the democracy of 800 million peasants). *Zhongguo Shehui Daokan* (Journal of Chinese Society), 5, 20–25.

Banaszak, Lee A. (1996). *Why movements succeed or fail: Opportunity, culture, and the struggle for woman suffrage*. Princeton, NJ: Princeton University Press.

Bao Yonghui. (1991). Cunmin zizhi fuhe bu fuhe Zhongguo guoqing? (Does villagers' autonomy accord with China's conditions?). *Xiangzhen Luntan* (Township Forum), 11–13.

Barbalet, J. M. (1988). *Citizenship*. Minneapolis: University of Minnesota Press.

Beckwith, Karen. (2000). Hinges in collective action: Strategic innovation in the Pittston coal strike. *Mobilization*, 5(2), 179–99.

Beech, Hannah. (2004, March 1). Nothing left to lose. *Time (Asia)*. Accessed, June 1, 2004, at http://www.time.com/time/asia/magazine/article/0,13673,501040301–593608,00.html.

Bernhardt, Kathryn. (1992). *Rents, taxes, and peasant resistance: The lower Yangzi region, 1840–1950*. Stanford: Stanford University Press.

Bernstein, Thomas P. (2003). Unrest in rural China: A 2003 assessment. Paper presented at the Conference on Reassessing Unrest in China, Washington, DC, December 11–12.

Bernstein, Thomas P., and Xiaobo Lü. (2000). Taxation without representation: The central and local states in reform China. *China Quarterly*, 163, 742–63.

Bernstein, Thomas P., and Xiaobo Lü. (2003). *Taxation without representation in contemporary rural China*. Cambridge: Cambridge University Press.

Bianco, Lucien. (2001). *Peasants without the party: Grass-roots movements in twentieth-century China*. Armonk, NY: M. E. Sharpe.

Blecher, Marc. (1995). Collectivism, contractualism and crisis in the Chinese countryside. In Robert Benewick and Paul Wingrove (Eds.), *China in the 1990s* (pp. 105–19). Vancouver: UBC Press.

Blecher, Marc. (2002). Hegemony and workers' politics in China. *China Quarterly*, 170, 283–303.

Bøckman, Harald. (2004). The background and potential of Chinese village compacts (*xiang gui min yue*). Unpublished paper. Accessed, July 2, 2004, at http://www.sum.uio.no/research/democracy/network/andrepapers/Bockman.pdf.

Brandtstädter, Susanne, and Gunter Schubert. (2005). From the villages? Democratic thought and practice in rural China. Unpublished paper. University of Manchester, United Kingdom, and University of Tübingen, Germany. Forthcoming in *Democratization*.

Brockett, Charles D. (1991). The structure of political opportunities and peasant mobilization in Central America. *Comparative Politics*, 23(3), 253–74.

Brown, M. Mitchell. (2003). From the perspective of leadership: The strategies and tactics of national advocacy organizations. Paper presented at the Midwest Political Science Association Meeting, Chicago, April 2–6.

Burns, John P. (1988). *Political participation in rural China*. Berkeley: University of California Press.

Bibliography

Burstein, Paul, Rachel L. Einwohner, and Jocelyn A. Hollander. (1995). The success of political movements: A bargaining perspective. In J. Craig Jenkins and Bert Klandermans (Eds.), *The politics of social protest: Comparative perspectives on state and social movements* (pp. 275–95). Minneapolis: University of Minnesota Press.

Cai Dingjian (Ed.). (2002). *Zhongguo xuanju qingkuang de baogao* (Reports on the election situation in China). Beijing: Falü chubanshe.

Cai, Yongshun. (2000). Between state and peasant: Local cadres and statistical reporting in rural China. *China Quarterly*, 163, 783–805.

Cai, Yongshun. (2002). The resistance of Chinese laid-off workers in the reform period. *China Quarterly*, 170, 327–44.

Cai, Yongshun. (2003). Collective ownership or cadres' ownership? The nonagricultural use of farmland in China. *China Quarterly*, 175, 662–80.

Cai, Yongshun. (2004). Managed participation in China. *Political Science Quarterly*, 119(3), 425–51.

Calhoun, Craig. (1994). *Neither gods nor emperors: Students and the struggle for democracy in China*. Berkeley: University of California Press.

Cao Jinqing. (2000). *Huanghe bian de Zhongguo: Yige xuezhe dui xiangcun shehui de guancha yu sikao* (China along the Yellow River: A scholar's observations and reflections on rural society). Shanghai: Shanghai Wenyi Chubanshe.

Carter Center Report on Chinese Elections. (2000). Observation of village elections in Fujian and the conference to revise the national procedures on villager committee elections. Atlanta, GA: Carter Center.

Chan, Alex. (2002). From propaganda to hegemony: *Jiaodian Fangtan* and China's media policy. *Journal of Contemporary China*, 11(30), 35–51.

Chan, Sylvia. (1998). Village self-government and civil society. In Joseph Y. S. Cheng (Ed.), *China Review, 1998* (pp. 236–58). Hong Kong: Chinese University Press.

Chen, Feng. (2000). Subsistence crises, managerial corruption and labour protests in China. *China Journal*, 44, 41–63.

Chen, Feng. (2003). Industrial restructuring and workers' resistance in China. *Modern China*, 29(2), 237–62.

Chen, Jie, and Yang Zhong. (2002). Why do people vote in semicompetitive elections in China? *Journal of Politics*, 64(1), 178–97.

Chen Lumin. (2001). Dou shi pufa re de huo (The disaster is all due to the legal education campaign). *Minzhu yu Fazhi* (Democracy and Legal System), 11, 31–33.

Chen, Xi. (2003). The transformation of state socialism and rising demands for citizenship rights in China, 1977–2002. Unpublished paper. Department of Political Science, Columbia University.

Chen, Xi. (2004). Chinese petitioners' tactics and their efficacy. Paper presented at the Conference on Grassroots Political Reform in Contemporary China. Fairbank Center, Harvard University. October 29–31.

Cheng Tongshun. (1994). Dangqian Zhongguo nongmin de zhengzhi canyu (Political participation of current Chinese peasants). Unpublished Master's thesis. Nankai University, Tianjin, China.

Cho, Young Nam. (2003). Public supervisors and reflectors: Role fulfillment of the Chinese people's congress deputies in the market socialist era. *Development and Society*, 32(2), 197–227.

Citrin, Jack, and Christopher Muste. (1999). Trust in government. In John P. Robinson, Phillip R. Shaver, and Lawrence S. Wrightsman (Eds.), *Measures of political attitudes* (pp. 465–532). New York: Academic Press.

Cody, Edward. (2005, August 1). A Chinese city's rage at the rich and powerful. *Washington Post Foreign Service*, p. A01.

Collier, David, and Steven Levitsky. (1997). Democracy with adjectives. Conceptual innovation in comparative research. *World Politics*, 49(3), 430–51.

Collier, David, and James E. Mahon Jr. (1993). Conceptual "stretching" revisited: Adapting categories in comparative analysis. *American Political Science Review*, 87(4), 845–55.

Collier, David, and James Mahoney. (1996). Insights and pitfalls: Selection bias in qualitative research. *World Politics*, 49(1), 56–91.

Cress, Daniel M., and David A. Snow. (2000). The outcomes of homeless mobilization: The influence of organization, disruption, political mediation, and framing. *American Journal of Sociology*, 105(4), 1063–1104.

Cui, Vivien. (2005, August 1). Beijing warns against abusing petition system to disrupt order. *South China Morning Post*. Accessed, September 13, 2005, at http://66.102.7.104/search?q=cache:61It1RwHqx4J:pekingduck.org/archives/petitions.doc.

Dagger, Richard. (1981). Metropolis, memory, and citizenship. *American Journal of Political Science*, 25(4), 715–37.

Dang Guoying. (2002). Qingnian nongmin shi dangjin Zhongguo zuida de zhengzhi (Young farmers are worth the most serious political attention in contemporary China). Accessed, February 17, 2002, at http://www.chinesenewsnet.com.

Davis, Sarah. (2005, August 25). China's angry petitioners. *Asian Wall Street Journal*, p. A7.

della Porta, Donatella. (1999). Protest, protesters, and protest policing: Public discourse in Italy and Germany from the 1960s to the 1980s. In Marco Giugni, Doug McAdam, and Charles Tilly (Eds.), *How social movements matter* (pp. 66–96). Minneapolis: University of Minnesota Press.

della Porta, Donatella. (2002). Comparative politics and social movements. In Bert Klandermans and Suzanne Staggenborg (Eds.), *Methods of social movement research* (pp. 286–313). Minneapolis: University of Minnesota Press.

della Porta, Donatella, and Mario Diani. (1999). *Social movements: An introduction*. Oxford: Blackwell.

Diamant, Neil J. (2000). Conflict and conflict resolution in China: Beyond mediation-centered approaches. *Journal of Conflict Resolution*, 44(4), 523–46.

Diamant, Neil J. (2001). Making love "legible" in China: Politics and society during the enforcement of civil marriage registration, 1950–1966. *Politics and Society* 29(3), 447–80.

Diamant, Neil J., Stanley B. Lubman, and Kevin J. O'Brien (Eds.). (2005). *Engaging the law in China: State, society, and possibilities for justice*. Stanford: Stanford University Press.

Bibliography

Ding Guoguang. (2001). Jiejue nongmin zengshou jianfu wenti yi ke bu rong huan (Allow no delay in increasing peasant incomes and reducing peasant burdens). In Zhang Youcai (Ed.), *Caishui gaige zongheng* (Perspectives on tax and finance reform) (pp. 433–40). Beijing: Jingji Kexue Chubanshe.

Duan Xianju, Tan Jian, and Chen Peng. (2000). "Yingxiong" hai shi "diaomin"? ("Heroes" or "shrewd, unyielding people"?). *Banyuetan (Neibuban)* (Fortnightly Chats) (Internal Edition), 2, 8–13.

Duan Zhiqiang and Tang Jinsu. (1989). Gansusheng nongcun jiceng zuzhi zhuangkuang diaocha baogao (Investigation report of the current situation of grass-roots rural organizations in Gansu Province). Unpublished report. Ministry of Civil Affairs, Beijing.

Edin, Maria. (2003). State capacity and local agent control in China: CCP cadre management from a township perspective. *China Quarterly*, 173, 35–52.

Edin, Maria. (2004). Taking an aspirin: Implementing fees and tax reforms at the local level. Paper presented at the Conference on Grassroots Political Reform in Contemporary China. Fairbank Center, Harvard University. October 29–31.

Edwards, R. Randle, Louis Henkin, and Andrew J. Nathan. (1986). *Human rights in contemporary China*. New York: Columbia University Press.

Einwohner, Rachel L. (1999). Gender, class and social movement outcomes. *Gender and Society*, 13(1), 56–76.

Ennis, James G. (1987). Fields of action: Structure in movements' tactical repertoires. *Sociological Forum*, 2(3), 520–33.

Esherick, Joseph W., and Jeffrey N. Wasserstrom. (1990). Acting out democracy: Political theater in modern China. *Journal of Asian Studies*, 49(4), 835–65.

Euchner, Charles C. (1996). *Extraordinary politics: How protest and dissent are changing American democracy*. Boulder, CO: Westview Press.

Ewick, Patricia, and Susan Silbey. (2003). Narrating social structure: Stories of resistance to legal authority. *American Journal of Sociology*, 108(6), 1328–72.

Falkenheim, Victor C. (1978). Political participation in China. *Problems of Communism*, 27(3), 18–32.

Fan Yu. (1998). Cunweihui xuanju weifa xu jiuzheng (Law-breaking activities in village elections must be corrected). *Gaige Neican* (Internal Reference on Reforms), 20, 14–15.

Fang Guomin. (1993). Dui dangqian nongcun jiti shangfang qingkuang de diaocha fenxi (Investigation and analysis of the current situation of groups seeking audiences at higher levels). *Xiangzhen Luntan* (Township Forum), 12, 36–37.

Felstiner, William, Richard Abel, and Austin Sarat. (1980–81). The emergence and transformation of disputes: Naming, blaming, claiming. *Law and Society Review*, 15(3–4), 631–54.

Field, Daniel. (1976). *Rebels in the name of the tsar*. Boston: Houghton Mifflin.

Fox, Jonathan. (1993). *The politics of food in Mexico: State power and social mobilization*. Ithaca, NY: Cornell University Press.

Frazier, Mark W. (2004). After pension reform: Navigating the "third rail" in China. *Studies in Comparative International Development*, 39(2), 45–70.

Gale, Richard P. (1986). Social movements and the state: The environmental movement, countermovement, and government agencies. *Sociological Perspectives*, 29(2), 202–40.

Gamson, William A. (1968). *Power and discontent*. Homewood, IL: Dorsey.

Gamson, William A. (1990). *The strategy of social protest* (2nd ed.). Belmont, CA: Wadsworth Publishing Company.

Gamson, William A. (1998). Social movements and cultural change. In Marco G. Giugni, Doug McAdam and Charles Tilly (Eds.), *From contention to democracy* (pp. 57–77). Lanham, MD: Rowman & Littlefield.

Gamson, William A., and David S. Meyer. (1996). Framing political opportunity. In Doug McAdam, John D. McCarthy, and Mayer N. Zald (Eds.), *Comparative perspectives on social movements: Political opportunities, mobilizing structures, and cultural framings* (pp. 275–90). Cambridge: Cambridge University Press.

Geertz, Clifford. (1973). *The interpretation of cultures*. New York: Basic Books.

Gerring, John. (2001). *Social science methodology: A criterial framework*. Cambridge: Cambridge University Press.

Giddens, Anthony. (1982). *Profiles and critiques in social theory*. Berkeley: University of California Press.

Gilley, Bruce. (2001, April 5). Arm the people with a book. *Far Eastern Economic Review*. Accessed, April 19, 2001, at http://www.feer.com/_0104_05/p028region.html.

Gilley, Bruce. (2001). *Model rebels: The rise and fall of China's richest village*. Berkeley: University of California Press.

Giugni, Marco. (1998). Was it worth the effort? The outcomes and consequences of social movements. *Annual Review of Sociology*, 24, 371–93.

Giugni, Marco. (1999). How social movements matter: Past research, present problems, future developments. In Marco Giugni, Doug McAdam, and Charles Tilly (Eds.) *How social movements matter* (pp. xxiii–xxxiii). Minneapolis: University of Minnesota Press.

Giugni, Marco, Doug McAdam, and Charles Tilly (Eds.). (1999). *How social movements matter*. Minneapolis: University of Minnesota Press.

Giugni, Marco, and Florence Passy. (1998). Contentious politics in complex societies. In Marco G. Giugni, Doug McAdam and Charles Tilly (Eds.), *From contention to democracy* (pp. 81–108). Lanham, MD: Rowman & Littlefield.

Goldberg, Ellis. (1986). *Tinker, tailor, and textile worker: Class and politics in Egypt, 1930–1952*. Berkeley: University of California Press.

Goldman, Merle, and Elizabeth J. Perry. (2002). *Changing meanings of citizenship in modern China*. Cambridge, MA: Harvard University Press.

Goldstone, Jack A. (2003). Introduction: Bridging institutionalized and noninstitutionalized politics. In Jack A. Goldstone (Ed.), *States, parties, and social movements* (pp. 1–24). Cambridge: Cambridge University Press.

Goldstone, Jack A., and Charles Tilly. (2001). Threat (and opportunity): Popular action and state response in the dynamics of contentious action. In Ronald R. Aminzade et al. (Eds.), *Silence and voice in the study of contentious politics* (pp. 179–94). Cambridge: Cambridge University Press.

Bibliography

Gonganbu Disi Yanjiusuo "Quntixing Shijian Yanjiu" Ketizu. (2001). Woguo fasheng quntixing shijian de diaocha yu sikao (Investigation and reflection on mass incidents in our country). *Neibu Canyue* (Internal Reference), 31, 18–25.

Goodwin, Jeff, and James M. Jasper. (1999). Caught in a winding, snarling vine: The structural bias of political process theory. *Sociological Forum*, 14(1), 27–53.

Gramsci, Antonio. (1971). *Selections from the prison notebooks.* Ed. Quintin Hoare and Geoffrey Nowell Smith. New York: International Publishers.

Gray, Robert P. (2001). Cadre corruption, village elections, and Chinese soap operas: The Communist Party's new conception of rural citizenship. In Ministry of Civil Affairs, PRC, and the Carter Center, USA, *Collection of English papers presented at the international symposium on villager self-government and rural social development in China* (pp. 73–92). Beijing, China, September 2–5. Also available at http://www.chinaelections.org/Eng/readnews. Accessed, May 24, 2004.

Guo Tu Ziyuanbu. (2004, February 11). Guanyu zuohao "lianghui" qijian guo tuziyuan xinfang gongzuo de jinji tongzhi (Urgent notice on handling work well concerning letters and visits on land and resources during the "two meetings"). Accessed, June 2, 2004, at http://www.law-lib.com/law/law_view.asp?id= 82351.

Guo, Xiaolin. (2001). Land expropriation and conflicts in rural China. *China Quarterly*, 166, 422–39.

Hao Fu and Chen Lei. (2002). Yifa zhi cun de ling lei zhi fa (A deviant way of governing a village according to law). *Fazhi Shijie* (Legal World), 8, 18–21.

Hastings, Justin V. (2005). Perceiving a single Chinese state: Escalation and violence in Uighur protests. *Problems of Post-Communism*, 52(1), 28–38.

Hay, Douglas. (1975). Property, authority and the criminal law. In Douglas Hay, Peter Linebaugh, John G. Rule, E. P. Thompson, and Cal Winslow (Eds.), *Albion's fatal tree: Crime and society in eighteenth-century England* (pp. 17–63). London: Allen Lane.

He, Baogang. (2005). Village citizenship in China: A case study of Zhejiang. *Citizenship Studies*, 9(1), 205–19.

Heilmann, Sebastian. (1996). Turning away from the cultural revolution. Occasional paper, 28. Stockholm: Center for Pacific Areas Studies at Stockholm University.

Herbst, Jeffrey. (1989). How the weak succeed: Tactics, political goods and institutions in the struggle for land in Zimbabwe. In Forrest D. Colburn (Ed.), *Everyday forms of peasant resistance* (pp. 198–220). Armonk, NY: M. E. Sharpe.

Hirsch, Susan F., and Mindie Lazarus-Black. (1994). Performance and paradox: Exploring law's role in hegemony and resistance. In Lazarus-Black and Hirsch (Eds.), *Contested states: Laws, hegemony, and resistance* (pp. 1–31). New York: Routledge.

Hobsbawm, E. J. (1973). Peasants and politics. *Journal of Peasant Studies*, 1(1), 3–22.

Hollander, Jocelyn A., and Rachel L. Einwohner. (2004). Conceptualizing resistance. *Sociological Forum*, 19(4), 533–54.

Howell, Jude. (1998). Prospects for village self-governance in China. *Journal of Peasant Studies*, 25(3), 86–111.

Hu Kui and Jiang Shu. (2003, December 11). Xinfang hongliu (A torrent of letters and visits). *Liaowang Dongfang Zhoukan* (Oriental Outlook Weekly), 4, 30–35.

Huang Haiyan. (2004). Wang Xingfu: "Zan bu shi 'diaomin'" (Wang Xingfu: "I'm not a 'shrewd, unyielding person'"). *Banyuetan (Neibuban)* (Fortnightly Chats) (Internal Edition), 8, 8–12.

Hunt, Alan. (1990). Rights and social movements: Counter-hegemonic strategies. *Journal of Law and Society*, 17, 309–28.

Hurst, William. (2004). Understanding contentious collective action by Chinese laid-off workers: The importance of regional political economy. *Studies in Comparative International Development*, 39(2), 94–120.

Hurst, William, and Kevin J. O'Brien. (2002). China's contentious pensioners. *China Quarterly*, 170, 345–60.

International Republican Institute. (1997). Election observation report: Fujian. Washington, DC: International Republican Institute.

Jakobson, Linda. (2004). Local governance. Village and township direct elections. In Jude Howell (Ed.), *Governance in China* (pp. 97–120). Lanham, MD: Rowman & Littlefield.

Jasper, James M. (1997). *The art of moral protest*. Chicago: University of Chicago Press.

Jasper, James M. (2004). A strategic approach to collective action: Looking for agency in social-movement choices. *Mobilization*, 9(1), 1–16.

Javeline, Debra. (2003). *Protest and the politics of blame: The Russian response to unpaid wages*. Ann Arbor: University of Michigan Press.

Jenkins, J. Craig, and Bert Klandermans. (1995). The politics of social protest. In J. Craig Jenkins and Bert Klandermans (Eds.), *The politics of social protest: Comparative perspectives on states and social movements* (pp. 3–35). Minneapolis: University of Minnesota Press.

Jenkins, J. Craig, and Charles Perrow. (1977). Insurgency of the powerless: Farm worker movements (1946–1972). *American Sociological Review*, 42(2), 249–68.

Jennings, M. Kent. (1997). Political participation in the Chinese countryside. *American Political Science Review*, 91(2), 361–72.

Jiang Zuoping, Li Shuzhong, and Yang Sanjun. (2001). Jianfu zuzhi wajie ji (The dissolution of burden reduction organizations). *Banyuetan (Neibuban)* (Fortnightly Chats) (Internal Edition), 8, 73–76.

Jiang Zuoping and Yang Sanjun. (1999). Chuanhuan si wei "lingxiu" niang cheng yi chang fengbo (Subpoenaing four "leaders" results in an incident). *Banyuetan (Neibuban)* (Fortnightly Chats) (Internal Edition), 2, 8–12.

Jing, Jun. (2000). Environmental protests in rural China. In Elizabeth J. Perry and Mark Selden (Eds.), *Chinese society: Change, conflict and resistance* (pp. 143–60). London: Routledge.

Johnson, Ian. (2004). *Wild grass: Three stories of change in modern China*. New York: Pantheon Books.

Kaye, Lincoln. (1997, November 6). Fade to black. *Far Eastern Economic Review*, 56–58.

Bibliography

Keane, Michael. (2001). Redefining Chinese citizenship. *Economy and Society*, 30(1), 1–17.

Kelliher, Daniel. (1997). The Chinese debate over village self-government. *China Journal*, 37, 63–86.

Kennedy, John James. (2002). The face of "grassroots democracy" in rural China: Real versus cosmetic elections. *Asian Survey*, 42(3), 456–82.

Kennedy, John James. (2004). The implementation of village elections and tax-for-fee reform in rural northwest China. Paper presented at the Conference on Grassroots Political Reform in Contemporary China. Fairbank Center, Harvard University, October 29–31.

Kerber, Linda K. (1997). The meanings of citizenship. *Journal of American History*, 84(3), 833–54.

Kernen, Antoine. (2003a). Demonstrations by state workers in China: Pressures and structure of political opportunity. Unpublished paper. University of Geneva, Switzerland.

Kernen, Antoine. (2003b). Worker protest in China: Toward a new public management of social conflicts. Unpublished paper. University of Geneva, Switzerland.

Kiecolt, K. Jill. (2000). Self change in social movements. In Sheldon Stryker, Timothy J. Owens, and Robert W. White (Eds.), *Self, identity, and social movements* (pp. 110–31). Minneapolis: University of Minnesota Press.

Kitschelt, Herbert P. (1986). Political opportunity structures and political protest: Anti-nuclear movements in four democracies. *British Journal of Political Science*, 16(1), 57–85.

Klandermans, Bert. (1997). *The social psychology of protest*. Oxford: Blackwell.

Koopmans, Ruud. (1999). Political. Opportunity. Structure. Some splitting to balance the lumping. *Sociological Forum*, 14(1), 93–105.

Koopmans, Ruud. (2005). The missing link between structure and agency: Outline of an evolutionary approach to social movements. *Mobilization*, 10(1), 19–35.

Koopmans, Ruud, and Susan Olzak. (2004). Discursive opportunities and the evolution of right-wing violence in Germany. *American Journal of Sociology*, 110(1), 198–230.

Koopmans, Ruud, and Paul Statham. (1999a). Political claims analysis: Integrating protest event and political discourse approaches. *Mobilization*, 4(2), 203–21.

Koopmans, Ruud, and Paul Statham. (1999b). Ethnic and civic conceptions of nationhood and the differential success of the extreme right in Germany and Italy. In Marco Giugni, Doug McAdam, and Charles Tilly (Eds.), *How social movements matter* (pp. 225–51). Minneapolis: University of Minnesota Press.

Kriesi, Hanspeter, Ruud Koopmans, Jan W. Duyvendak, and Marco G. Giugni. (1995). *New social movements in Western Europe: A comparative analysis*. Minneapolis: University of Minnesota Press.

Kurzman, Charles. (1996). Structural opportunity and perceived opportunity in social-movement theory: The Iranian revolution of 1979. *American Sociological Review*, 61(1), 153–70.

Kymlicka, Will, and Wayne Norman. (1995). Return of the citizen: A survey of recent work on citizenship theory. In Ronald Beiner (Ed.), *Theorizing citizenship* (pp. 283–322). Albany: SUNY Press.

Landry, Pierre, and Yanqi Tong. (2005). Disputing the authoritarian state in China. Paper presented at the 101st annual meeting of the American Political Science Association, Washington, DC, September 1–4.

Lazarus-Black, Mindie, and Susan F. Hirsch (Eds.). (1994). *Contested states: Law, hegemony and resistance.* New York: Routledge.

Lee, Ching Kwan. (2000). The "revenge of history": Collective memories and labor protests in north-eastern China. *Ethnography*, 1(2), 217–37.

Lee, Ching Kwan. (2001). From the specter of Mao to the spirit of the law: Labor insurgency in China. *Theory and Society*, 31(2), 189–228.

Lee, Ching Kwan. (2004). Is labor a political force in China? Paper presented at the Conference on Grassroots Political Reform in Contemporary China. Fairbank Center, Harvard University, October 29–31.

Levi, Margaret, and Laura Stoker. (2000). Political trust and trustworthiness. *Annual Review of Political Science*, 3, 475–507.

Li Changping. (2003, March 1). Cong "diaomin" dao "gongmin" (From "shrewd, unyielding people" to "citizens"). *Nanfeng Chuang* (Window on the Southern Wind), 3(A), 42–46.

Li Chao. (2002). Min gao guan, kanke qi zai liu shen, guan baisu, yuan yu renda jiandu (An administrative lawsuit lasts seven years and six trials, and the government loses owing to the supervision of a people's congress). *Minzhu yu Fazhi* (Democracy and Legal System), 5(A), 40–41.

Li Fan. (2003). *Zhongguo nongcun minzhu fazhan baogao 2002* (2002 report on developments in grass-roots democracy in China). Xi'an: Xibei Daxue Chubanshe.

Li Jingyi. (1992). Nongcun zhiluan qishi lu (Reflections on overcoming disorder in the countryside). Unpublished paper written by a county Party secretary in Hebei. A shortened version appeared in *Hebei Nongcun Gongzuo* (Hebei Rural Work), 8 (August 1992), 14–15.

Li Junde. (2000). Jianfu yingxiong za cheng le fanzui xianyiren (How heroes of reducing peasant burdens became crime suspects). *Banyuetan (Neibuban)* (Fortnightly Chats) (Internal Edition), 2, 13–14.

Li Kang. (1994). Jiceng zhengquan yu jiceng shequ (Grass-roots government and grass-roots community). In Li Xueju, Wang Zhenyao, and Tang Jinsu (Eds.), *Zhongguo xiangzhen zhengquan de xianzhuang yu gaige* (Current situation and reform of Chinese township government) (pp. 267–74). Beijing: Zhonguo Shehui Chubanshe.

Li Ke and Fan Rongjun. (1998, March 19). Jiujie quanguo renda yici huiyi juxing jizhe zhaodai hui Zhu Rongji zongli deng da zhongwai jizhe wen (Premier Zhu Rongji responds to questions of Chinese and foreign journalists at a press conference convened at the first session of the ninth NPC). *Renmin Ribao* (People's Daily), 1.

Li, Lianjiang. (1999). The two-ballot system in Shanxi province: Subjecting village Party secretaries to a popular vote. *China Journal*, 42, 103–118.

Bibliography

Li, Lianjiang. (2001). Elections and popular resistance in rural China. *China Information*, 15(2), 1–19.

Li, Lianjiang. (2003). The empowering effect of village elections in China. *Asian Survey*, 43(4), 648–62.

Li, Lianjiang. (2004). Political trust in rural China. *Modern China*, 30(2), 228–58.

Li, Lianjiang, and Kevin J. O'Brien. (1996). Villagers and popular resistance in contemporary China. *Modern China*, 22(1), 28–61.

Li, Lianjiang, and Kevin J. O'Brien. (1999). The struggle over village elections. In Merle Goldman and Roderick MacFarquhar (Eds.), *The paradox of China's post-Mao reforms* (pp. 129–44). Cambridge, MA: Harvard University Press.

Li Renhu and Yu Zhenhai. (1993). Yangzhao xiang gengming fengbo (The disturbance over changing the name of Yangzhao township). *Banyuetan (Neibuban)* (Fortnightly Chats) (Internal Edition), 6, 32–36.

Li Xiuyi. (1992). Guanyu shiban nongmin xiehui de ruogan wenti (A few questions regarding the trial establishment of peasant associations). *Zhongguo Nongcun Jingji* (Chinese Rural Economy), 6, 15–18.

Lian Jimin. (2000). Min gao guan renda jiandu zuo houdun (People's congress supervision supports ordinary people suing officials). *Minzhu yu Fazhi* (Democracy and Legal System), 7, 28–30.

Liebman, Benjamin L. (1998). Class action litigation in China. *Harvard Law Review*, 111(6), 1523–41.

Liebman, Benjamin L. (2005). Watchdog or demagogue? The media in the Chinese legal system. *Columbia Law Review*, 105(1), 1–157.

Linders, Annulla. (2004). Victory and beyond: A historical comparative analysis of the outcomes of abortion movements in Sweden and the United States. *Sociological Forum*, 19(3), 371–404.

Lipsky, Michael. (1968). Protest as a political resource. *American Political Science Review*, 62(4), 1144–58.

Lipsky, Michael. (1980). *Street-level bureaucracy: Dilemmas of the individual in public services*. New York: Russell Sage.

Liu Jing and Lin Yanxing. (2003). Nongmin kai xuanchuan che jingxuan, hao xi wei he yan za le (Farmers drive a propaganda vehicle while campaigning, how was the high drama ruined?). *Banyuetan (Neibuban)* (Fortnightly Chats) (Internal Edition), 7, 20–22.

Liu Shuyun and Bai Lin. (2001). "Kang shui daibiao" zhuanbian wei "bang shui ren" ("Tax-resistance representatives" are changed into "tax-collection helpers"). *Banyuetan (Neibuban)* (Fortnightly Chats) (Internal Edition), 8, 70–72.

Liu Weihua. (1999). Shuji shi ge bai jia zi (The Party secretary is a scoundrel). In Zhao Shukai (Ed.), *Nongcun, nongmin* (The Countryside and the peasantry) (pp. 22–26). Unpublished paper. Qinghua University.

Liu, Yawei. (2000). Consequences of village elections in China. *China Perspectives*, 31, 19–35.

Lü, Xiaobo. (1997). The politics of peasant burden in reform China. *Journal of Peasant Studies*, 25(1), 113–38.

153

Lü, Xiaobo. (2000). *Cadres and corruption: The organizational involution of the Chinese Communist Party*. Stanford: Stanford University Press.

Lu Yunfei. (1993). Qieshi jiaqiang xinwen yulun jiandu de falü baozhang (Earnestly strengthen legal protection of supervision through news and public opinion). *Minzhu yu Fazhi* (Democracy and Legal System), 9, 8.

Luehrmann, Laura M. (2003). Facing citizen complaints in China, 1951–1996. *Asian Survey*, 43(5), 845–66.

Lynch, David J. (2004, September 14). Discontent in China boils into public protest. *USA Today*. Accessed, December 8, 2004, at http://www.usatoday.com/news/world/2004-09-14-china-protest_x.htm.

Ma Changshan. (1994). Cunmin zizhi zuzhi jianshe de shidai yiyi jiqi shijian fancha (The epoch-making significance and the imperfect practice of building villagers' self-governing organizations). *Zhengzhi yu Falü* (Politics and Law), 2, 19–20.

Ma, Josephine. (2004, June 8). Three million took part in surging protests last year. *South China Morning Post* (Hong Kong).

Ma Zhongdong. (2000). Huan gei wo yige gongmin de quanli (Return me my citizenship rights). *Fazhi Shijie* (Legal World), 1, 36–37.

McAdam, Doug. (1982). *Political process and the development of black insurgency, 1930–1970*. Chicago: University of Chicago Press.

McAdam, Doug. (1983). Tactical innovation and the pace of insurgency. *American Sociological Review*, 48(6), 735–54.

McAdam, Doug. (1989). The biographical consequences of activism. *American Sociological Review*, 54(5), 744–60.

McAdam, Doug. (1996). The framing function of movement tactics. In Doug McAdam, John D. McCarthy, and Mayer N. Zald (Eds.), *Comparative perspectives on social movements: Political opportunities, mobilizing structures, and cultural framings* (pp. 338–55). Cambridge: Cambridge University Press.

McAdam, Doug. (1999). The biographical impact of activism. In Marco Giugni, Doug McAdam, and Charles Tilly (Eds.), *How social movements matter* (pp. 117–46). Minneapolis: University of Minnesota Press.

McAdam, Doug, John D. McCarthy, and Mayer N. Zald. (1988). Social movements. In Neil Smelser (Ed.), *Handbook of sociology* (pp. 695–737). Thousand Oaks, CA: Sage.

McAdam, Doug, John D. McCarthy, and Mayer N. Zald. (1996). Introduction: Opportunities, mobilizing structures, and framing processes. In McAdam, McCarthy, and Zald (Eds.), *Comparative perspectives on social movements: Political opportunities, mobilizing structures, and cultural framings* (pp. 1–20). Cambridge: Cambridge University Press.

McAdam, Doug, and Dieter Rucht. (1993). The cross-national diffusion of movement ideas. *Annals of the American Academy of Political and Social Science*, 528, 56–74.

McAdam, Doug, Robert J. Sampson, Simon Weffer, and Heather MacIndoe. (2005). "There will be fighting in the streets": The distorting lens of social movement theory. *Mobilization*, 10(1), 1–18.

Bibliography

McAdam, Doug, and Yang Su. (2002). The war at home: Antiwar protests and congressional voting, 1965 to 1973. *American Sociological Review*, 67(5), 696–721.

McAdam, Doug, Sidney Tarrow, and Charles Tilly. (2001). *Dynamics of contention*. Cambridge: Cambridge University Press.

McCammon, Holly J., Ellen M. Granberg, Karen E. Campbell, and Christine Mowery. (2001). How movements win: Gendered opportunity structures and U.S. women's suffrage movements, 1866 to 1919. *American Sociological Review*, 66(1), 49–70.

McCann, Michael W. (1994). *Rights at work: Pay equity reform and the politics of legal mobilization*. Chicago: University of Chicago Press.

McCarthy, Susan. (2000). Ethno-religious mobilization and citizenship discourse in the People's Republic of China. *Asian Ethnicity*, 1(2), 107–16.

McCubbins, Mathew D., and Thomas Schwarz. (1984). Congressional oversight overlooked: Police patrols versus fire alarms. *American Journal of Political Science*, 28(1), 165–79.

Mahoney, James, and Gary Goertz. (2004). The possibility principle: Choosing negative cases in comparative research. *American Political Science Review*, 98(4), 653–69.

Manion, Melanie. (2000). Chinese democratization in perspective: Electorates and selectorates at the township level. *China Quarterly*, 163, 764–82.

Mansbridge, Jane J. (1986). *Why we lost the ERA*. Chicago: University of Chicago Press.

Mao Zedong. (1971). *Selected readings from the works of Mao Tse-Tung*. Peking: Foreign Languages Press.

Markoff, John. (1996). *Waves of democracy: Social movements and political change*. Thousand Oaks, CA: Pine Forge Press.

Marshall, T. H. (1976). *Class, citizenship, and social development*. Westport, CT: Greenwood Press.

Marwell, Gerald, Michael T. Aiken, and N. Jay Derath III. (1987). The persistence of political attitudes among 1960s civil rights activists. *Public Opinion Quarterly*, 51(3), 359–75.

Mathiesen, Thomas. (1965). *The defences of the weak: A sociological study of a Norwegian correctional institution*. London: Tavistock.

Matsuda, Mari J. (1987). Looking to the bottom: Critical legal studies and reparations. *Harvard Civil Rights – Civil Liberties Review*, 22, 323–99.

Meyer, David S., and Debra C. Minkoff. (2004). Conceptualizing political opportunity. *Social Forces*, 82(4), 1457–92.

Meyer, David S., and Suzanne Staggenborg. (1996). Movements, countermovements, and the structure of political opportunity. *American Journal of Sociology*, 101(6), 1628–60.

Meyer, David S., and Nancy Whittier. (1994). Social movement spillover. *Social Problems*, 41(2), 277–98.

Michelson, Ethan. (2004). Causes and consequences of grievances in China. Paper presented at the Conference on Socioeconomic Rights in China. Dickinson College, April 16–18.

Michelson, Ethan. (2005). Justice from above or justice from below? Lessons from rural China for the study of disputing. Unpublished paper. Department of Sociology, Indiana University, Bloomington.

Migdal, Joel S. (2001). *State-in-society: Studying how states and societies transform and constitute one another*. Cambridge: Cambridge University Press.

Migdal, Joel S., Atul Kohli, and Vivienne Shue (Eds.). (1994). *State power and social forces*. Cambridge: Cambridge University Press.

Minkoff, Debra C. (1999). Bending with the wind: Strategic change and adaptation by women's and racial minority organizations. *American Journal of Sociology*, 104(6), 1666–1703.

Minzner, Carl. (2005). Xinfang: An alternative to the formal Chinese judicial system. Unpublished paper. Forthcoming in *Stanford Journal of International Law*.

Morris, Aldon D. (1992). Political consciousness and collective action. In Aldon D. Morris and Carol Mueller (Eds.), *Frontiers in social movement theory* (pp. 351–73). New Haven, CT: Yale University Press.

Mueller, Carol. (1999). Claims "radicalization?" The 1989 protest cycle in the GDR. *Social Problems*, 46(4), 528–47.

Nathan, Andrew J. (1985). *Chinese democracy*. Berkeley: University of California Press.

Naughton, Barry, and Dali Yang. (2004). *Holding China together: Diversity and national integration in the post-Deng era*. Cambridge: Cambridge University Press.

Nongmin chengdan feiyong he laowu guanli tiaoli. (Regulations concerning peasants' fees and labor). (1991). In *Zhonghua renmin gongheguo guowuyuan gongbao* (Bulletin of the State Council of the People's Republic of China, January 1, 1992), 1430–35.

O'Brien, Kevin J. (1994a). Agents and remonstrators: Role accumulation by Chinese people's congress deputies. *China Quarterly*, 138, 359–80.

O'Brien, Kevin J. (1994b). Implementing political reform in China's villages. *Australian Journal of Chinese Affairs*, 32, 33–59.

O'Brien, Kevin J. (1996). Rightful resistance. *World Politics*, 49(1), 31–55.

O'Brien, Kevin J. (2001). Villagers, elections, and citizenship in contemporary China. *Modern China*, 27(4), 407–35.

O'Brien, Kevin J. (2002). Collective action in the Chinese countryside. *China Journal*, 48, 139–54.

O'Brien, Kevin J. (2003). Neither transgressive nor contained: Boundary-spanning contention in China. *Mobilization*, 8(3), 51–64.

O'Brien, Kevin J. (2004). Discovery, research re-design, and theory-building. Unpublished paper. Forthcoming in Maria Edin and Stig Thøgersen (Eds.), *Doing Fieldwork in China*. Copenhagen and Honolulu: Nordic Institute of Asian Studies and University of Hawaii Press.

O'Brien, Kevin J., and Lianjiang Li. (1995). The politics of lodging complaints in rural China. *China Quarterly*, 143, 756–83.

O'Brien, Kevin J., and Lianjiang Li. (1999). Selective policy implementation in rural China. *Comparative Politics*, 31(2), 167–86.

Bibliography

O'Brien, Kevin J., and Lianjiang Li. (2000). Accommodating "democracy" in a one-party state: Introducing village elections in China. *China Quarterly*, 162, 465–89.

O'Brien, Kevin J., and Lianjiang Li. (2004). Suing the local state: Administrative litigation in rural China. *China Journal*, 51, 75–95.

Ocko, Jonathan K. (1988). "I'll take it all the way to Beijing": Capital appeals in the Qing. *Journal of Asian Studies*, 47(2), 291–315.

Oi, Jean C. (2004). Realms of freedom in post-Mao China. In William C. Kirby (Ed.), *Realms of freedom in modern China* (pp. 264–84). Stanford: Stanford University Press.

Pan, Philip P. (2005, August 27). Who controls the family? *Washington Post Foreign Service*, p. A1.

Pan, Philip P. (2005, September 7). Rural activist seized in Beijing. *Washington Post Foreign Service*, p. A22.

Parris, Kristen. (1999). Entrepreneurs and citizenship in China. *Problems of Post-Communism*, 46(1), 43–61.

Pastor, Robert A., and Qingshan Tan. (2000). The meaning of China's village elections. *China Quarterly*, 162, 490–512.

Peaceful village election broken up by more than 30 armed police in Dazu village, Ningbo. (2004, February 26). *China Labour Action Express*, 43. Accessed, June 1, 2004, at http://www.china-labour.org.hk/iso/article.adp?article_id=5258& category_name=Rural%20workers.

Pei, Minxin. (1997). Citizens v. mandarins: Administrative litigation in China. *China Quarterly*, 152, 832–62.

Peng Fangzhi. (1999). Anningcun de diaocha (Investigation of Anning village). In Zhao Shukai (Ed.), *Nongcun, nongmin* (The countryside and the peasantry). Unpublished paper. Beijing Normal University.

Peng Fei. (2000). Shi nongmin zhapian, haishi zhengfu keng nong? (Do farmers cheat the government, or does the government frame farmers?). *Fazhi yu Xinwen* (Legality and News), 12, 4–7.

Peng Zhen. (1987). Speech to the fifth joint meeting of delegation leaders and members of the Law Committee of the Sixth National People's Congress, April 6, 1987. Unpublished report. Ministry of Civil Affairs, Beijing.

Perry, Elizabeth J. (1984). Collective violence in China, 1880–1980. *Theory and Society*, 13(3), 427–54.

Perry, Elizabeth J. (1985). Rural violence in socialist China. *China Quarterly*, 103, 414–40.

Perry, Elizabeth J. (1994). Trends in the study of Chinese politics: State-society relations. *China Quarterly*, 139, 704–13.

Perry, Elizabeth J. (2003a). *Challenging the mandate of heaven: Social protest and state power in China*. Armonk, NY: M. E. Sharpe.

Perry, Elizabeth J. (2003b). "To rebel is justified": Cultural revolution influences on contemporary Chinese protest. In Kam-Yee Law (Ed.), *The Chinese cultural revolution reconsidered: Beyond purge and holocaust* (pp. 262–81). New York: Palgrave.

Perry, Elizabeth J., and Li Xun. (1997). *Proletarian power: Shanghai in the cultural revolution*. Boulder, CO: Westview.

Perry, Elizabeth J., and Mark Selden. (2003). *Chinese society: Change, conflict, and resistance* (2nd ed.). London: Routledge.

Piven, Frances Fox, and Richard A. Cloward. (1992). Normalizing collective protest. In Aldon D. Morris and Carol McClurg (Eds.), *Frontiers in social movement theory* (pp. 301–25). New Haven, CT: Yale University Press.

Potter, Pitman. (1994). Riding the tiger: Legitimacy and legal culture in post-Mao China. *China Quarterly*, 138, 325–58.

Prazniak, Roxann. (1980). Tax protest at Laiyang, Shandong, 1910: Commoner organization versus the county political elite. *Modern China*, 12(2), 41–71.

Pye, Lucian W. (1991). The state and the individual: An overview interpretation. *China Quarterly*, 127, 443–66.

Ragin, Charles. (1987). *The comparative method*. Berkeley: University of California Press.

Rankin, Mary Backus. (1982). "Public opinion" and political power: *Qingyi* in late nineteenth century China. *Journal of Asian Studies*, 41(3), 453–84.

Renmin Ribao Pinglunyuan. (2005, July 28). Weihu wending, cujin fazhan (Uphold stability, promote development). *Renmin Ribao* (People's Daily), 1.

Riesenberg, Peter. (1992). *Citizenship in the western tradition*. Chapel Hill: University of North Carolina Press.

Rochon, Thomas R. (1988). *Between society and state: Mobilizing for peace in Western Europe*. Princeton, NJ: Princeton University Press.

Rochon, Thomas R. (1998). *Culture moves: Ideas, activism, and changing values*. Princeton, NJ: Princeton University Press.

Rochon, Thomas R., and Daniel A. Mazmanian. (1993). Social movements and the policy process. *Annals of the American Academy of Political and Social Science*, 528, 75–87.

Rosenberg, Gerald N. (1991). *The hollow hope: Can courts bring about social change?* Chicago: University of Chicago Press.

Rucht, Dieter. (1990). The strategies and action repertoires of new movements. In Russell Dalton and Manfred Kuechler (Eds.), *Challenging the political order: New social and political movements in western democracies* (pp. 156–75). New York: Oxford University Press.

Rueschemeyer, Dietrich. (2003). Can one or a few cases yield theoretical gains? In James Mahoney and Dietrich Reuschemeyer (Eds.), *Comparative historical analysis in the social sciences* (pp. 305–36). Cambridge: Cambridge University Press.

Santoro, Wayne, and Gail McGuire. (1997). Social movement insiders: The impact of institutional activists on affirmative action and comparable worth policies. *Social Problems*, 44(4), 503–20.

Sawyers, Traci M., and David S. Meyer. (1999). Missed opportunities: Social movement abeyance and public policy. *Social Problems*, 46(2), 187–206.

Scalmer, Sean. (2002). Reinventing social movement repertoires: The "Operation Gandhi" experiment. Unpublished paper. Accessed, January 12, 2004, at http://polsc.anu.edu.au/Seminars2002.html.

Bibliography

Schock, Kurt. (1999). People power and political opportunities: Social movement mobilization and outcomes in the Philippines and Burma. *Social Problems*, 46(3), 355–75.

Schock, Kurt. (2005). *Unarmed insurrections: People power movements in nondemocracies*. Minneapolis: University of Minnesota Press.

Schultz, David A. (1998). *Leveraging the law: Using the courts to achieve social change*. New York: Peter Lang.

Scott, James C. (1976). *The moral economy of the peasant: Rebellion and subsistence in southeast Asia*. New Haven, CT: Yale University Press.

Scott, James C. (1977). Hegemony and the peasantry. *Politics and Society*, 7(3), 267–96.

Scott, James C. (1985). *Weapons of the weak: Everyday forms of peasant resistance*. New Haven, CT: Yale University Press.

Scott, James C. (1989). Everyday forms of resistance. In Forrest D. Colburn (Ed.), *Everyday forms of peasant resistance* (pp. 3–33). Armonk, NY: M. E. Sharpe.

Scott, James C. (1990). *Domination and the arts of resistance*. New Haven, CT: Yale University Press.

Sewell, William H., Jr. (1990). Collective violence and collective loyalties in France: Why the French Revolution made a difference. *Politics and Society*, 18(4), 527–52.

Sewell, William H., Jr. (1996). Three temporalities: Toward an eventful sociology. In Terence J. McDonald (Eds.), *The historic turn in the human sciences* (pp. 245–80). Ann Arbor: University of Michigan Press.

Shafir, Gershon. (1998). Introduction: The evolving tradition of citizenship. In Shafir (Ed.), *The citizenship debates* (pp. 1–28). Minneapolis: University of Minnesota Press.

Shapiro, Ian. (2002). Problems, methods, and theories in the study of politics, or what's wrong with political science and what to do about it. *Political Theory*, 30(4), 588–611.

Shi, Tianjian. (1997). *Political participation in Beijing*. Cambridge, MA: Harvard University Press.

Shi, Tianjian. (1999a). Village committee elections in China: Institutionalist tactics for democracy. *World Politics*, 51(3), 385–412.

Shi, Tianjian. (1999b). Voting and nonvoting in China: Voting behavior in plebiscitary and limited-choice elections. *Journal of Politics*, 61(4), 1115–39.

Shi, Tianjian. (2000). Cultural values and democracy in the People's Republic of China. *China Quarterly*, 162, 540–59.

Shi, Ting. (2005, July 7). Acceptance of rights replacing reflex fear of protests. *South China Morning Post*. Accessed, September 13, 2005, at http://66.102.7.104/search?q=cache:n6iPes1YXocJ:pekingduck.org/archives/002633.

Shi Weimin and Lei Jingxuan. (1999). *Zhijie xuanju: Zhidu yu guocheng* (Direct elections: System and process). Beijing: Zhongguo Shehui Kexue Chubanshe.

Shixin haiyao feili (Not only breaking promises, but also using force). (1993). *Hebei Nongcun Gongzuo* (Hebei Rural Work), 6, 41–42.

Shue, Vivienne. (1988). *The reach of the state: Sketches of the Chinese body politic*. Stanford: Stanford University Press.

Singerman, Diane. (1995). *Avenues of participation: Family, politics, and networks in urban quarters of Cairo*. Princeton, NJ: Princeton University Press.

Skocpol, Theda, and Margaret Somers. (1980). The uses of comparative history in macrosocial inquiry. *Comparative Studies in Society and History*, 22(2), 174–97.

Smith, Steve. (2002). *Like cattle and horses: Nationalism and labor in Shanghai, 1895–1927*. Durham, NC: Duke University Press.

Solinger, Dorothy J. (1999). *Contesting citizenship in urban China: Peasant migrants, the state, and the logic of the market*. Berkeley: University of California Press.

Somers, Margaret R. (1993). Citizenship and the place of the public sphere: Law, community, and political culture in the transition to democracy. *American Sociological Review*, 58(5), 587–620.

Somers, Margaret R. (1994). Rights, relationality, and membership: Rethinking the making and meaning of citizenship. *Law and Social Inquiry*, 18(1), 63–112.

Soule, Sarah A. (1997). The student divestment movement in the United States and tactical diffusion: The shantytown protest. *Social Forces*, 75(3), 855–82.

Soule, Sarah A., and Susan Olzak. (2004). When do movements matter? The politics of contingency and the Equal Rights Amendment. *American Sociological Review*, 69(4), 473–97.

Steinberg, Marc W. (1995). "The great end of all government...": Working people's construction of citizenship claims in early nineteenth century England and the matter of class. *International Review of Social History*, 40(3) (Supplement), 19–50.

Stinchcombe, Arthur. (1978). *Theoretical methods in social history*. New York: Academic Press.

Strang, David, and John W. Meyer. (1993). Institutional conditions for diffusion. *Theory and Society*, 22(4), 487–511.

Straughn, Jeremy Brooke. (2005). "Taking the state at its word": The arts of consentful contention in the German Democratic Republic. *American Journal of Sociology*, 110(6), 1598–1650.

Su Yongtong. (2004, November 4). "Shangfangcun" de rizi (Days spent in the "complainants' village"). *Nanfang Zhoumo* (Southern Weekend), 13.

Suh, Doowon. (2001). How do political opportunities matter for social movements? Political opportunity, misframing, pseudosuccess, and pseudofailure. *Sociological Quarterly*, 42(3), 437–60.

Svensson, Marina. (2002). *Debating human rights in China: A conceptual and political history*. Lanham, MD: Rowman & Littlefield.

Szabo, Mate. (1996). Repertoires of contention in post-communist protest cultures: An East Central European comparative survey (Hungary, Slovakia, Slovenia). *Social Research*, 63(4), 1155–83.

Tang Jinsu and Wang Jianjun. (1989). Nanyi huibi de redian: Jinnian nongcun ganqun guanxi toushi (Hot issues that are hard to avoid: Perspectives on rural cadre-mass relations in recent years). Unpublished report of the Ministry of Civil Affairs. A shortened version appeared in *Difang Zhengzhi yu Xingzheng* (Local Politics and Administration), 3 (1990), 15–20; 4 (1990), 13–17.

Tang, Yuen Yuen. (2005). When peasants sue *en masse*: Large-scale collective ALL suits in rural China. *China: An International Journal*, 3(1), 24–49.

Bibliography

Tanner, Murray Scot. (1994). Law in China: The terra incognita of political studies. *China Exchange News*, 22, 21–22.

Tanner, Murray Scot. (2004). China rethinks unrest. *Washington Quarterly*, 27(3), 137–56.

Tanner, Murray Scot. (2005). Rethinking law enforcement and society: Changing police analyses of social unrest. In Neil J. Diamant, Stanley B. Lubman, and Kevin J. O'Brien (Eds.), *Engaging the law in China: State, society, and possibilities for justice* (pp. 193–212). Stanford: Stanford University Press.

Tarrow, Sidney. (1989). *Democracy and disorder: Protest and politics in Italy, 1965–1975.* New York: Clarendon Press.

Tarrow, Sidney. (1996). States and opportunities: The political structuring of social movements. In Doug McAdam, John D. McCarthy, and Mayer N. Zald (Eds.), *Comparative perspectives on social movements* (pp. 41–61). Cambridge: Cambridge University Press.

Tarrow, Sidney. (1998). *Power in movement* (2nd ed.). Cambridge: Cambridge University Press.

Tarrow, Sidney. (2005). *The new transnational activism.* Cambridge: Cambridge University Press.

Thaxton, Ralph A. (1997). *Salt of the earth: The political origins of peasant protest and communist revolution in China.* Berkeley: University of California Press.

Thireau, Isabelle, and Hua Linshan. (2003). The moral universe of aggrieved Chinese workers. *China Journal*, 50, 83–103.

Thøgersen, Stig. (2000). Cultural life and cultural control in rural China: Where is the Party? *China Journal*, 44, 129–44.

Thompson, E. P. (1971). The moral economy of the English crowd in the eighteenth century. *Past and Present*, 50, 76–136.

Thompson, E. P. (1975). *Whigs and hunters: The origins of the Black Act.* New York: Pantheon Books.

Thompson, E. P. (1991). *Customs in common.* New York: New Press.

Thornton, Patricia M. (2002). Framing dissent in contemporary China: Irony, ambiguity and metonymy. *China Quarterly*, 171, 661–81.

Thornton, Patricia M. (2003). The new cybersects: Resistance and repression in the reform era. In Elizabeth J. Perry and Mark Selden (Eds.), *Chinese society* (2nd ed., pp. 247–70). London. Routledge.

Thornton, Patricia M. (2004). Comrades and collectives in arms. Tax resistance, evasion, and avoidance strategies in post-Mao China. In Peter Hays Gries and Stanley Rosen (Eds.), *State and society in 21st century China: Crisis, contention, and legitimation* (pp. 87–104). New York: Routledge.

Tian Yuan. (1993). Zhongguo nongcun jiceng de minzhu zhilu (The pathway to grass-roots democracy in rural China). *Xiangzhen Luntan* (Township Forum), 6, 3–4.

Tilly, Charles. (1976). Rural collective action in modern Europe. In Joseph Spielberg and Scott Whitehead (Eds.), *Forging nations: A comparative view of rural ferment and revolt* (pp. 9–40). East Lansing: Michigan State University Press.

Tilly, Charles. (1978). *From mobilization to revolution*. Reading, MA: Addison-Wesley.

Tilly, Charles. (1981). *As sociology meets history*. New York: Academic Press.

Tilly, Charles. (1984). *Big structures, large processes, huge comparisons*. New York: Russell Sage.

Tilly, Charles. (1986). *The contentious French: Four centuries of popular struggle*. Cambridge, MA: Harvard University Press.

Tilly, Charles. (1993). Contentious repertoires in Great Britain, 1758–1834. *Social Science History*, 17(2), 253–80.

Tilly, Charles. (1995). *Citizenship, identity, and social history*. Cambridge: Cambridge University Press.

Tilly, Charles. (1998). Where do rights come from? In Theda Skocpol (Ed.), *Democracy, revolution, and history* (pp. 55–72). Ithaca, NY: Cornell University Press.

Tilly, Charles. (1999). From interactions to outcomes in social movements. In Marco Giugni, Doug McAdam, and Charles Tilly (Eds.), *How social movements matter* (pp. 253–70). Minneapolis: University of Minnesota Press.

Tilly, Charles. (2002). *Stories, identities, and political change*. Lanham, MD: Rowman & Littlefield.

Townsend, James R. (1967). *Political participation in communist China*. Berkeley: University of California Press.

Turner, Bryan S. (1992). *Citizenship and social theory*. London: Sage.

Turton, Andrew. (1986). Patrolling the middle-ground: Methodological perspectives on "everyday peasant resistance." In James C. Scott and Benjamin J. Tria Kerkvliet (Eds.), *Everyday forms of peasant resistance in South-East Asia* (pp. 36–49). London: Frank Cass.

Unger, Jonathan. (2000). Power, patronage, and protest in rural China. In Tyrene White (Ed.), *China briefing, 2000* (pp. 71–94). Armonk, NY: M. E. Sharpe.

Unger, Jonathan. (2002). *The transformation of rural China*. Armonk, NY: M. E. Sharpe.

Verdery, Katherine. (1999). Fuzzy property: Rights, power and identity in Transylvania's decollectivization. In Michael Burawoy and Katherine Verdery (Eds.), *Uncertain transition: Ethnographies of change in the postsocialist world* (pp. 53–82). Lanham, MD: Rowman & Littlefield.

Voss, Kim, and Rachel Sherman. (2000). Breaking the iron law of oligarchy: Union revitalization in the American labor movement. *American Journal of Sociology*, 106(2), 303–49.

Wang, Gungwu. (1991). *The Chineseness of China*. Hong Kong: Oxford University Press.

Wang Wanfu. (1992). Mo rang qunzhong "xunzhao gongchandang" (Don't make the masses "look for the Communist Party"). *Hebei Nongcun Gongzuo* (Hebei Rural Work), 9, 33.

Wang, Xiangwei. (2005, July 4). Mainland official hails bloody riots as a sign of democracy. *South China Morning Post*. Accessed, September 13, 2005, at http://www.zonaeuropa.com/20050705_1.html.

Bibliography

Wang Xinqing, Liu Zhenying, Wang Yanbin, and Jiang Xia. (1998, January 10). Zhongyang nongcun gongzuo huiyi zai Jing zhaokai (The central meeting on the countryside held in Beijing). *Renmin Ribao* (People's Daily), 1.

Wang, Xu. (1997). Mutual empowerment of state and peasantry: Grassroots democracy in rural China. *World Development*, 25(9), 1431–42.

Wang Zhiquan. (2002). WTO neng gei nongmin dailai shenmo? (What can the WTO bring farmers?). *Fazhi Shijie* (Legal World), 4, 4–8.

Wang Zirui and Wang Songmiao. (2001). Yueji shangfang qineng yancheng? (How can the government severely punish those who bypass levels when lodging complaints?). *Renmin Xinfang* (People's Letters and Visits), 12, 31.

Wasserstrom, Jeffrey. (1992). The evolution of the Shanghai student protest repertoire: Or, where do correct tactics come from? In Frederic Wakeman Jr. and Wen-hsin Yeh (Eds.), *Shanghai sojourners* (pp. 108–44). Berkeley: Institute of East Asian Studies, Chinese Research Monograph Series.

Weatherley, Robert. (1999). *The discourse on human rights in China*. New York: St. Martin's Press.

Wedeman, Andrew. (1997). Stealing from the farmers: Institutional corruption and the 1992 IOU crisis. *China Quarterly*, 152, 805–31.

Wedeman, Andrew. (2001). Incompetence, noise and fear in central-local relations in China. *Studies in Comparative International Development*, 35(4), 59–83.

Wei shenmo guojia zhengce falü zai Sichuan Linshui xian zhixing bu xia qu? Shi shui gei le tamen falü wai de tequan? (Why can't state policies and laws be enforced in Linshui county, Sichuan? Who gives them extra-legal privileges?). (2003, June 22). Unpublished letter of complaint concerning land appropriation signed by 515 villagers, Dongwai village and Nanwai village, Dingping township.

Wen Jiabao. (2004, March 17). Zhengfu gongzuo baogao (Government work report). Delivered at the second plenum of the Tenth National People's Congress. *Renmin Ribao* (People's Daily), 1.

White, Tyrene. (2003). Domination, resistance and accommodation in China's one-child campaign. In Elizabeth J. Perry and Mark Selden (Eds.), *Chinese society* (2nd ed., pp. 183–203). London: Routledge.

Whiting, Susan H. (2001). *Power and wealth in rural China: The political economy of institutional change*. Cambridge: Cambridge University Press.

Whiting, Susan H. (2004). The cadre evaluation system at the grassroots: The paradox of party rule. In Barry J. Naughton and Dali L. Yang (Eds.), *Holding China together: Diversity and national integration in the post-Deng era* (pp. 101–19). Cambridge: Cambridge University Press.

Whittier, Nancy. (1995). *Feminist generations: The persistence of the radical women's movement*. Philadelphia: Temple University Press.

Willis, Paul E. (1977). *Learning to labour: How working class kids get working class jobs*. Westmead, England: Saxon House.

Winkler, Edwin A. (2002). Chinese reproductive policy at the turn of the millennium: Dynamic stability. *Population and Development Review*, 28(3), 379–418.

Wittgenstein, Ludwig von. (1958). *Philosophical investigations*. Trans. G. E. M. Anscombe. New York: Macmillan.

Wong, R. Bin. (1997). *China transformed: Historical change and the limits of European experience*. Ithaca, NY: Cornell University Press.

Wood, Elisabeth Jean. (2003). *Insurgent collective action and civil war in El Salvador*. Cambridge: Cambridge University Press.

Wright, Teresa. (2001). *The perils of protest: State repression and student activism in China and Taiwan*. Honolulu: University of Hawaii Press.

Wright, Teresa. (2002). The Chinese Democratic Party and the politics of protest in the 1980s–1990s. *China Quarterly*, 172, 906–26.

Wu Xinghua. (1997, February 15). Hunan sifa xitong weihu nongmin quanyi, qunian wei nongmin wanhui jingji sunshi 1.96 yi yuan (Law enforcement systems in Hunan defended peasants' rights and recovered 196 million yuan in economic losses for peasants last year). *Renmin Ribao* (People's Daily), 1.

Xi Ling. (1993). Nongmin fudan wei shenmo chengwei lao da nan wenti (Why peasant burdens have become a long-standing, big and difficult problem). *Jiage Yuekan* (Price Monthly), 8, 9–10.

Xiang Wen. (2000). Nongmin yulun lingxiu shi yingxiong haishi diaomin? (Are peasant public opinion leaders heroes or shrewd, unyielding people?). *Zhongguo Shehui Daokan* (Guide to Chinese Society), 4, 6–9.

Xiao Han. (2002, January 1). Xianzai jiu zuo ge gongmin (Be a citizen now). *Nanfeng Chuang* (Window on the Southern Wind), 1(A), 14–17.

Xiao Tangbiao. (2002). Zhongguo nongcun jiceng quanwei jichu de bianqian yu yanxu (Changes and continuities in the basis of grassroots authority in rural China). In Jing Yuejin (Ed.), *Zhengzhi xue yu bianhua zhong de Zhongguo* (Political science and China in transition) (pp. 349–65). Beijing: Renmin Daxue Chubanshe.

Xinhuashe. (1996, May 7). Zhongban guoban zhuanfa guanyu jianqing nongmin fudan de "yijian" (The General Office of the Central Party Committee and the General Office of the State Council transmit an "opinion" on reducing peasant burdens). *Renmin Ribao* (People's Daily), 1.

Xinhuashe. (1996, December 9). Guowuyuan Bangongting fachu tongzhi renzhen zuohao jianqing nongmin fudan gongzuo (The General Office of the State Council issues a circular, the work on reducing peasant burdens must be done seriously). *Renmin Ribao* (People's Daily), 2.

Yan, Yun-xiang. (1995). Everyday power relations. Changes in a north China village. In Andrew G. Walder (Ed.), *The waning of the communist state: Economic origins of political decline in China and Hungary* (pp. 215–41). Berkeley: University of California Press.

Yang, Dali L. (1996). *Calamity and reform in China: State, rural society and institutional change since the great leap famine*. Stanford: Stanford University Press.

Yang, Guobin. (2000a). Achieving emotions in collective action: Emotional processes and movement mobilization in the 1989 Chinese student movement. *Sociological Quarterly*, 41(4), 593–614.

Yang, Guobin. (2000b). The liminal effects of social movements: Red Guards and the transformation of identity. *Sociological Forum*, 15(3), 379–406.

Bibliography

Yang Haikun. (1994). Baituo xingzheng susong zhidu kunjing de chulu (The way out of the difficult situation in the administrative litigation system). *Zhongguo Faxue* (Chinese Legal Science), 3, 51–56.

Yang Hao. (1999). Nongmin de huhuan (Farmers' cries). *Dangdai* (Modern Times), 6, 63–90.

Yang Shouyong and Wang Jintao. (2001). "Wending cun" wei he chu le da luanzi? (Why did a big disturbance occur in a "stable village"?). *Banyuetan (Neibuban)* (Fortnightly Chats) (Internal Edition), 1, 40–42.

Yang Xuewu. (2001). Ling ren tongxin de zaoyu (Deplorable mistreatment). *Nanfeng Chuang* (Window on the Southern Wind), 4, 39.

Yardley, Jim. (2005, April 25). A hundred cellphones bloom, and Chinese take to the streets. *New York Times*, 1.

Yep, Ray. (2004). Can "tax-for-fee reform" reduce rural tension in China? The process, progress, and limitations. *China Quarterly*, 177, 42–70.

Yu Jianrong. (2000). Liyi, quanwei he zhixu: dui cunmin duikang jiceng zhengfu de quntixing shijian de fenxi (Interests, authority, and order: An analysis of collective incidents in which villagers resist grass-roots government). *Zhongguo Nongcun Guancha* (Survey on Rural China), 4, 70–76.

Yu Jianrong. (2001). *Yuecun zhengzhi* (Politics in Yue village). Beijing: Shangwu Yinshuguan.

Yu Jianrong. (2003). Nongmin youzuzhi kangzheng jiqi zhengzhi fengxian (Organized peasant contention and its political risks). *Zhanlue yu Guanli* (Strategy and Management), 3, 1–16.

Yu Jianrong. (2004). Dangdai nongmin weiquan huodong dui Zhongguo zhengzhi de yingxiang (The impact of peasants' rights' defense activities on Chinese politics). Unpublished paper. Chinese Academy of Social Sciences, Beijing.

Yu Jianrong. (2004, October 19). Guanyu woguo xinfang zhidu de diaocha (An investigation of the letters and visits system in our country). *Zhongguo Shehui Kexueyuan Yaobao Xinxi Zhuanbao* (Special Report of the Chinese Academy of Social Sciences), no. 51.

Yu, Verna. (2004, November 27). 1000 villagers in clash with police. *South China Morning Post* (Hong Kong).

Yu Xin. (1993). "Luan tanpai" reng wei xiu ("Arbitrary apportionments" still have not stopped). *Minzhu yu Fazhi* (Democracy and Legal System), 9, 26–27.

Zald, Mayer N. (1992). Looking backward to look forward: Reflections on the past and future of the resource mobilization program. In Aldon D. Morris and Carol McClurg Mueller (Eds.), *Frontiers of social movement theory* (pp. 326–48). New Haven, CT: Yale University Press.

Zald, Mayer N. (2000). Ideologically structured action: An enlarged agenda for social movement research. *Mobilization*, 5(1), 1–16.

Zelin, Madeleine. (1984). *The magistrate's tael: Rationalizing fiscal reform in eighteenth century Ch'ing China*. Berkeley: University of California Press.

Zeng Yesong. (1995). Jingdong Zhongnanhai de shinian yuanan (A ten-year-long unjust verdict that disturbs Zhongnanhai). *Zhongguo Nongmin* (China's Farmers), 5, 34–37.

Zhang Chenggong. (1993). Cunzhang si yu chunjie (Village heads die at spring festival), *Landun* (Blue Shield), 3, 23–27.

Zhang Cuiling. (2002). Zenyang duidai zheli de nongmin shangfang – Anhui Chengzhuang shijian diaocha baogao (How to deal with farmers lodging complaints – An investigative report on Anhui's Chengzhuang incident). *Fazhi yu Xinwen* (Legality and News), 1, 4–8.

Zhang Sutang and Xie Guoji. (1995, March 29). Shahai shangfang cunmin guofa nanrong, Henan siming cun ganbu bei chujue (National law does not tolerate murder of villagers who lodge complaints – Four village cadres in Henan are executed). *Renmin Ribao (Haiwaiban)* (People's Daily)(Overseas Edition), 4.

Zhang, Wu. (2005). Peasant power in China: A comparative study of peasant protest in Hunan in the 1990s. Paper presented at the 101st Annual Meeting of the American Political Science Association, Washington, DC, September 1–4.

Zhang Yinghong. (2002). Gei nongmin yi xianfa guanhuai (Give farmers constitutional protection). *Nanfeng Chuang* (Window on the Southern Wind), 1, 42–44.

Zhao, Dingxin. (2001). *The power of Tiananmen: State-society relations and the 1989 Beijing student movement.* Chicago: University of Chicago Press.

Zhao Ling. (2004). Significant shift in focus of peasants' rights activism. Interview with rural development researcher Yu Jianrong of the Chinese Academy of Social Sciences. Accessed, September 16, 2004, at http://www.chinaelections.org/en/readnews.asp?newsid={A0B4FFF9-1F57-460D-BBB3-824B59420C2F}&classname=News%20Highlights.

Zhao Ling. (2004, November 4). Guonei shou fen xinfang baogao huo gaoceng zhongshi (The first report on the letters and visits system has caught the attention of high levels). *Nanfang Zhoumo* (Southern Weekend), 12.

Zhao Shukai. (2003). Shangfang shijian he xinfang tixi: Guanyu nongmin jin jing shangfang wenti de diaocha fenxi (Petitioning incidents and the letters and visits system: Investigation and analysis of the issue of farmers who lodge complaints in Beijing). *Sannong Zhongguo* (Chinese Agriculture, Countryside, and Farmers). Accessed, May 28, 2005, at http://www.ccrs.org.cn/NEWSgl/ReadNews.asp?NewsID=5777.

Zhao Shukai. (2004). Lishixing tiaozhan: Zhongguo nongcun de chongtu yu zhili (An historical challenge: conflicts and governance in rural China). In Ru Xin, Lu Xueyi, Li Peilin, Huang Ping, and Lu Jianhua (Eds.), *2004 nian: Zhongguo shehui xingshi yuce yu fenxi* (2004: Forecasts and analyses of social trends in China) (pp. 212–23). Beijing: Shehui Kexue Wenxian Chubanshe.

Zheng, Wang. (2000). Gender, employment and women's resistance. In Elizabeth J. Perry and Mark Selden (Eds.), *Chinese society: Change, conflict and resistance* (pp. 62–82). London: Routledge.

Zhengdingxian Minzhengju. (1991). Shixing cunmin daibiao huiyi zhidu jiakuai nongcun jiceng minzhu jincheng (Implement the villagers' representative congress system, quicken the construction of rural grass-roots democracy). Unpublished report. Zhengding County Bureau of Civil Affairs. 8pp.

Bibliography

Zhengfu gongzuo baogao. (2004, March 17). Government work report delivered by Premier Wen Jiabao at the second plenum of the Tenth National People's Congress. *Renmin Ribao* (People's Daily), 1.

Zhonggong Hebei Shengwei Zhengce Yanjiushi Ketizu. (1999). Yingxiang wending de yinsu yu baochi wending de jizhi (Factors affecting stability and mechanisms for maintaining stability). *Neibu Wengao* (Internal Manuscripts), 4, 27–28, 32.

Zhonggong Sichuan Shengwei Zuzhibu Ketizu. (2002). Zenyang zhengque chuli quntixing tufa shijian (How to correctly handle collective and abrupt incidents). *Banyuetan (Neibuban)* (Fortnightly Chats) (Internal Edition), 1, 29–32.

Zhonggong Zhongyang Bangongting and Guowuyuan Bangongting. (1998, June 1). Guanyu zai nongcun pubian shixing cunwu gongkai he minzhu guanli zhidu de tongzhi (Circular on broadly implementing village openness and democratic management systems in the countryside). *Renmin Ribao* (People's Daily), 1.

Zhonggong Zhongyang Bangongting and Guowuyuan Bangongting. (2002, July 18). Jinyibu zuohao cunmin weiyuanhui huanjie xuanju gongzuo (Further improve the work of electing villagers' committees). *Renmin Ribao* (People's Daily), 1.

Zhonggong Zhongyang Zuzhibu Ketizu. (2001). *Zhongguo diaocha baogao, 2000–2001: Xin xingshi xia renmin neibu maodun yanjiu* (Investigation report on China, 2000–2001: Research on contradictions among the people under the new situation). Beijing: Zhongyang Bianyi Chubanshe.

Zhongguo Jiceng Zhengquan Jianshe Yanjiuhui. (1994). *Zhongguo nongcun cunmin weiyuanhui huanjie xuanju yanjiu baogao* (Research report on rural China's villagers' committee re-elections). Beijing: Zhongguo Shehui Chubanshe.

Zhongguo Nongcun Cunmin Zizhi Zhidu Yanjiu Ketizu. (1994). *Study on the election of villagers' committees in rural China*. Beijing: Zhongguo Shehui Chubanshe.

Zhongyang Zhengfawei Yanjiushi. (2001). *Weihu shehui wending diaoyan wenji* (Collected essays on maintaining social stability). Beijing: Falü Chubanshe.

Zhou Decai. (2002). Lun Zhongguo renquan jiefang yu heping tongyi (On the liberation of human rights in China and peaceful reunification). Unpublished paper by a protest leader. Beijing.

Zhou, Guangyuan. (1993). Illusion and reality in the law of the late Qing: A Sichuan case study. *Modern China*, 19(4), 427–56.

Zhou, Kate Xiao, and Lynn T. White III. (1995). Quiet politics and rural enterprise in reform China. *Journal of Developing Areas*, 29, 461–90.

Zhou Qingyin and Wang Xinya. (2000a). Shi hong hai shi hei (Red or black). *Banyuetan (Neibuban)* (Fortnightly Chats) (Internal Edition), 2, 17–21.

Zhou Qingyin and Wang Xinya. (2000b). Yi shu bu yi du (Better channeling than blocking). *Banyuetan (Neibuban)* (Fortnightly Chats) (Internal Edition), 2, 22–26.

Zhou Zhanshun. (1999). Qunzhong xinfang xin dongxiang (New trends in letters and visits of the masses). *Banyuetan (Neibuban)* (Fortnightly Chats) (Internal Edition), 2, 54–55.

Zhu Anshun. (1999). Ruci jian fang wei na ban? (Why did they build new houses?). In Zhao Shukai (Ed.), *Nongcun, nongmin* (The countryside and the peasantry) (pp. 320–25). Unpublished paper. Qinghua University.

Zhu Kexin. (1993). Yiqian babai sanshiyi ci gaozhuang (Lodging 1831 complaints). *Minzhu yu Fazhi* (Democracy and Legal System), 9, 2–6.

Zolberg, Aristide. (1972). Moments of madness. *Politics and Society*, 2(2), 183–207.

Zweig, David. (1997). *Freeing China's farmers: Rural restructuring in the reform era*. Armonk, NY: M. E. Sharpe.

Zweig, David. (2000). The "externalities of development": Can new political institutions manage rural conflict? In Elizabeth J. Perry and Mark Selden (Eds.), *Chinese society: Change, conflict and resistance* (pp. 120–42). London: Routledge.

Zweig, David. (2001). Democracy and (in)stability in rural China: A dialectical relationship. Paper presented at the 97th annual meeting of the American Political Science Association, San Francisco, August 30–September 2.

Zwerman, Gilda, and Patricia Steinhoff. (2005). When activists ask for trouble: State-dissident interactions and the new left cycle of resistance in the United States and Japan. In Christian Davenport, Hank Johnston, and Carol Mueller (Eds.), *Repression and mobilization* (pp. 85–107). Minneapolis: University of Minnesota Press.

Index

Index

compliant villagers, xii
consentful contention, 2, 17, 18
Constitution (1982), 6
    article 111 on self-governance at
      village level, 32
    as a formally ratified central policy, 6
    not used to back up claims of rightful
      resisters, 60
    popular sovereignty and rule by law
      as constitutional principles, 126
    protecting citizens against state
      organs violating the law, 31
contained claims, 51, 63, 66. *See*
    boundary-spanning claims;
    transgressive claims
contention, 93. *See* collective action;
    mediated contention; rightful
    resistance; protests; riots; violence
    confrontational forms of, 77, 91
    consequences of, 95, 96, 99
    contained, 51, 63, 99
    dynamics of, 63, 95
    popular, 52, 64, 95, 96, 99, 141
    repertoires of, xiv, 10, 63, 67, 69, 76,
      77
    rights-based, 10
    transgressive forms of, 21
contentious conversation, 4, 56, 62
contentious politics, xiii, xiv, xv, xvi, 2,
    48, 63, 65, 113
    critique of students of, 64
    impact of, 99
    indirect outcomes of, 97
    research implications of, 91
    studying causality in, 97
corruption, 42, 100, 141
    of cadres, 53
    government campaign against, 9, 45,
      72, 113
    opposition to, 137
    protests against, 72, 116
    as spur to rightful resistance, xi, 6,
      120
Cultural Revolution
    openings for popular action during,
      30

protest legacies of, 9, 135
protest tactics during, 10
worker-rebel defiance in Shanghai,
    89

Dangshan county, Anhui province
    repression in, 35
    rightful resistance in, 79
    tax-for-fee reform in, 34
defeats, 21
    acceptance of as common response,
      105
    as contributing to confrontation
      among protest leaders, 91,
      105
    as contributing to protest leaders
      giving up, 80
    as contributing to tactical escalation,
      80, 94
    increase as rightful resisters scale the
      official hierarchy, 90
    repeated failures as escalating to
      violence, 3
    when mediators do not act, 81
democracy, 51
    discussed by Chinese villagers,
      12
    lack of in China, 108
    multiparty, 108
    people's, 30, 128
    rightful resistance in democratic
      countries, 23
    socialist, 9, 13, 62
    Western theories of, 118
Deng Xiaoping, 6
Department of Labor (U.S.), 21
diaomin, xi, 55
dingzihu, xi
disaggregating the state, 51, 66. *See*
    anthropology of the state;
    state-society relations

East Germany
    consentful contention in, 17
    petition drives in, 2
    protesters in, 18

Index

173

Index

Mao Zedong
  his campaigns against corrupt
    grass-roots cadres, 10
  impressed with peasant activism in
    Hunan, 111
  protest leaders influenced by, 137
mass mobilization, 72
Mathiesen, Thomas, 16
McAdam, Doug, 27, 50, 51, 64, 91
McCann, Michael, 18, 19, 22, 23
McCarthy, John, 27
media
  as elite ally, 13, 29, 46, 58, 61, 62, 101
  penetration of into the countryside,
    11
  response to rightful resistance, 98
  use by rightful resisters, 39, 108,
    128
  in the West, 77
mediated contention. *See* contention;
  rightful resistance
  as contributing to tactical escalation,
    80
  definition of, 69
  disenchantment with, 89
  failure of to produce redress, 81, 83,
    86, 89
  as opposed to direct action, 76, 91
  participants in, 82
  used to obtain "red-headed
    documents," 82
migrant workers
  enhanced policy awareness of, 40
  not treated as full citizens, 119
  protest leaders who become, 88, 108,
    135, 136
  as spreaders of news about popular
    action, 78
Ministry of Agriculture, 82
Ministry of Civil Affairs
  appeals and letters to, 54
  on center-local divide, 28
  involvement with elections, 101
  as protesters' ally, 13, 58, 100
Minzner, Carl, 135

misimplementation. *See*
  implementation
  of central policies, 28, 41, 45, 47, 60,
    90, 99, 100, 109
  of judicial decisions in South Africa,
    16
misperceptions, 47. *See* opportunities,
  perceptions of
Montgomery bus boycott (U.S.), 51
moral economy
  claims, 23
  protests as distinguished from
    rightful resistance, xii

nail-like individuals, xi. *See* recalcitrants
National People's Congress
  appeals to, 81, 92
  decisions by, 57
  Peng Zhen's speech to, 14
  protesters' access to blocked, 81
  as protesters' ally, 59
Ningxiang county, Hunan province
  popular support for rightful
    resistance in, 111
  protests in, 72
  rightful resistance in, 67, 79
nongmin fudan, 6, 29, 70
nongnu, 122. *See* slaves
Norway, 16

object shift, xv, 91
openings. *See* opportunities
opportunities, xv
  affected by state fragmentation, 28
  definition of opportunity structure,
    49
  different from improved
    opportunities, 49
  expanding, 43, 93, 128
  for expression, 50
  Herbst, Jeffrey on, 2
  perceptions of, xv, 26, 27, 38, 43, 48
  political, xiv, xv, 20, 25, 27, 48, 93
  for popular classes, 52, 66
  rightful resistance as a product of, 4

175

Index

Made in the USA
San Bernardino, CA
09 January 2018